The Language of Children

SECOND EDITION

The Language of Children

Evolution and Development of
Secondary Consciousness and Language

SECOND EDITION

Mathilda Holzman

Tufts University, Medford, Massachusetts

BLACKWELL
Publishers

First published 1997

2 4 6 8 10 9 7 5 3 1

Blackwell Publishers Inc.
238 Main Street
Cambridge, Massachusetts 02142
USA

Blackwell Publishers Ltd
108 Cowley Road
Oxford OX4 1JF
UK

Library of Congress Cataloging-in-Publication Data

Holzman, Mathilda.
    The language of children : evolution and development of secondary
consciousness and language / Mathilda Holzman. — 2nd ed.
        p.   cm.
    Includes bibliographical references (p.) and index.
    ISBN 1–55786–516–7 (hardcover : alk. paper). — ISBN 1–55786–517–5
(pbk. : alk. paper)
    1. Children—Language. 2. Language acquisition. I. Title.
LB1139.L3H64   1997
372.6—dc20   96–26311
                                                                        CIP

British Library Cataloguing in Publication Data

A CIP catalogue record for this book is available from the
British Library.

Commissioning Editor: Alison Mudditt
Desk Editor: Sue Ashton
Production Controller: Lisa Eaton

Typeset in $10\frac{1}{2}$ on 13 pt Galliard
by Graphicraft Typesetters Ltd, Hong Kong
Printed in Great Britain by Hartnolls Ltd, Bodmin, Cornwall

This book is printed on acid-free paper

Contents

Figures

Tables

Preface

The first chapter of a book provides an opportunity for the writer to introduce prospective readers to her view of the subject. I take the opportunity in chapter 1 to explain myself so that readers may expect the heterogeneity of topics and issues addressed. Early in the book (chapters 2–4) I will be striving to place human beings and our use of language on the evolutionary trail with other animal species. The middle of the book, chapters 5 through 10, is concerned with the development of language, including literacy, by the human child. The last two chapters, on bilingualism and second-language learning (chapter 11) and sociolinguistics (chapter 12), are concerned with language in its social context. If this book had been written before the 1960s, these two chapters would not necessarily have been included. Events which occurred in the 1960s changed our society and affected the language we use, our awareness of language policy issues, and the sociolinguistics of children.

This edition of *The Language of Children* was written as a contribution to the research being done in the field, and should be useful in upper-level undergraduate and graduate courses. As the first edition was constructed to provide a broad introduction to the subject, and the new edition is written in a reader-friendly style, the book could be used in introductory courses. Besides college students, this book will be of interest to parents who become intrigued by their children's development of language and to people working with children as teachers, in day-care centers, pre-schools, and through the grades.

The domain I survey is too large to describe exhaustively. I have therefore chosen to look at particular aspects of the subject of each

chapter. Rather than simply relating the conclusions of research, however, I tell – briefly – what was involved in the research and how the
researchers discovered what they report. As I have not presented an
exhaustive survey of each topic, every chapter concludes with suggestions for further reading.

The first edition of *The Language of Children* appeared in 1984.
Times have changed since then, much is now known that wasn't then,
and my understanding and some conclusions about what is important
are different now. Nevertheless there are research studies and theories
that I wrote about then that remain important and interesting to me,
and I have borrowed from what I wrote then for this new edition.
I point this out to show how the study of human language development has evolved since its early beginnings in the 1960s.

Acknowledgments

This book was written after I became Professor Emerita in the Department of Child Study at Tufts University, in 1993, and I want to thank my department for providing me with an office and a friendly environment to work in. Colleagues at Tufts have been important contributors to my intellectual development in the biological, philosophical and linguistic aspects of this book, especially Nancy Milburn, Ben Dane, Helen Cartwright, Dan Dennett, and Calvin Gidney.

Colleagues in my field have been generous with their books and articles. I am particularly in debt to Elizabeth Bates, Steven Pinker, Katherine Nelson, and Patricia Marks Greenfield. Donna Christian, President of the Center for Applied Linguistics, has been my guide into the sociolinguistic reality of chapters 11 and 12.

Katie Trainor has been my research assistant during the preparation of this book, and she has also transcribed the manuscript in my terrible handwriting on to disk. I truly couldn't have done it without Katie. Kim Austen worked as my research assistant doing the analysis of Carol's and Jean's trip through the one-word period in chapter 6. My editors at Blackwell, Susan Milmo and Alison Mudditt, have given me guidance and useful evaluations from reviewers to whom they submitted my text.

Friends and family have listened and responded as I talked through the material I used for chapter 4. I thank them, particularly my husband, son David, and friend, Nancy Dorfman. Naturally, only I, and none of my helpful colleagues, relatives, and friends, bear responsibility for what I have written.

The author and publishers gratefully acknowledge the following for permission to reproduce copyright material.

Figure 2.1 is redrawn from E. O. Wilson, "Animal communication." Copyright © 1972 by Scientific American Inc. All rights reserved. Figure 3.1 is taken from R. J. Herrnstein et al., "Natural concepts in pigeons," *Journal of Experimental Psychology, Animal Behavior Processes*, 2(1976), pp. 285–311. Figure 3.2 is from A. J. Premack and D. Premack, "Teaching language to an ape." Copyright © 1972 by Scientific American Inc. All rights reserved. Figure 5.3 is redrawn from P. D. Eimas, "Perception of speech in early infancy." Copyright © 1985 by Scientific American Inc. All rights reserved. Figure 7.1 is reproduced from J. Berko, "The child's learning of English morphology," *Word*, 14(1958), pp. 150–77. Figures 8.1 and 8.2 are from J. Carrier and H. Leet, "Effects of context upon children's referential development," unpublished paper, Tufts University. Figure 8.3 is reproduced from M. Chandler et al., "Small scale deceit," by kind permission of the Society for Research in Child Development. Figure 9.1 is taken from E. Markman and J. Hutchinson, "Children's sensitivity to constraints on word meaning: taxonomic vs. thematic relations," by permission of Academic Press Inc. Table 5.3 is taken from J. Locke, *Phonological Acquisition and Change* (1983) by permission of Academic Press Inc. Tables 8.1–8.4 are reprinted from the 1977 Nebraska Symposium on Motivation by permission of the University of Nebraska Press. Copyright © 1978 by the University of Nebraska Press. Tables 9.1, 9.3, and 9.4 are reproduced by kind permission of the Society for Research in Child Development.

1
Introduction

This is a book about human beings and our use of language, the behavior that has set us apart from all other animals. Notice that I didn't say "our language." I said "our use of language." What is it about us that accounts for our having this amazing, flexible instrument, more expressive than a piano, and knowing, all of us from a very early age, how to use it? As we mature, we become able to use it to participate in the complex life of human beings, first in our homes, then in school and society.

Two closely related parts of our human endowment are, I believe, fundamentally responsible for human culture and, as they differ from relations among members of other animal species, relations among human beings. Human culture and social relations are not really separable entities. A distinction can be made between our evolutionary biological nature and the culture we humans have brought into being. Human beings are endowed with *secondary consciousness*, the capacity to take our own thoughts, feelings, and goals as objects of thought, as well as the thoughts, feelings, and goals of others. Because of this we are able to plan, to evaluate what we have done, and, therefore, to make changes in what we do.

As all of us have secondary consciousness, we have a basis for cooperating. Our social life does not have to have the inflexibility of animal societies in which the determinants of intra-species relations are instincts and physical power. We would not get very far cooperating and planning, however, if it were not also for our innate capacity to develop language. For language is the medium that makes communication, and hence cooperation, planning, and thinking together, possible. But language without secondary consciousness would not make us the language users we are but rather the kind that chimpanzees are. Their language use comes about through conditioning and is limited to responding to conditioned stimuli rather than being the result of intention, thinking, or wishing to communicate a feeling – all higher mental processes, part of our innate human endowment. This book is the result of my efforts to achieve an understanding of the evolutionary trail to human language use, its biosocial development in the young of our species and its subsequent development in family, school, and society.

The book begins with animals in the wild, addressing the signaling behavior of primates, other mammals, birds, and insects (chapter 2). I pick up the evolutionary trail to human language use with these species. Obviously, this is not the beginning, but it is far enough back to provide informative comparisons. We can see how using signals and signaling enables animals in the wild to provide information to other members of their species.

Next, we look at animals in contact with human beings as pets and experimental animals (chapter 3). We see that, in contact with people, animals are conditioned to emit and respond to signals not in their innate repertoires. We consider conditioning and how it is mediated by reward and punishment and does not require or give rise to higher mental operations like planning or other intentional processes. We then look at animal signal systems and signaling and human language and communication (chapter 4) and what is known about the evolutionary trail, given that we know nothing empirically about the origins of human language because spoken language – and that's all that there was until 3000 BC – leaves no fossil or artifactual record.[1] I try to describe how evolutionary biologists confront issues arising because of the lack of data on developments that must have taken place in communication in hominid species evolutionarily between the great apes and modern *Homo sapiens*.[2]

Since we don't have empirical data on the origins of human language, we look at the behavior of human infants to discover its similarities to and differences from the signaling behavior of other living animal species. We compare infants' behavior with their mothers to that of animals as pets or experimental subjects with their human keepers. There is continuity here, too. Infants become conditioned in the same way as pets. But, on the basis of my research and that of others, I conclude that it is not only the infants who become conditioned; competent language users respond to language-acquiring humans, in part, instinctively rather than intentionally, providing linguistic input appropriate to the infant's stage of language development. As language use has survival value for the human species, fostering its development in the young is a good candidate for being an instinctive behavior. It is like mothers finding their own babies the most lovable and attractive.

We see in chapter 6, "The One-word Period," that as infants become language users their linguistic capacity diverges radically from that of chimpanzees, who have been seen for some 25 years as the most promising species, other than *Homo sapiens,* for being able to acquire language. In chapter 7, we focus on the syntactic system, grounded in the biology of *Homo sapiens.* This is the part of language that is most probably innately based. Current theory is that blueprints for the four types of syntactic system known to exist in the world's languages are innately given. From attending to the language he or she hears, the infant is able to pick the relevant blueprint and acquire that syntactic system.

Chapter 8 takes up the communication skills of young children. All language use which is not the result of innate knowledge is learned and it is learned at the same time as the child's linguistic system is developing. Actually, some learned language-use behaviors begin to appear before the child's syntactic system. Some conversational rules – one person at a time and both get turns and that rising intonation at the end of an utterance signals that the conversation has not finished – are learned before the infant has spoken a word. Children learn how to communicate like mothers and fathers, the parental register, when they are about 4 years old. You can hear them in the doll corner in their nursery school "playing house." "I'll be the mother," says one. "I'll be the father," says another, speaking in a deep voice. They give evidence of their developing secondary consciousness or "theory of mind" as it has come to be called by cognitive developmental psychologists. Children by the age of 4 become capable of "pretend" play, acting out being firemen or doctors. They become able to intentionally deceive, the behavior which we would accept, if it were conclusively demonstrated, as proving that a non-human animal species had secondary consciousness.

Chapter 9 is about semantic development. If syntax is the skeleton of language, semantics is its flesh and blood. Language is living, organic.

We can analyze a discourse and describe both its syntax and its semantic characteristics. Semantic development begins as soon as the child starts to use words intentionally to give names to objects, actions, and qualities like "hot" and "sharp" in order to think or communicate about them. Semantic development is a many-faceted jewel of a topic, and I have selected a few facets to consider in order to provide more detailed descriptions. Chapter 9 begins with a consideration of vocabulary acquisition. Our impressively large vocabularies were not acquired by looking words up in dictionaries. How did it happen?

It happened as part of our life experience. In our minds, the words we know become organized, grouped. They are not a chronological or alphabetical or random list. Analysis of the several bases for organization and categorizing of words in our minds occupies much of the chapter. One comparison is between natural categories and scientific categories. Natural categories arise from our attempts to understand our everyday experience; scientific categories arise when our natural categories mislead us, for example, into categorizing whales as fish when it matters for our understanding of the world to know that whales are mammals.

Children's semantic development is constrained by their cognitive development so that their early verbal concepts may not match the adult's. We will take a brief look at the difficult – for children – concept of time past. Children's use and understanding of metaphor can be better explained today than in the 1980s and this is our next topic. Finally, we look at event memory and the development of scripts and autobiographical memory as organizers of contents of the mind. We see that researchers have found that animals are capable of generic memory but only human beings, because they have secondary consciousness, have autobiographical memory, the memory of specific episodes involving oneself.

Chapter 10 is about reading. We start by considering beginning reading and writing, two activities related through phonological awareness. Treating reading and writing as aspects of acquiring literacy rather than as discrete skills – the whole language approach – is touched on. The research that explains why 3- and 4-year-olds who are familiar with nursery rhymes experience early success in learning to read is the next topic in chapter 10, followed by the information-processing model of reading, which seems to me the most illuminating. This leads naturally into the problems that deaf children encounter in becoming English literate, and the similarity of ASL and logographic writing systems like Chinese. The chapter ends with a brief mention of some developments in our understanding based on research over the past two decades.

Chapter 11, on bilingualism and second-language learning, treats topics that are becoming of great interest because of conditions in the world at large, but pressingly in the United States with the possibility of the US becoming an English–Spanish bilingual nation, resulting from changes in US immigration laws since 1965 and as many as 300,000 undocumented persons attempting to settle in the US each year, most of them non-English speaking. These topics raise social and political issues that are not usually the subject of books such as this. Chapter 11 discusses these issues but no basis for settling them is discovered.

I conclude this book with a chapter on sociolinguistics, how society's construction of social reality is reflected in language use. The chapter begins with the Whorfian hypothesis that language patterns reality so that people can perceive only what language reveals, and the work of Eleanor Rosch that, in my opinion, led to the abandonment of the hypothesis by most. Next, culturally determined bases for categorizing objects, entities, and natural phenomena are briefly noted. Language use provides a window through which to observe the values of a society, and we will take a look. Proverbs, metaphors, and acceptably polite questions in various languages highlight cultural similarities and differences among speech communities. Whether a society has more formal or informal relations among its members is reflected in terms of address, personal pronouns, and politeness markers. Most human societies have a class structure with class membership depending on education, occupation, and ancestry. We will look at the effects of class on language use.

Next, we consider sex as a sociolinguistic variable, a topic receiving much attention as part of the development of the feminist movement. Finally, we take a look at language as the basis for ethnic stereotyping, unfortunately a problem in the 1990s in many countries of the world.

Suggested Reading

The topics discussed in this book are a selection from a range of possibilities. I have picked ideas and research which seem particularly interesting or important to me and I cannot claim to have presented a definitive and exhaustive analysis of any. I therefore conclude each of the following chapters with suggestions for further reading. I also urge readers interested in particular topics to read the books and articles that I have cited in text. Readers with an interest in my research are invited to write to me for data, protocols, and analyses.

Notes

1   Sumerian is seen by archeologists as leaving the earliest written record, closely followed by Egyptian (Professor Peter Reid, Tufts University, personal communications).
2   When I visited Lascaux in France, I noticed that in the paintings on the walls of the cave, in addition to the magnificent depictions of animals done 17,000 years ago, there were squiggles of black paint. Could this be writing?

2
Signal Systems of Animals in the Wild

Why does a book about the development of human language start with a consideration of animals in the wild? It has been thought that human language as it exists today – English, Chinese, Arabic, Turkish, and the many other tongues familiar and unfamiliar to us in the West – must have evolved from some more primitive human language. This more primitive human language, people have reasoned, would be like the signal systems of the other animal species with which this chapter is concerned. Hundreds of human languages have now been studied. Many having a spoken but not a written form have been investigated, including the languages of human societies which have extremely primitive technologies. But nowhere has a human society been found, no matter how primitive its technology, that does not have a developed spoken language based on the principle of combining words or their equivalents according to grammatical rules to form sentences or their equivalents.

The beginnings of human language are lost to us, as far as we know, because there were no written languages until fairly recently in human history. When a human society with a spoken language but not a written one dies out, its language dies with it. When I lived in Seattle, Washington, I knew anthropologists from the University of Washington who were gathering language samples from elderly informants, members of Northwest Indian tribes on the verge of extinction. The anthropologists were hurrying to tape-record the spoken languages before it was too late, before the last remaining speakers of the language died.

Even though it is not possible to investigate the continuity of human language and the signaling systems of the lower animals via a primitive human language, the relationship between animal signals and human language can still be examined. The reason it is of significant interest to me, a psycholinguist, is my conviction that our capacity for language use is the keystone of our human (as distinct from our animal) natures. Out of this conviction comes the curiosity to find out what lines of continuity with other animals' signals can be discovered. Human beings are the result of Darwinian evolution. To what extent can the evolutionary trail from animal signal systems and signaling to human language and communication be discovered?

Jane Goodall (1971) has written a book about chimpanzees she observed living in the wild in Africa. She called this book *In the Shadow of Man* which reflects her conviction that chimpanzees are next in the evolutionary line to humans. She discovered tool use and tool-making behaviors, information-transmitting behaviors, and even carnivorous behaviors on the part of chimpanzees analogous to human behavior.

There are similarities between human and animal behavior that touch and impress us all. Everyone knows of instances of courage, devotion to offspring, and cleverness on the part of animals. We are impressed by the amazing things that circus animals can be taught to do. And, yet, the reason the dog that can ride a bicycle or the horse that seems to count impresses us is that we are aware of the vast differences between animal culture and human culture – culture being understood here as intellectual and artistic activity and products.

The ability to use language to communicate is a crucial, maybe *the* crucial, element in human culture. Language use is a powerful and efficient means to share and store information. Although much information can be shared by word of mouth and stored in memory, the development of written language has made it possible to transcend barriers of space and time in transmitting information. In order to think about the relationship of human language use to animal signal systems we need to consider animal signals as a means of information transmission and storage in comparison to human languages. We also need to see what can be learned about animal species signaling as compared to human beings communicating.

Signaling and Communicating

Until now, I have avoided using the word *communication* in talking about the sharing or transmitting of information by animals. I want to be able to preserve the distinction made by J. C. Marshall (1970) between *informative behavior* and *communicative behavior*. My frequently spilling my glass of water at the dinner table would inform others of the fact that I am clumsy. But unless I *intended* my action to inform, it is not communicative behavior. Current research indicates that the signaling behavior of animals in the wild is informative but not communicative. The alarm cry of the sparrow emitted as a hawk flies overhead causes other birds and animals that fall prey to marauding birds to flee or seek cover. The flight behavior is part of an innate coordination, the stimulus for which is the alarm cry. But the alarm cry is not an intentional warning like "watch out" uttered by one boy to the other boys in the street as he sees the neighborhood bully coming round the corner.

Instead, the alarm cry of the sparrow is also part of an innate coordination; in this case, the cry is in response to an environmental stimulus. The sight of the hawk causes a sensation of fright in the sparrow, which always results in the sparrow's emitting an alarm cry. Human beings also have innate coordinations of this sort. If someone were to sneak up behind you and jab you with a pin, you would emit a noise of discomfort. The noise would be involuntary, caused by the unexpected painful jab. Anyone within earshot would be informed that you had been hurt, even though your cry was not intended. In terms of the definitions of this chapter, your cry would be informative but not intentional and therefore not communicative.

Most human vocalizations are intended, but animal signals – chemical, vocal, and visual – are involuntary, part of an innate coordination. The animal cannot help emitting the signal. It is caused by the sensation in the animal evoked by the external stimulus. A secondary ground for accepting the innate coordination explanation for the sparrow's alarm cry, rather than an explanation based on the sparrow's intending to warn other birds, stems from Lloyd Morgan's canon of parsimony. This is the principle that one should attribute to an organism no more intelligence, consciousness, or rationality than will suffice to account for its behavior.

It is Lloyd Morgan's canon that tips the scale because we cannot get inside the heads of animals to ascertain whether a behavior is voluntary. The deceptive behavior of the bob white, dragging her wing as if it were broken to get a predator to go after her and away from the chicks in the nest, is an instinctive response to the sight of the predator. It is accepted that this behavior is adaptive for the species and is the result of natural selection.

The Sign Stimulus

Following Tinbergen (1951), cited by Marshall (1970), ethologists have distinguished informative exchanges among members of animal species from other regular behavior patterns by means of the sign stimulus concept. A sign stimulus is part of an animal's appearance or behavioral repertoire, which includes vocalizations, that reliably elicits a particular type of response from another animal of the same species. The primary function of sign stimuli is to elicit behavior that ensures the continuation of the species. Sign stimuli have evolved, then, as specific releasers of adaptive behavior patterns. The theory is that species with innate signaling coordinations in their repertoires, which serve to ensure continuation of the species in its environment of biological adaptation, have greater survival potential than other species. Evidence for the theory comes from demonstrating in a range of cases what the sign stimulus is. This involves presenting, by itself, the behavior or part of the animal's appearance that is the sign stimulus candidate to see if it will evoke the expected, adaptive response. The technique has been successfully exploited by Tinbergen, Lorenz, Ohreson, Marler, and many others in isolating sign stimuli for adaptive responses in insects, fish, birds, and mammals (Marshall, 1970).

Playing the sparrow's alarm cry on a remote-controlled tape-recorder near an area where sparrows are feeding is an example of the technique. If the recorded cry causes the sparrows to fly away (the adaptive response), then the alarm cry is a sign stimulus. This procedure does not prove that the sparrow, when it gives the alarm cry, does not intend to warn the other sparrows. But making the assumption that the alarm cry is a specific releaser, or an innate, involuntary behavior, places the burden of proof on those who claim that the informative behaviors of animals in the wild are intentional. The best way to prove that informative behavior on the part of animals is intentional would be to demonstrate an intention to misinform, in other words, to present examples of animals lying. Thus far, no scientifically acceptable evidence of animals in the wild intentionally misinforming other animals has been produced. However, scientists continue to report findings of deceptive behavior – in fireflies, birds in the rain forests of Peru, and chimpanzees in Africa, for example – and it is possible that there will be sufficient irrefutable evidence of intentional rather than instinctive deceptive behavior to change our understanding of animal signaling.

Although I say that animals don't lie, I am always being given examples of misinforming behavior on the part of people's pets or animals seen in zoos. Actually, I used to attribute an intention to misinform to the dogs in our neighborhood who, in play with other dogs, growl, chase, and jump on each other. They are pretending aggressive behavior, and this seems like a possible intentional behavior. One prominent piece of behavior I had observed in these pretend fights is a little jump, ending with the dog crouched on its forelegs and standing on its hind legs. It turns out that this is called a "playbow" and evidence for its "evolution as a stereotyped mammalian display" has been reported (Berkoff, 1977). It is a sign stimulus signaling that what follows is play. It is highly stereotyped behavior that has been observed in infant coyotes, infant wolves, infant wolf–malamute hybrids, and domestic dogs. There are no important differences in bows performed by pups of different ages and the first bows performed by pups who have been hand-reared and have never interacted with another animal or seen a bow. The playbow fulfills the requirements for a sign stimulus, making it possible for canines to play at aggression. We do not know why such play is adaptive behavior for coyotes, wolves, and dogs. It is clear that playing is more adaptive than real fighting, but the function of interaction among animals of the same species for other than mating, hunting, or other survival-serving behaviors is not clear.

Ritualization

A signal or sign stimulus indicating that an animal's behavior is sexual rather than aggressive is certainly adaptive. The displays that signal sexual readiness must be quite clear so that they do not signal aggressiveness. The concept of ritualization, originated by Julian Huxley, is used to explain the evolution of displays that are clear indicators of sexual readiness to species members, even though difficult for human investigators to interpret. E. O. Wilson (1972) has described the ritualization of a dance fly's courtship behavior. Dance flies are carnivorous species classified together as the family, *Empididae*. Many of the species engage in a courtship in which the male makes a simple approach to the female after which copulation takes place. Among other species, the male first captures an insect and presents it to the female before copulation. This appears to reduce the chance that the female will eat the male instead of copulating with it. In still other species, the male attaches threads of silk to the insect he is presenting to the female. This makes his offering more distinctive in appearance, a step toward ritualization. Further steps can be observed in other dance flies. In one species, the male wraps his offering in a silk sheet. In another, the size of the insect presented to the female is reduced, but the wrapping is such that it does not appear to be partially empty. The male of another species does not bother to catch an insect and presents an empty silken wrapping to the female. This last behavior would be very hard for scientists to interpret if the other species of the dance fly did not exist so that the ritualization of the male's behavior could be observed.

Chemical Signals

Chemical signals called pheromones are involved in the social behavior of many animals. Anyone who has had a dog for a pet is aware of the importance of pheromones (smells) in the social life of the dog. E. O. Wilson has demonstrated that the social life of insects is mediated largely by pheromones. He studied a type of ant whose behavior evoked a feeling of fellowship in entomologists (persons who study insects). Those ants bury their dead. They do not exactly bury, but they carry dead ants to a spot somewhat removed from the ant hill. Wilson was able to demonstrate that the sign stimulus for the burying behavior was a pheromone given off by dead ants. He smeared a lively ant with the candidate pheromone and, shortly after, two ants picked up the lively ant and carried it to the burial spot. They put the lively ant down, and it promptly returned to the ant hill and was again picked up and taken to the burial spot. This time, when it returned to the ant hill, it was ignored. The pheromone odor had disappeared. Ants use pheromones to leave a trail of scent when returning from a food source to their hill. Other ants in the hill are attracted by the odor and follow the trail back to the food source. Pheromones lose

Figure 2.1 Stages of aggressive display in the rhesus monkey and green heron (redrawn from E. O. Wilson, "Animal communication." Copyright © 1972 by Scientific American Inc. All rights reserved)

their potency after a short time, so the trail to an exhausted food source disappears; more generally, the air is cleared so that new chemical information can appear and not be confused with old information.

Intensity

It has been shown in the green heron and the rhesus monkey that the stronger the aggressive display, the more probable it is that the opponent will retreat. Three stages of increasing aggressiveness for the rhesus monkey and green heron are shown in figure 2.1. This increase in signal intensity seems analogous to human behavior. The misbehaving child may sense how likely it is that an irate parent is going to resort to spanking by the loudness of the parent's scolding. The child has become conditioned to loudness of voice as an indicator of how angry the parent is. Some people may get quieter as they get angry, but this occurs only when the expression of anger is under voluntary control. In animals, the strength of the aggressive display depends only on the intensity of the sign stimulus and the consequent state aroused in the animal making the display. The likelihood of a flight response by a species member depends on the intensity of the display of the animal making the display.

Signals vary not only in intensity but also in the type of information conveyed. We have considered signals that indicate an aggressive state, sexual readiness, or alarm on the part of the signaler. Recent research of Robert Seyforth and Barbara Cheney described by Diamond (1992) demonstrates that vervet monkeys have different alarm calls signaling the presence of eagles, lions, and snakes. Diamond refers to these calls as words, the names of the three animals. Students of human language acquisition would not agree. A word is an abstract symbol, used in many different ways. The three calls are just alarm calls. They are never heard except as an involuntary response accompanying the monkey's fright.

Contextual Sources of Information and Responses to Signals

If the information in a signal is inadequate to determine a response, the animal receiving the signal instinctively makes use of contextual information to respond. For example, in conflicts between great skuas, various postures and movements are elements of the signal, in addition to the call. If the signaling bird is not facing its antagonist, the antagonist does not get enough information to be able to escape if need be, and the distance between signaler and recipient, a contextual variable, accounts for whether the antagonist will flee (Leger, 1992). Leger defines context as "the set of events, conditions, and changeable recipient characteristics that modify the effect of a signal on recipient's behavior" (Leger, 1992: 296). Habituation is a well-studied form of contextual effect. Playbacks of a recorded call or song have been used to study response, and repeated playbacks have demonstrated habituation. Recipients cease responding to a call that is repeated. To avoid habituation, experimenters impose long delays between playbacks of a call or song whose effect on recipients is being studied.

How Many Signals?

As the number of studies of animal species in the wild increases, there will undoubtedly be changes in the estimated number of signals different animal species possess. There may well be differences in the way signals are defined. For example, green herons and rhesus monkeys each have three gradations of their aggressive displays. Shall we say that each species has an aggressive display with three gradations or that each species has three different aggressive displays? The decision will influence the number of signals the species is reported to have. However, the important differences between the signal systems of animals in the wild and human language do not rest on whether the animal species with the largest known number of signals has 36, as reported by Wilson (1972) for the rhesus monkey, or 343, the number of intermediate, graded calls of the chimpanzee which Marler (1976), cited by Bonner (1980), has grouped into 13 categories of vocalizations.

In chapter 3, the signaling behavior of vertebrate animals as experimental animals in contact with human beings will be examined, along with evidence that the signaling repertoires of vertebrate animals can be vastly increased. The important differences, however, are that animal signals are innate, involuntary, and limited in number, while human language use is learned, intentional, and comprised of an infinite number of messages. More will be said on this topic in the course of the book.

The Effect of Female Behavior on Male Cowbird Song

In the past few years we have begun to see research that challenges our ideas about the strictly stereotypical nature of the stimulus–response coordination in animal signaling. In addition to the role of context in determining the response to a signal, signals, particularly bird song, are being seen as not totally stereotyped. The male cowbird song – only male birds sing – is influenced by female response. Females don't sing, but signal by visual display, a wing stroke elicited by specific vocalizations. The wing strokes elicit copulatory behavior by the male (West and King, 1988).

It can be said that the female has a tutorial role in the development of the male cowbird's song. Male cowbirds housed with non-singing female cowbirds made vocal changes which related directly to female preferences signaled by wing stroke. The wing stroke resembles the initial wing movement of a copulating posture, and it occurs very rapidly while the male's one-second song is still in progress. The evidence that the wing stroke indeed signals the female's readiness to copulate was obtained the following spring when the experimenters played back the versions of the song that had elicited wing strokes in six females who had been in the experiment relating wing strokes to vocal changes in the male's song and to two additional females. These were interspersed with versions that had not elicited wing strokes, but only wing stroke songs produced consistently high levels of copulatory responses. Wing strokes were clearly conspicuous to males and they immediately made use of the information in the females' displays to produce songs that induce copulatory behavior in females.

Although we have accepted, for many years, that human beings can teach animals to carry out activities foreign to their life in the wild, it is only recently that researchers have provided impeccable studies that give evidence of play in the stimulus–response coordinations of animals in the wild.

Further Reading

Diamond, J. (1992) *The Third Chimpanzee* (New York: Harper Collins).
  Diamond is interested in the evolutionary trail. I found chapters 1, 2, 8, and 9 important and interesting.
Goodall, J. (1971) *In the Shadow of Man* (Boston: Houghton Mifflin).
  Goodall spent many years observing chimpanzees, how their society was organized, how it functioned and how family (mother and offspring) relationships developed.

3

Animals in Contact with People

Clever Hans was a horse which stamped his hoof the correct number of times when his master said a number (Pfungst, 1911). Hans and his master went about the German countryside early in the century demonstrating Clever Hans' ability to count. This was not an act of charlatanism because Hans' master believed Hans could indeed count. Eventually it was demonstrated that Hans could count only if his master performed with him and only if Hans could see his master. Hans was actually stamping his hoof as long as his master maintained a tense stance. When Hans got to the correct number of stamps, his master unconsciously would relax a bit and take a breath; Hans would respond by ceasing to stamp. Hans' clever behavior is understood as a result of conditioning. The positive reinforcement came from the affectionate approval, including lumps of sugar perhaps, given to Hans by his master when Hans was successful.

I begin this chapter with Hans because his case can serve as the example against which to evaluate instances of information exchange between human beings and experimental animals or pets. One fact in the case of Clever Hans that gives it particular relevance to naturalistic development of communication and the topic of this book is that Hans' master did not realize that he was conditioning Hans' behavior; he thought he was teaching Hans to count.

Hoover, a harbor seal brought to the New England Aquarium in Boston in 1971, talked in a friendly, raspy voice with the As of New England. He pronounced his name "Hoovah." He said, "Come ovuh heah," and "Hello dere." He talked only when he wanted to, most often in the spring. The Aquarium kept records that documented Hoover's behavior following his arrival as a 4-month-old pup. On November 12, 1978, seven years later, he said "Hoover" in his New England dialect. Animal trainers at the Aquarium were sure Hoover did not know what he was saying and could not figure out what function his talking served.

Then, in 1984, George and Alice Swallow of Cundys Harbor, Maine, visited Hoover at the Aquarium. The Swallows had taken care of Hoover, a very young seal, for almost 4 months after his mother was shot by a fisherman. They put him in their bathtub and when he refused a bottle, ground up a mackerel in a food grinder and force-fed him. After a day he began to eat like a vacuum cleaner so they called him Hoover. He was a great pet. Neighborhood children liked to take him riding in a wheelbarrow. When he outgrew the bathtub, the Swallows put Hoover in a freshwater pond behind their house. Mr Swallow never tried to teach Hoover to talk or rewarded him with fish for any behavior he displayed, but he said he had hollered at Hoover a lot, "Come over here!" "Get out a here!" Every evening when he got home, Mr Swallow would get out of his car, hit his hand hard against the side and yell, "Hey, stupid!" Hoover would climb out of the pond and waddle up to Mr Swallow, who would say, "Hello, there." One day, Hoover made a noise that sounded like "Hello dere." A few days later, Mr Swallow said, "Some kids told me my seal kept saying hello to them." After a while, Mr Swallow could ask Hoover his name and he would say, "Hoover." The Swallows regretfully gave Hoover to the Aquarium because he had begun eating more fish than they could afford.

When the Swallows came to visit Hoover at the Aquarium, Mr Swallow yelled, "Hey, stupid," and Hoover came over and took Mr Swallow's hand in his mouth and tried to pull him into the seal pool. Hoover sounded exactly like Mr Swallow except, when he said "Hoover," he sounded more like the daughter of a neighbor who used to hang around the Swallow's house and tell Hoover what his name was.

According to Dr Bruce Moore, a Canadian psychologist interested in mimetic behavior, interviewed at the Aquarium, Hoover's behavior is like that of mimetic birds who imprint themselves on human speech. They imprint themselves on the way the voice sounds as well as the words. The ethologist Konrad Lorenz (1970) was able to get goslings to imprint themselves on him rather than a parental goose by being the first animate being they saw moving after they were born. They lined up and followed him as her ducklings followed Mrs Mallard in Robert McCloskey's *Make Way for Ducklings* (1941). According to Lorenz, imprinting must take place within 48 hours of an animal's birth. After this period, animals will flee rather than follow. Imprinting would be adaptive in the wild where it is most probable that the first animate being a newborn bird or animal will see is a parent, unless the baby is a turtle or some other animal whose mother lays a clutch of eggs and leaves them never to return.

Imprinting is an instinctive response to a stimulus, the sight, sound, smell of it. Lorenz thought size, shape, and movement were crucial to the goslings imprinting on him. The adaptive function connects juveniles with care-giving adults of their species. At the Catskill Game Farm in New York animals are bred for zoos, and species are raised in proximity to species they would not encounter in the wild. On a visit, I watched a peacock spread his beautiful fan of a tail, a courtship gesture, in front of a prairie dog sitting on its haunches. I concluded that the peacock, when it was newly hatched, had imprinted on a prairie dog neighbor and had grown up mistaken in its species identity.

Imprinting is a non-intentional, infant response, functional in inducing contact with and care-giving from adults where offspring are hatched from eggs and therefore not in immediate and prolonged contact with their mothers as are land-dwelling mammals. Conditioned responses are also non-intentional; they are governed by positive and negative reinforcement, pleasure and pain. I assume that, for the most part, responses that result in positive reinforcement and that avoid negative reinforcement are the outcome of evolutionary selection and contribute to survival of the species as does imprinting.

Conditioning versus Intentionality

I said above that Clever Hans' behavior was conditioned behavior. Conditioning is the means by which the signaling repertoire of animals is increased when they are in contact with people. Conditioning is also the means by which the innate signaling repertoires of human infants are increased. It is a learning process in which what is learned is the connection between a signal, behavior, and pleasant or unpleasant consequences called positive and negative reinforcement. For Clever Hans, the signal was his master's relaxing a bit and taking a breath;

the behavior was Hans' ceasing his stamping; and the pleasant consequences were his master's affectionate approval and the sugar lump. Conditioned behavior is not intentional. Hans did not think to himself when his master drew a breath, "time to stop stamping because Master has relaxed, and if I stop he'll love me and give me a sugar lump." Instead, the conditioned response, the behavior, comes to be elicited by the signal because of the connection between the signal and pleasant consequences. The conditioned response is a coordination between signal and response like the innate coordinations of signal–response of animals in the wild.

In the case of both positive and negative reinforcement, the subject being conditioned has to engage in the behavior before it can be positively or negatively reinforced. When a subject is being conditioned with positive reinforcement, each time the subject produces the behavior the trainer rewards it. Since people and animals seek rewards, the rewarded behavior will become more frequent so that it becomes a habit in the kind of circumstances in which it was conditioned. Actually, the behavior does not have to be rewarded every time it is produced, just often enough that the subject being conditioned will keep trying for the reward.

In the case of conditioning with negative reinforcement, like spankings, the aim is to eliminate a misbehavior on the subject's part. If the child or pet had not been producing the misbehavior there would not be any reason for the negative reinforcement. I will use the example of a child stopping a misbehavior to avoid a spanking. The loudness of a parent's voice directing the child to stop is the signal. The negative reinforcement (spanking) has been paired a few times with the signal (loudness of voice) following the misbehavior, and subsequently hearing the signal is enough to cause the child to inhibit the behavior, avoiding the unpleasant consequence.

Conditioning is non-intentional learning. It cannot be proved that a particular response is produced by a person as the result of conditioning rather than intentionally. What we do, rather, is to look at the subject's past history which perhaps contains an account of the experience which led to the conditioning, as with Clever Hans. We also investigate the limitations of the subject's ability to produce the behavior in circumstances other than the ones in which it might have been conditioned, again as with Hans, and finally we invoke Lloyd Morgan's canon (see chapter 2). Conditioning is a learning process requiring less in the way of higher mental processes than intentional learning. So it will be the explanation preferred to intentional learning in instances in which conditioning will account for acquisition of a new response by a subject.

Pets

When our cat, Lucy, stands in front of the refrigerator and meows, I give her something to eat; when she stands in front of the door and meows, I let her out. She has been conditioned to produce these behaviors, meowing in particular locations, because I have correctly responded, thereby providing positive reinforcement. This happened in the natural course of events. I did not set out to condition Lucy to emit these informative behaviors. It might be said on Lucy's behalf that she probably did not set out to condition me either, but I do respond correctly to her signals. I am not sure how I became conditioned. I did not notice it happening. As I think about it, I realize that I avoid negative reinforcement. By letting her out when she meows at the front door, I avoid having to clean out the cat box, or clean up an even worse mess. The positive reinforcement for feeding her after she meows at the refrigerator must come from the fulfillment of a care-giving impulse. I do not know whether she has attempted to elicit other behaviors from me by vocalizing. If she has, I have not understood, and she has ceased trying.

In chapter 2, I distinguished between communicative behavior, which is intentional, and signaling, which is an involuntary response elicited by a stimulus such as a particular smell or seeing a predator. Where does the kind of conditioned signaling behavior that Lucy displays belong? Once again, it cannot be proved that the behavior is not intentional, but the explanation that assumes the least in the way of higher mental processes on Lucy's part says that conditioned signaling behavior is like innate animal signals; it is unintentional and is the result of having become conditioned to an internal sensation through positive reinforcement. Lucy's meowing in front of the refrigerator is a conditioned response to the internal sensation of hunger, acquired because food has been given her, reliably, when she has meowed in front of the refrigerator.

It is more difficult for me to make the assumption that her meowing at the front door is nothing but a conditioned response. In my thinking, Lucy's wanting to go out is associated with her being housebroken, but Lucy also uses a cat box in the house. The signaling behavior of animals in the wild is a simple response behavior. The animal has only one possible response to a stimulus. The sparrow that gives the alarm cry also flies off, but these are parts of the same response. The sparrow does not fly away occasionally without giving the alarm cry, or give cry and not fly away. However, Lucy sometimes meows at the front door and at other times uses the cat box. She has two possible responses to the sensation. Which response she makes could reflect conditioning to particular temperatures. Perhaps this is the case as I have noticed that she meows at the front door only in the warm months of the year and does not step out of the house between the end of October and the beginning of May.

Maybe I am wrong about the internal sensation that elicits Lucy's meowing at the front door. All I know is that she meows at the front door, and I let her out. If I were to watch her each time she goes out to see what she does, I would be able to check the hypothesis that her meowing to get out is a response to her being housebroken. I have not watched, so what I have is a plausible but unconfirmed hypothesis. Lucy's meow at the door could be the response to various internal sensations such as a sexual urge or the urge to hunt. Both of these urges can be satisfied outdoors but not in the house. In order to settle the question in a way that would be entirely satisfactory to the empirical scientist, I would have to observe Lucy's behavior after she gets out of the house a sufficient number of times to see what her habitual patterns of behavior are. But finding that Lucy's meowing at the door is her response to several different internal sensations rather than just one would still leave unresolved the question of the intentionality of her meow at the door. Her behavior is consistent with both the explanation that it is conditioned and that it is intentional. The conditioning explanation makes less of an assumption of higher mental processes on Lucy's part; therefore, I will stand by the conditioning explanation.

The question of intentionality versus conditioning as the explanation for a behavior is important because intentionality is a defining characteristic of human language use. One claim that fond pet owners frequently make is that their pets understand what they say. I have an English friend who says to her dog, "Die for the Queen," whereupon the dog rolls over on its back with its feet in the air, the appropriate response. This anecdote is useful in helping people to take an objective view of pets' understanding of language. Few would claim that my friend's dog hears the sentence, "Die for the Queen," figures out what it implies for his behavior and acts accordingly. Once the question is raised as to what the dog is responding to and how he learned his response, it can be seen that the utterance has signal properties to which the dog is responding. The utterance has to have a particular sound pattern; try "Die for the Queen" first as a command then as a question, and note the different pitch patterns. For the command, pitch falls at the end of the utterance. For the question, pitch rises. Pitch pattern is one of the variables distinguishing different signals that trainers use with animals. Another is the length of the signal. "Heel!" and "Die for the Queen!" differ in length. Another very important part of the signal is the trainer's accompanying gesture or bodily movement. Animals probably do respond to actual word differences. Dogs can differentiate "Down" from "Heel." However, the difference in the trainer's accompanying gesture may be more significant than the sound difference.

Experimental Animals

When human beings interact with experimental animals, the situation is like the interaction of trainers and pets. The human experimenter aims to teach the experimental animal(s). Over the years there has been controversy among animal behavior research psychologists about what animals have learned in animal-learning experiments. Here again, the behavioral scientist will abide by Lloyd Morgan's canon and interpret the animal's learning in a way that assumes the least intelligence necessary to account for the animal's behavior, as I did, for example, in interpreting the dog's response to "Die for the Queen." Experimental psychologists have taught rats to run mazes, cats to open doors, and many other kinds of animal to produce many other kinds of behavior. These experiments are investigations of the learning abilities of species members.

The other, and perhaps more basic, question is what are the species members born already knowing? A prominent psychologist said not long ago that we, that is members of the species *Homo sapiens*, are born knowing everything we'll ever know except the facts. This is an extreme nativist position and contrasts diametrically with the empiricist idea that purpose, strong effort, and practice make it possible for most human beings to learn widely and well, acquiring knowledge and skills. The nativist says contact with the world serves a priming function, clueing the human being to what he or she innately knows.

Richard Herrnstein began his scientific career influenced by the work of B. F. Skinner, committed to conditioning as the paradigm of learning. He continues to use the Skinnerian vocabulary – stimulus, response, generalization gradient, and so on – and the conditioning paradigm to investigate innate knowledge in his preferred research subject, the pigeon.

All vertebrates are capable of treating different stimulus objects as equivalent. Asking the reader to pick the spoons out of the silverware drawer would be an example of requesting that stimulus objects be treated as equivalent. In order to respond, the reader would also need to be able to differentiate spoons from forks and knives. All vertebrates are capable of differentiation. Species differ in the range of equivalence classes they can form, which is a biological given for a species. The capacity to form equivalence classes is a cognitive ability but not a linguistic ability, and it can be observed in animal species for which no linguistic claims have been made.

Fascinating findings concerning the capacities of pigeons to treat stimulus objects as equivalent are described by Herrnstein et al. (1976). Hernnstein and his fellow researchers were not interested in teaching pigeons to form equivalence classes; rather, they wanted to find out how pigeons naturally, visually, discriminated objects like trees from other objects that from a distance might be mistaken for trees. They wanted to investigate the kind of stimulus objects that the experimenters thought might be equivalent to trees for pigeons but which the pigeons would actually differentiate from trees.

The experimental subjects in this research were 11 male pigeons which had been raised on the seventh floor of Harvard University's behavioral sciences building and had never been outdoors. The stimuli were color slides projected on the front wall of a standard pigeon chamber. The pigeon being tested was conditioned to peck at a key in the presence of positive stimuli, such as a picture of a house with branches of two trees visible, and not to peck in the presence of negative stimuli, such as a vine with many leaves climbing on a cement wall.

Three experiments were carried out; they concerned the pigeon's ability to differentiate pictures of trees from non-trees, naturally lying water from non-water, and one particular person from others. Typical pictures that were correctly classified as trees and non-trees are shown in figure 3.1. The pigeon's striking ability to classify naturally occurring stimulus objects that are significant to its biological adaptation is a cognitive ability, totally separate from the use of language, although sometimes mistaken for a linguistic ability, but an ability, I believe, essential to lexical development (understanding word meanings and relationships of word meanings).

In the course of his or her language development, each human being creates a mental lexicon or dictionary. One category of lexical items (words) comprises nouns which are either proper or common. Proper nouns are names of individual persons, animals, countries, or states, etc. Dick and Jane are usually human names. Jumbo and Secretariat are names of two famous animals and maybe others I do not know about. Common nouns are the names for equivalence classes. People (men, women, boys, girls), animals (fish, monkeys, birds, etc.), places (meadows, mountains, forests, etc.). Cities and countries name equivalence classes where individual members may, like Chicago, have proper names or, like a rock, a pebble, a boulder, not. Notice that rock, pebble, and boulder are themselves class names.

Being able to form equivalence classes or to categorize makes it possible to organize experience adaptively. The equivalence classes or categories, edible and non-edible, are essential to biological adaptation. To survive, a species must have members of these classes innately.

Herrnstein concluded that the equivalence classes he discovered in his pigeons had to be innate since his pigeons had not had experience sufficient to generate them. He has proposed (Herrnstein, 1982, 1990) that sensory systems, including the pigeon's visual system, are an outcome of natural selection. Generalization gradients – what I have called equivalence classes – favor perceiving invariances which pick out significant classes of objects and events in the species environment of biological adaptation, perceiving objects as equivalent even though the sensory stimulation from the stimulus is changing. The leopard, although it becomes a blur of feet and fur as it races toward its prey, is perceived by a gazelle as the same animal sighted standing far away five minutes earlier.

Because the capacity for innate categorization is seen in pigeons and

Figure 3.1
Tree and non-tree slides
(from Herrnstein et al.,
1976)

humans (and all vertebrates) it has substantial biological generality and must be neurophysiologically simple because pigeons have simple brains. It cannot be based on physical dimensions, Herrnstein concludes, because his pigeons were incapable of forming the classes "bottles and non-bottles," and "wheeled vehicles and non-wheeled vehicles." Although his pigeons were able to form the class "slides with a particular woman in the picture," they were unable to do so with cartoons of Charlie Brown which an electronic pattern recognition device could pick out. Herrnstein writes "Categorization is more arbitrary from the point of view of physical measurement and more adaptive from the point of view of biology than biologists and psychologists have thought" (Herrnstein, 1990: 145).

Linguistic Apes

Over the past 30 years, beginning with the research of David Premack (1971), studies of the linguistic abilities of the great apes – chimpanzees, gorillas, and orang-utans – have generated a great deal of work from researchers and attention from linguists, psycholinguists, and psychologists not themselves directly involved in the research. If it were true that apes could be language users like us, we would be able to better understand and investigate evolutionary change and our relationship to other primates. Most of the research that has so fascinated us has been inter-species communication with apes and humans. There are the Gardners and Washoe and other chimpanzees (1971, 1989), the Premacks and Sarah (1971), and the long-running research of the Rumbaughs (see Rumbaugh and Rumbaugh, 1977; Savage-Rumbaugh et al., 1993).

Generally, studies of language development and competence are based on language production: what words and longer utterances subjects can produce. Studies of hearing human beings are based on spoken language. Research with other primates has been based on the production of ASL (American Sign Language) signs or the use of visual symbols for words. Language production data have been preferred to comprehension data because they are more reliable. Subjects' comprehension of language is hard to separate from comprehension based on being part of and observing what is going on. When a young child grabs the cookie mother holds out to her as she says, "Here's a cookie for you," it's hard to know if the child is responding to the mother's words or behavior. The same caveat holds for chimpanzees. The reason researchers want to study comprehension is that comprehension and production of language do not always develop together. It is commonly thought that comprehension precedes production and that comprehension is a better predictor of the course of language development than production because production is affected by variables that do not have anything to do with language development *per se*. My favorite example is the young child who is unwilling to speak until she is sure she is doing it right. She is comprehending, monitoring, and checking her grammatical hypotheses silently until the day she is satisfied with her understanding and begins speaking in sentences.

It would have been a mistake to have concluded during the months when this child was saying nothing that she was not acquiring language. She clearly had been. The challenge to the researcher is to devise language comprehension tasks that are effective and not vitiated by the subject's non-linguistically acquired information. The current research of Savage-Rumbaugh et al. (1993) concerns language comprehension in ape and child. Their interest is in the linguistic abilities of their chimpanzee and child subjects. Human children figure as model examples of linguistic development. Since it is known that human children become competent language users, it is useful to compare development in apes with development in children. To the extent that it can be shown that development in the two species is similar, a case is made that to that extent the language capacity of the apes is the same as that of humans. In papers published in 1979 and 1985, Professor Herbert Terrace concluded that the findings of all animal language research were consistent with the conclusion that apes were capable of associating an object with an arbitrary symbol, a particular plastic chip (the Premack's chimpanzee, Sarah) or an ASL sign (the Gardner's Washoe). The ability to form paired associates is not sufficient for the development of language. Paired associates are linked by reinforcement so that the ape has no flexibility in using the sign or the plastic chip. In order for a being to become a language user, the ASL signs or differently shaped plastic chips have to become abstract symbols, freed from the particular circumstances in which they were initially paired with particular stimulus objects, events or qualities.

1 "Here's your *bottle*." The positive reinforcement from drinking her milk links the baby's bottle and the word.
2 "*Up* you go." Mother says as she lifts the baby out of her crib. Again, positive reinforcement. *Up* is often treated as a verb by very young children.
3 "That's *hot*, don't touch it." The negative reinforcement from touching the hot stove inhibits the infant's approach to the stove and then to other objects and substances mother calls hot. Stimulus generalization gives rise to the equivalence class whose members are labeled *hot*.

Human children just beginning to acquire language form paired associates, words and stimuli paired by reinforcement. But humans, sometimes very rapidly, decontextualize words so that they become abstract symbols no longer restricted to the particular context in which they were acquired (see chapter 6). Recent research findings reported by Savage-Rumbaugh et al. (1993) are interpreted by them to imply that early language acquisition in their four apes and two human subjects proceeded similarly. The young of both species learn how to:

(a) Decode sounds into word units.
(b) Map these word units into real world cause and effect relations.
(c) Reconstruct the rules governing the combinatorial usage of different classes of these word units.
(d) Use these relations and units in a productive manner to change the behavior of others . . . . (Savage-Rumbaugh et al., 1993: 24)

It is (d) that is crucial. Savage-Rumbaugh et al. state that the role of reward in children's acquisition of language has not yet been addressed. They propose that it is possible that language is learned by humans because it is beneficial rather than "something that is a loosely constrained manifestation of genetic programming . . .". In plainer English, language is learned through positive and negative reinforcement in humans as in apes – to the extent that language is learned by apes. The starting point for both species, they state, is the learning of inter-individual routines in which mother and infant participate.

When I was carrying out my research on early language acquisition, I remember thinking that, for the first-born infant whose mother is the principal care-giver, life with mother is like being in a play put on every day. Life conforms to highly predictable routines with mother: feeding, bathing, napping, riding in the baby carriage, occurring daily. Being in a play requires the rote learning of one's lines and actions, attending to the cues from the actions and lines of the other actors. In the mother–baby drama, baby has to look only to mother for cues, and there are many. I would agree with Savage-Rumbaugh et al. that this rote/social-cue supported aspect of language acquisition is not beyond the capacity of apes. But this is only a part of what beginning human language users do. Most importantly, human infants are interested in learning the names of objects, actions, and people, in the absence of wanting the object, itself, as Helen Keller poignantly recalls in her autobiography and has also been reported time and again in the language acquisition literature. Long before young children can produce a grammatical question like "What's this?," "Dis?" or "Dat?" said by the beginning English speaker sometimes turns out to be a request for information – the object's name – rather than the object itself. The evidence is that, for example, when the mother looks in the direction in which the child (Carol) is pointing as she says "Dis," and replies, "This is curtains," Carol is content. When the child wants the object, not just the name, she will continue asking for it.

What Savage-Rumbaugh et al. (1993) report about language comprehension by ape and child is only part of the story for humans. Instrumental learning through reinforcement, conditioning, or by rote memorization – the monkey see, monkey do kind of learning – is certainly part of the development of human language use. The nouns we use to name objects, people, and actions are for the most part arbitrary and learned by imitation. *Chaise* (French) and *chair* (English), *mesa* (Spanish) and *table* (English) are pairs which label the same object in different languages.

There are some rules for converting words in one syntactic category into another, like adding "ly" to the adjective to form the adverb. For example, sincere becomes sincerely; kind, kindly; slow, slowly. There are always exceptions. Kindness is the noun form for kind, and slowness for slow, but sincerity for sincere. There is no rule-governed relationship between word and meaning, so it must be learned by rote.

To me, the most telling comparison of language development of Kanzi, Savage-Rambaugh's bonobo ape, and Alia, the human child, her main research subjects, is the course of their mean length of utterance over the experimental period, nine months for Kanzi, six months for Alia. Alia's MLU (mean length of utterance) increased from 1.91 to 3.19. Kanzi's remained at 1.5. MLU is a measure of production rather than comprehension. I am convinced that infant early language development depends on either comprehension of the speech the infant hears or ASL, the signs she sees used meaningfully. But without samples of syntactically developed, productive language use it is not possible to rule out explanations for comprehension based on conditioning, rote learning, and contextual information. Over nine months in his ninth year, Kanzi's MLU remained constant at 1.5, even though he had heard language being used from the age of six months, while Alia's MLU increased from 1.91 to 3.19 over six months from her 19th to her 25th month. The research of Savage-Rumbaugh et al. provides evidence of the evolutionary path from bonobo to human in the development of language. Kanzi appears to have some comprehension of word order as a grammatical marker and of the ostensive meaning of nouns and verbs. He is not always accurate in carrying out the behaviors indicated by the experimenter, but neither is Alia. Many of the behaviors can be accurately carried out by Kanzi and Alia without their complete understanding of the experimenter's utterance. Requests that begin with "Can you" like "Can you put the blanket on the doggy?" are scored correct if Kanzi or Alia puts the blanket on the dog. In ordinary discourse, "Can you" functions either as a politeness marker (see chapter 12) or as a beginning of a request for information, "Can you give me a ride tomorrow," "Can you go fishing tomorrow?" If the "Can you?" sentence is a polite request for action from the hearer, she does not need to understand "Can you?" to correctly carry out the behavior.

Another reservation I have regarding Savage-Rumbaugh et al.'s interpretation of experimental results concerns scoring. For example, one of the experimenter's directives to Kanzi (1993: 160) is "Take your ball to the hammock." Kanzi picked up his ball and went to the other keyboard (the utterances are written in a symbol system called lexagrams on a keyboard). The experimenter said "To the hammock." Kanzi put his ball in the microwave. Error correction by the experimenter: the door of the microwave opened and Kanzi is shown what to do. We are not informed if he did so. Kanzi's response is scored partially correct (PC). All that is really correct is the object and the action, the ball and taking it somewhere. Alia, in response to "Take your ball to the table," said something not clear to the experimenter, picked up the ball, went to the window, looked out the window, put the ball on the table, and got on a chair so that she could put the ball on the television. Savage-Rumbaugh does not say Alia actually did this. Alia's response was also scored PC. The correct response was actually included in her activity. She gave evidence of understanding table as well as ball and take.

When Kanzi was directed to "Put the rock in the water," he did so. When Alia was so directed, she shook her head yes, picked up the container of water, said something the experimenter did not understand, and poured the water into a bowl. She then picked up the rock and put it in the bowl. Both responses were scored correct. Alia's response was elaborated, but complied with the directive in contrast to Kanzi's performance with the ball. I am not sure that Kanzi's ability to comprehend speech extends beyond the pairing of some words with their sound and/or lexagram and remembering some routines in which the words occur.

In addition to the cognitive abilities to treat objects as equivalent and to learn to differentiate objects, most primates have the ability to relate categories to each other and respond to the relationship between objects rather than the object itself. So they can be taught to order three stimulus objects by size, for example (Lenneberg, 1967).

Sarah and the other linguistic apes have another capacity; they are able to associate a sound or meaningless token with a class of object. In human beings this becomes the ability to label or name. Because apes lack the vocal abilities of human beings and at the same time are extremely dextrous, all contemporary linguistic apes are being taught some kind of visual manipulatory, rather than auditory, system. The Premack's used colored plastic tokens to stand for words. Their method of teaching was conditioning with positive reinforcement in the form of food Sarah likes. For example, Sarah was first conditioned to pair objects that were alike. Two apples and a banana were placed in front of her and she was rewarded for moving the apples close to each other and away from the banana. Then she was conditioned to place a gold-colored plastic token with jagged edges between an apple and a banana (figure 3.2). These responses were conditioned to other objects, including corks and bottle tops, keys and rubber bands. Following this, Sarah was conditioned to replace a purple token with

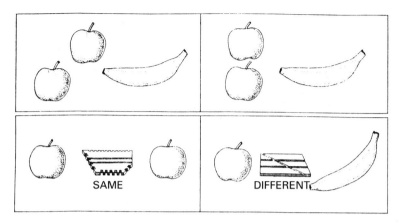

a hole in it, lying *between two corks*, with a jagged-edged, gold-colored token. If a purple token with a hole was lying *between a cork and a bottle top*, Sarah was conditioned to replace the purple token with a smooth-edged, red token. This is a straightforward conditioning procedure in which the Premacks used bananas, raisins, apples, and others of Sarah's preferred foods (including chocolate) as the positive reinforcement. The difficulty with the Premacks' work was their interpretation of it. To them, the jagged-edged, gold-colored token stood for the word *same*; the smooth-edged, red token for the word *different*; and they wanted to impute the same linguistic status for the tokens to Sarah. They wanted to credit Sarah with understanding "apple same (as) apple" and "apple different (from) banana" in the presence of fruit and the tokens. This is imputing a linguistic interpretation to behavior that is fully consistent with the interpretation that it is conditioned. It would not be possible to condition Sarah's behavior in this way if it were not for her innate capacity to see objects as equivalent (two apples) and different (an apple and a banana). This is a cognitive capacity and, as we have seen, highly developed in the pigeon. It is not a linguistic capacity. In chapter 6, a human being, Genie, will be described who has cognitive abilities more than adequate to language development but has not been able to acquire a human language. As far as Sarah is concerned, and the Premack's have concurred, the information exchange with her using objects and plastic tokens is not language use, but the achievements of other linguistic apes, notably Kanzi, remain to be evaluated.

Further Reading

Terrace, H., Petito, R. and Sanders, J. (1979) "Can an ape create a sentence?," *Science*, 206: 891–902.

4

From Signals and Signaling to Syntactic Language and Communication

When we compare human use of language and animal use of signals we separate what is being done and how. Human beings communicate (the what) using syntactic language (the how). Animals signal (the what) using the fixed repertoire of signals which are innate (the how). The innate repertoire of signals may be altered through conditioning in animals in contact with people as pets or experimental animals (see chapter 3). Both what is being done and how it is being done are different in animals and humans. Until recently, the contrast between what is being done by other animals and by human beings has been, usually, starkly drawn. Animals involuntarily emit informative signals, each innately coordinated to a particular stimulus because it was adaptive during the animal's period of biological adaptation so that the lines of species members lacking the signal were adaptively disadvantaged and died out. Human beings intentionally communicate using syntactic language. The basic units of languages like English are the morphemes (words and grammatical markers attached to words). For example, /s/, which makes singular nouns like *cat* plural. The other basic unit is the sentence (a rule-governed word-string).

Today we are gaining understanding of what is involved in communicating, as opposed to signaling, and the mental development of human beings that makes us capable of communicating rather than just signaling. We and other animals have primary consciousness, we see and hear, and our bodies are sensitive to touch, pressure, cold, and so on. We have sensations of hunger, thirst, sleepiness, and other biological drives like sex. Primary consciousness is absolutely essential to survival on Earth for animals employing voluntary behavior to fulfill needs. Voluntary implies that the animal has a choice in fulfilling needs. Choice begins with some species of wasps. For animals lower in the phylogenetic order, behavior that is not mandatory does not occur – no choice. What is not prescribed is proscribed.

In addition, human beings have secondary or higher-order consciousness which means that we are conscious of being conscious. We can think about aspects of our consciousness. I can say to myself, "I feel envious of Mary because she is so smart and understands problems that I don't." I am conscious that I have this negative feeling for Mary and I know why. Because I can think about my own mental processes, my thoughts and feelings, I can impute thoughts and feelings to others and think about these, especially people I know well. I can make predictions about what people will do based on my understanding of how they think, what they believe, and so on. Using syntactic language rather than a signal system makes it possible for human beings to communicate precise and elaborate messages tailored to the demands of a particular situation.

Evidence and Theories Concerning the Evolutionary Trail

What follows is an account of the ideas of important thinkers, and what their writings suggest about the evolution from signaling and signal systems to communicating and syntactic language.

In chapters 2 and 3 we considered the informative behaviors of animals in the wild and in contact with human beings. Animals signal to others of their species as part of an involuntary response to a stimulus that arouses fear: for example, the alarm squawk of the sparrow at the sight of the shadow of a hawk overhead, or the submissive retreat of the chimp about to grab a banana, in the face of the bared teeth and threatening posture of a higher-ranking male reaching for the same banana. The medium is the species' signal system including vocal, visual, and chemical elements. The stimulus–response coordinations are innate but both stimuli and responses can be conditioned through reward and punishment. That is, an animal can learn to give a response (rolling over on its back) to a stimulus (an order from its trainer to "Die for the Queen") if the trainer is competent and the reinforcement – praise, tasty food – is adequate. The trainer "shapes" the response by rewarding the animal's responses that are moving toward the trainer's goal. The animal uses the trainer's word stress, other sound cues, and visual cues from the trainer to learn, but it learns in order to get the praise, the hunk of meat, or whatever the positive reinforcer is. An unrelated stimulus can be paired with the natural stimulus and a response conditioned to it, as Pavlov demonstrated when he conditioned dogs to salivate to a sound which the dogs had heard just before food was given to them.

Sometime between the ages of 2 and 4–7, human beings give evidence of self-awareness. They become able to think about themselves, about their thoughts and feelings. The sparrow has a sensation of fear, given the shadow of the hawk, but the young human being [Joel, aged 2] says "[Mos]quito bite leg," pointing to the red bump on his leg. He sees the spot, knows it's his leg. Of course, he also knows something about mosquito behavior. But the difference between communicating and signaling lies in self-awareness and intentional communication as opposed to the sparrow's sensation of fear and accompanying involuntary squawk.

How did we get from there to here? The communicating ability of the human species evolved, but how? We cannot trace the evolution because *Homo sapiens*, our species, is the only living hominid species. To study morphological evolution (the evolution of organs and structures), there is the fossil record to examine, but mental processes and spoken language leave no fossil record, and, since the Neanderthals and Cro-Magnons no longer exist, we cannot compare ourselves to Neanderthal, a human being but not an example of *Homo sapiens*, or to Cro-Magnon, *Homo sapiens* but an example that lived many thousand years ago and was culturally less developed than we – and left no written records. All human societies extant today have fully developed human languages with a system of speech sounds that are combined to form the equivalent of words and a system of rules for combining words into well-formed strings in their language. In English and many other languages the basic strings are sentences, but the sentence is not the only type of rule-governed string.

Since all existing human societies have fully developed spoken language, and since spoken language and mental processes leave no fossil record, we cannot study their evolution as physical evolution is studied. I am not an evolutionary biologist and will borrow from ones I have read to lay out an account of what evolved that differentiates us from our closest living relatives, the great apes.

> Evolution occurs through the differential selection of traits with survival value in the habitat adopted by the animals. The word habitat implies more than simply the physical environment of an animal. It includes the presence of other animals that may be predators or competitors for food . . . and animals of its own species that may interact with it. The structure of the animal's behavior will be adapted to all these features in ways that in past generations have been most successful in transmitting the gene complexes into the future. (Crook, 1980: 8)

For years, the fact that human beings are language users seemed to me the root cause of the enormous differences between our life and that of all other animal species. As I began to read about evolution and the development of human language use, I had to take account of Darwin's dictum that evolution proceeds incrementally and not in great jumps like that between animals instinctively using signal systems that are informative and our using syntactic language, intentionally, to communicate. I describe, in detail, animal signal systems and signaling in chapters 2 and 3, but I want here to sketch some ideas about the evolutionary course to human language use that my reading of Darwin (1871), Edelman (1987, 1989), Piatelli-Palmarini (1980), Gould (1980) and others makes reasonable to me. I learned that "an organ built under the influence of selection for a specific role may be able as a consequence of its structure to perform many other unselected functions as well" (Gould, 1980: 50). Darwin (1871: 172) illustrates the principle using the swimbladder in fishes. Originally for flotation, it came to serve the widely different function of respiration. Birds' feathers evolved originally for warmth and subsequently proved useful for flying. The selected functions are adaptations; the unselected, exaptations (see also Piatelli-Palmarini, 1980, who mentions insect wings selected for thermal exchange and turned into organs of flight).

Human language use requires two evolutionary developments: secondary consciousness, making possible communication rather than signaling, and syntactic language, which makes combining morphemes (the smallest meaning-bearing units of language) possible so novel messages can be created. Signals of an animal signal system cannot be combined to create a new signal. Vervet monkeys give different alarm cries at the sight of eagles, leopards, and snakes. Escape patterns from the three predators are different: if it is a leopard, run up a tree; if an eagle, run into a bush; if a snake, stand erect on your hind legs and look for the snake (Diamond, 1992). Since escape patterns differ, it is biologically adaptive for the different alarm cries to have evolved. It might also be adaptive for the vervets to be able to combine two of the alarm cries, for the eagle and the leopard for example, to signal the presence of both predators, should both be in the monkey's vicinity. No one has produced evidence that this happens or any findings at all to suggest signals can be combined. Research *has* been carried out to demonstrate, by playing each of the three alarm calls from a tape-recording on separate occasions and videotaping the behavior of the monkeys on hearing the call, that the recordings elicit the appropriate escape behaviors (Diamond, 1992). Signals can be more or less intense (see chapter 2 for examples) but their association to a stimulus type cannot change. A squawk that signals a danger always signals that particular danger. The squawk's loudness depends on how frightening the stimulus for the squawk is.

I propose that secondary consciousness was the adaptive evolutionary event and language the exaptation because secondary consciousness is adaptive for the individual and can be functional for the individual without language, while language use requires secondary consciousness because language use is intentional rather than involuntary as instinctive signaling is. Being able to take one's own mental processes and those of others as objects of thought (secondary consciousness) makes it possible for a person (Mary) to think about how she could induce another person (Anne), for example, to falsely believe that extraordinary wealth would come to her (Anne) as the result of giving her store of "money" to Mary. This is the trick that the cat and the fox played on Pinocchio when they induced him to plant his coins so a tree bearing coins as fruit would grow. Having secondary consciousness makes it possible for a person to plan to manipulate other people's beliefs to the planner's benefit, clearly a beneficial adaptation for the individual which will gradually become a species characteristic through natural selection (Cosmides and Tooby, 1992).

Secondary consciousness without language can be adaptive for the individual if the individual (Rover) can think of a way without using language to make others (Spot and Fido) believe something that is false. Rover knows where a turtle has laid some eggs, and he has actually eaten one. He and Spot and Fido love turtle eggs and eat them whenever they find them. Spot and Fido smell turtle egg on Rover and are staying close, drawn by the smell. Rover suddenly discovers that he has secondary consciousness. He can take his own mental processes as an object of thought; and he thinks, non-verbally, running a silent movie before his mind's eye, I smell turtle egg smell on me. Spot and Fido must smell turtle egg smell on me, too. If I lie down and pretend to take a nap, they will think there are no more eggs and they will go away. Then I'll eat the rest of the eggs. Rover tries to induce the false belief by his behavior. Fido and Spot, not being endowed with secondary consciousness, are fooled by Rover's behavior because they are unable to think that Rover might be tricking them by pretending he's eaten so much he has fallen asleep.

Psychological evolution is different from morphological evolution (organs or structures) because it is observable only through behavior and the products of behavior. There is no structure like feathers whose evolution can be traced; rather, there are the human behaviors, intentional communication and language use and their evolution to think about and understand.

Until this century it was the origin of language that was the object of attention. For me, at least, the person who understood and explained communication is H. P. Grice (1957, 1968). Human communication depends on secondary consciousness, being able to think about one's own mental processes – thoughts, beliefs, emotions, intentions – and the mental processes of others. Instead of the sparrow's involuntary squawk, the concomitant of the fear evoked by the sight of a hawk overhead, there is the human intentional warning to others, "Look out! There's a bear, rattlesnake, dangerous human being." When a person (John) warns another (Jim), Jim believes that John has warned, "There's a bear," because he, John, believes there is a bear which threatens him, Jim. Human communication depends on being able to intend to deliver a message, to understand that we humans share that ability and generally can be trusted to communicate what we believe to be true.

This last is what makes intentionally misinforming (lying) successful.

If, generally, people did not communicate what they believe to be true and expect others to do the same, lying would not pay off because no messages would be trusted. The biological instincts and power and coercion would drive human behavior. Socially created laws and institutions would not be possible. Ultimately communication, as here characterized, is what makes cooperation, and the give and take of non-authoritarian social life, possible.

How, evolutionarily, did we get from the involuntary, informative squawk to intentional, voluntary communication? I have said that secondary consciousness is essential. How did it evolve? For the ensuing description, I have relied on Povinelli (1993). Povinelli has written about "the evolution of the capacity for self conception and mental state attribution" (1993: 494), what I have called secondary consciousness. Darwin knew that he had to confront the fact of the discontinuity between animal and human consciousness, but he saw as a requirement of his theory of evolution that he be able to show varying degrees in other animal species of what became secondary consciousness in humans (Darwin, 1871, as cited in Povinelli, 1993). "If natural selection resulted in the origin of new species through the gradual accumulation of small adaptations, then the absence of those gradual differences between the most closely related species was evidence against his theory of natural selection" (Povinelli, 1993: 494). If Darwin postulated that mental evolution was determined differently from physical evolution his theory could easily be challenged by those who saw the difference between man and beast as reflecting a divine spark, the human soul. Darwin noted the easily perceived differences in mental prowess between fish and the higher apes and suggested that it was vaster than that between apes and men. As Povinelli has it, Darwin searched for psychological as well as physical continuity in evolution, but evidence is harder to come by because psychology does not fossilize. We can only find evidence of psychological evolution in differences among living species. The only extant *hominid* is our species, *Homo sapiens*, so we make comparisons with our closest living relatives, the great apes.

In 1970, Gordon Gallup discovered that chimpanzees are capable of recognizing themselves in a mirror. Orang-utans are also capable of self-recognition. Since then, evidence of self-recognition has been sought and *not* found in 20 other non-human primates, including gorillas. Self-recognition provides evidence of self-awareness, a prerequisite to being able to take one's mental processes as objects of thought and, on this basis, to attribute mental processes to other humans.

Povinelli presents comparative data on self-awareness of chimpanzees and young children. This is relevant to work on young children's "theory of mind" to be presented in chapter 8. Povinelli concludes that Gallup (Gallup and Suarez, 1986) "could predict that self-recognition is an empirical marker of the beginning of a complex developmental sequence involving multiple feedback between self and social attribution (attributing mental processes to one's self and to others)" (Povinelli, 1993: 503), what I would call development of secondary consciousness in any particular human being. Self-recognition is not present in very young humans. In the home movies of friends, we saw their 3-year-old son pick up their cat and throw it down the hill in front of their house. He said, as he looked at himself in the movie, "Look at that bad boy throwing McCavity down the hill!" He recognized the family cat, but not himself, even though he was wearing the Davy Crockett coonskin hat which he wore most of the time. Empirical research concerning development of secondary consciousness in children is presented in chapter 8.

The transition from signals to language can only be approached theoretically, buttressing hypotheses with reasoning. The first requirement for there to be a transition is for signaling to become intentional as well as involuntary. It then becomes possible for a cry elicited by the sight of a feared predator to be uttered when the utterer is not afraid but wants to warn others because they are in danger, or the utterer wants them to believe that they are. If the utterer intends to warn he must be aware that he would interpret the cry as signaling danger and believe that the others hearing his cry will be afraid and flee. The others do not need to have secondary consciousness for the warning to succeed. The cry could be the involuntary cry as far as its effect on their behavior is concerned. But, invoking natural selection, the individuals without secondary consciousness are adaptively disadvantaged, and their lines will die out leaving all the species members having secondary consciousness. The species members endowed with secondary consciousness can then conventionalize signals so they no longer need be replicas of the involuntary signal.

The early evolution of conventionalized signals may be similar to that of facial expressions which originally were the involuntary concomitants of an action; for example, the facial expression now used to indicate disgust was caused by the action of ridding the mouth of a foul-tasting substance. When it became possible to conventionalize signals so they no longer needed to be analogues of instinctive signaling behaviors, signals could be arbitrary symbols and they could undergo change, as long as users understood the relation between symbol and meaning. Symbols could be combined to create new meanings. Symbols standing for phonemes (the smallest units in a language which influence meaning) could be combined to create new morphemes (words and grammatical affixes like the "s" appended to the end of a noun to make it plural). Words can be combined to create sentences of great variety of meaning as long as the conventions governing word and sentence formation "work." In English, word order is central to sentence formation and meaning. "The dog bit the cat," and "The cat bit the dog" have opposite meanings. We understand this because of word order. In other languages, Russian for example, case marker affixes on words grammatically mark the biter and the bitten, the subject and object of the verb, marked in English by word order. The case marker in Russian for subject is word-final "a," for object, "u."

Sobaka kusala koshku.
(subj.)   (obj.)
The dog bit the cat.

Sobaka koshku kusala.
(subj.) (obj.)
The dog the cat bit.

Kusala koshku sobaka.
        (obj.) (subj.)
Bit the cat the dog.

Koshka kusala sobaku.
(subj.)   (obj.)
The cat bit the dog.

The grammatical intuitions of the competent speaker of a language tell her or him that a sentence is well formed, grammatically correct (Chomsky, 1965). Secondary consciousness is required to judge the correctness of a verbal string one hears in terms of one's grammatical intuition; for example, I hear a person saying, "That ain't no good," which doesn't sound right to me, violates my intuition of grammatical correctness. If I want to "judge" why, I think, "ain't" isn't standard English and "ain't" and "no" make a double negative, not grammatical in English. So on two counts this sentence fails as standard English, my language.

In my attempt to construct a plausible picture of the development from animal signaling to human language use, I have also learned from the analysis of Edelman (1989), who deals with higher consciousness (secondary consciousness) and human language and is a Nobel laureate evolutionary neural biologist. First, he considers the adaptive advantage to a being of primary consciousness which links satisfying biological needs to the being's ability to explore and act on its environment. For Edelman, categorization and memory are crucial aspects of primary consciousness. All vertebrates have the innate ability to categorize, although in species with primary consciousness only, categorizing (this is edible, that is not, for example) is done without explicit awareness. What can be categorized varies enormously over species and as the result of learning. The ability to categorize makes it possible for a vertebrate animal to seek what it needs for survival in its environment. According to Edelman, "Although its behavior is undoubtedly altered by long term changes in learning, it has no means of reviewing explicitly its present perceptions in terms of analogues in the past or in terms of anticipated analogues ... It has no direct awareness and is not conscious of being conscious" (1989: 186). In order to be conscious of being conscious (secondary consciousness), to be self-aware, it is essential to have long-term memory. Long-term memory is necessary to be able to call on past experience. We may say, then, that the sense of self cannot exist without long-term memory. As I write this, I am chilled by understanding that the fate of human beings who lose long-term memory because of blows to the head, strokes, or Alzheimer's disease is to lose their selfhood, to no longer be conscious of being conscious.

However, a necessary concomitant to long-term memory for selfhood is the ability to categorize. "The ability to categorize is indispensable in using previous experience to guide the interpretations of new experience, i.e. without categorization memory is virtually useless" (Jackendoff, 1983). Being "conscious of being conscious" requires evolution of neural structures (parts of the brain) that make it possible to image the distinction between the self and the non-self.[1] For example, I construct in imagination a little event sequence in which I meet my friend, Mary, and we talk about a mutual acquaintance whom we haven't seen for awhile. Edelman (1989) sees the evolution of such symbolic structures (mental images with verbal labels) as essential to the emergence of long-term memory based on a notion of the past. He further posits that neural development making such symbolic structures possible is required for the development of syntactic semantic language, human language.

The transition from having just primary consciousness to also having higher consciousness is seen in chimpanzees which:

> do display some evidence of self awareness. The emergence of this trait suggests that chimpanzees have, at least, the beginnings of higher order (secondary) consciousness with some capacity to form a self model in relation to a world model. True language is thus probably not necessary for the emergence of higher order consciousness although it is required for its later elaborations. (Edelman, 1989: 187)

In order for higher consciousness to further evolve:

> a conceptual self category must [exist], be stable and therefore must accumulate. It can arise (as in chimpanzees) but cannot develop further without being freed to some extent from current activities and their distractions. Successful development of self awareness requires a means of long term storage of relations that are symbolic, standing for states of memory that are related to communication with other individuals of the same species. (Edelman, 1989: 187)

Edelman posits that the self–non-self concept has to be social, not biological. It is this, I believe, that makes it difficult for him to be entirely consistent about which came first, self-awareness or language. The stable and growing social self–non-self concept needs language according to Edelman. I agree that it is certainly helped by language, if only because of long-term memory storage and retrieval. If long-term memory is a type of filing cabinet, language provides the labels for the file folders. But the first person with secondary consciousness which enabled him to get an adaptive advantage by engendering false beliefs in others, probably didn't have so much in his long-term memory that he was unable to function without language. I propose that he could manage with mental images, perhaps something like a silent movie portraying his stories. In his group's presence, placing their supplies in a cave and then sneaking back to the cave at night and moving the supplies to a place not known to the others is a possible scenario for an event sequence stored in mental pictures.

Speech (and Why)

How did the vocal–auditory channel evolve as our preferred medium of communication and speech as our means? Why not a visual–gestural language like ASL (American Sign Language), for example? Researchers report that children acquiring ASL acquire signs earlier than children acquiring English acquire words, and further that English-acquiring infants learn to wave "bye-bye" or nod their heads to indicate "no" before learning the words. The adaptive superiority of spoken over gestural language is not speed of early acquisition. Using speech rather than gestures to communicate frees the hands so that it is possible to work with our hands and talk at the same time, an adaptive advantage. Being able to communicate without having to see each other is a further advantage, as is being able to find out in which direction the speaker is from you by turning your head to discover the direction of your ear in which it is easiest to hear the speaker. Even very young babies do this. The auditory–vocal channel provides total feedback (as long as only one message is conveyed at a time). Both speaker and hearer hear the speaker's message, unlike gestural language where, even though communication must be face to face, unless there is a well-placed mirror, the communicator will not be able to see all her own gestures. These advantages also hold for auditory as opposed to gestural signal systems. But the characteristics of language as opposed to signal system, as we have seen, are finally what makes a language so vastly superior to signals as a system for providing precise and elaborate information.

A First Look at the Analysis of Human Language Use

The need to separate analysis of human language use into linguistic (the syntactic–semantic meaning of sentences in the language) and speech-act analysis became apparent as English philosophers considered Bertrand Russell's analysis of the sentence, "The present King of France is bald." The interest of philosophers analyzing language lies in establishing the truth or falsity of the propositional content of sentences. The problem with "The present King of France is bald" is that, in Russell's time, France was no longer a monarchy. This being the case, Russell said, the proposition is not based in reality and, therefore, is meaningless. Some philosophers found this conclusion unsatisfactory because as a sentence in the English language, "The present King of France is bald," has meaning even though, in reality, France is now a republic rather than a monarchy. Such reasoning led to distinguishing the semantic–syntactic meaning of a sentence in the language from the utterer's meaning – what the person who said the sentence meant by saying it. When mothers ask their children, "When are you going to learn to tie your shoes?" or "How many times do I have to tell you to close the door?," "Next year" and "Seven" are not appropriate answers. "I'm trying" and "I'm sorry" are possible responses to utterer's meaning, which is what one should respond to when utterer's meaning and syntactic–semantic meaning (literal meaning) are not the same. Children too young to produce well-formed questions understand this (Holzman, 1973). Conceptualizing verbalizations as *speech acts* as well as *linguistic entities* begins with J. L. Austin. In his book, *How to do Things with Words* (1962), he examines the difference between statements like:

1   I have been faithful all my life.
2   There is a cow in the backyard.

and performatives like:

3   I promise that I will serve you faithfully all of my life.
4   I sentence you to ten years in prison (said by the judge to the prisoner standing before him in court at the conclusion of the trial).

The statements are reports about phenomena that the person making the statement is communicating. Statements always express a proposition. In the two examples, "I have been faithful all my life" and "There is a cow in the backyard," the propositional content is all there is to the statements. Propositions specify an idea, person, or object, for example, and make a comment about it. In (1), "I" is the person specified or referred to, and "have been faithful all my life" is the comment the proposition makes or the predicating expression. In (2), "a cow" is the object specified, and "is in the backyard" is the comment or predicating expression. Performatives are acts that are accomplished simply by saying the words in the appropriate circumstances (that is, one cannot pass sentence unless one is a judge who has just tried a suspect). Performatives do not express propositions. "I promise that I will serve you faithfully" makes a promise to the person addressed, and "I sentence you to ten years" sentences the person addressed to prison. Austin was interested in the fact that propositions can be analyzed to determine whether they are true or false, while performatives cannot be so analyzed. Instead, there are *conditions* that must be met for them to be successfully carried out. There are *appropriateness* conditions, such as being a judge addressing a suspect, and *sincerity* conditions, which means that a promise must be sincere or it is not a promise. But there is no way to talk meaningfully about true and false sentencing to prison or promising to serve. If the person passing sentence is not a judge in a court addressing the prisoner, the appropriateness condition for the speech act is not met. If a person is lying when making a promise, the sincerity condition for carrying out the speech act is not met. The various speech acts have sets of conditions that must be met for the successful carrying out of the speech act.

The idea of the speech act was developed and made more directly relevant to the study of language development during the 1960s by J. R. Searle, another philosopher of language. Searle (1969) conceptualized speaking a language as "performing speech acts – acts such as making statements, giving commands, asking questions, making promises, and so on." Speech acts are understood by the hearer because they are performed in accordance with the rules that govern their success, and these rules are learned along with the other aspects of language use. Searle saw that it was not necessary to all speech acts that they contain a performative verb. The legal speech acts, "I *sentence* you to jail," "I *pronounce* you husband and wife," require the performative verb. But the speech act of warning, for example, does not.

5 I'll break your neck if you don't pay me back my money.
6 I warn you that I will break your neck if you don't pay me back my money.

That is, (5) is just as much a warning as (6), although it lacks the performative "I warn."

This insight led to Searle's analyzing language use as performance of speech acts with two principal components: what he referred to as *illocutionary force* and *propositional content*. For the purposes of my research in language development, I have found that distinguishing utterer's meaning or function of the speech act from its syntactic–semantic meaning, its meaning in the (English) language, makes it possible to conceptualize the continuity between animal signal systems and human language in a clear way. Recall, I said that my friend's dog responded to utterer's meaning (roll over) when my friend said "Die for the Queen" without understanding "Die for the Queen" as an English sentence. The distinction between utterer's meaning and syntactic–semantic meaning of the sentence in the English language roughly corresponds to Searle's illocutionary force and propositional content. Utterer's meaning is exactly the same as illocutionary force. Propositional content is closely related to semantic–syntactic meaning but is not identical to it.

Note

1 The capacity to develop the distinction is present at birth because it is innate. CNS maturation and/or experience in the environment are necessary for its development. The idea that the human infant initially lacks a sense of the boundaries of her body, i.e. a sense of herself as an entity separate from her mother, is an example of the distinction.

Further Reading

Barkow, J., Cosmides, L. and Tooby, J. (eds) (1992) *The Adapted Mind* (New York: Oxford University Press).
  Evolutionary psychology and the generation of culture.
Braine, M. D. S. (1994) "Is nativism sufficient?," *Journal of Child Language*, 21: 9–31.
  Braine analyzes the past and present state of the empiricism–nativism issue.
Edelman, G. (1987) *Neural Darwinism* (New York: Basic Books).
Edelman, G. (1989) *The Remembered Present* (New York: Basic Books).
  Deeply thought-provoking books about the evolution of the human mind.

Gomila, A., Sussman, H. M., Pinker, S. and Bloom, P. (1994) "Natural language and natural selection: commentary and responses," *Behavioral and Brain Sciences*, 17: 180–5.
    Authors' hypothesis about evolution of language.
Searle, J. (1994) *The Rediscovery of the Mind*. Cambridge, Mass.: MIT Press.
    The human brain is not a computer. Lucid presentation.

5

The Prelinguistic Infant

A Greek myth describes how Zeus was suffering from a terrible head-ache which ceased when Pallas Athena, goddess of wisdom, sprang forth, grown and in full armor, from his head. Steven Pinker, in *The Language Instinct* (1994), quotes a tabloid headline "Baby born talking describes heaven." Developing to the mature stage where one might be arrayed in full armor and wise like Pallas Athena or be able to describe heaven takes time and experience.

I used to think that human beings used language, while other species did not, simply because human beings have larger brains and are generally more intelligent than other species. But the evidence is that human brains, unlike the brains of other primates, have elements specialized to process linguistic information. A disposition to acquire language use has evolved in human beings (like the disposition in pigeons and other animals to categorize). In addition to the disposition to use language, areas specialized to language functions (Broca's and Wernicke's areas) exist in the human brain.

The Brain: Localization and Lateralization of Functions

In most human beings, the language areas are on the left side of the brain (figure 5.1). The brain has two hemispheres approximately the same size and shape, fitted together like the two halves of a walnut. The hemispheres are connected by a bundle of nerve fibers called the corpus callosum, a pathway that permits the two hemispheres of the brain to be in communication. The outer surface of the hemispheres is

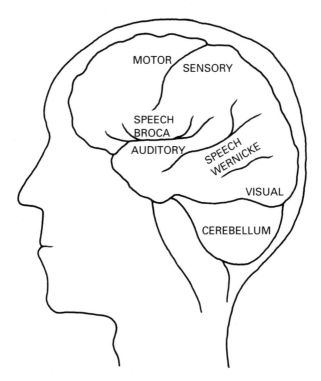

Figure 5.1 Left hemisphere of the human brain

called the cerebral cortex. The cortex is the "gray matter" of the brain, gray because it consists of nerve cells. Beneath the cortex is the "white matter," mostly nerve fibers that connect the nerve cells of the cortex with other nerve fibers, which finally connect the cortical nerve cells with the nerve cells of sense organs and muscles of the body.

The cortex is the part of the brain that controls seeing, hearing, and the other senses, and exerts voluntary control over the muscles and therefore over the voluntary actions of the body. All involuntary activity, like breathing and blood circulation, is regulated by subcortical parts of the brain. The sensory and muscular activities of the right side of the body are controlled by the left hemisphere, and vice versa, because the principal bundles of nerve fibers cross in the brain.

The areas of the left hemisphere where control of particular right-side functions is localized are shown in figure 5.1. The area marked "motor," along the line drawn from the top of the cortex, is the *motor cortex* where all voluntary movements of the right leg, arm, fingers, eye, and so on, are controlled. If a person suffers a stroke (a failure of the heart and circulation that causes damage to the brain), and the person's right side is paralyzed, we know that the motor cortex of the left hemisphere was injured by the stroke. Injury to Broca's and Wernicke's areas would interfere with speech production and comprehension, respectively. There are no areas in the right hemisphere corresponding to the speech areas. Language is a left hemisphere function in the great majority of human beings. (Some left-handed people have the language area in the right hemisphere.)

As the child develops, the two hemispheres of the brain become specialized for certain functions: language in the left hemisphere, along with music and other serial-ordered phenomena; spatial organization and spacial pattern recognition, including recognition of faces, and perception of environmental (non-speech) sounds (like automobiles, water flowing, and footsteps) in the right hemisphere. We say that these functions are *lateralized* in the brain. As yet it has not been determined when lateralization is complete. Evidence appears when individuals who have had a stroke or sustained a severe head wound on the left side of the head recover. A severe injury or a stroke kills nerve cells of the cortex. These dead nerve cells are not replaced. The human central nervous system, unlike the rest of the human body, does not regenerate cells. We are born with all the nerve cells of the central nervous system that we will ever have. That is the reason why people do not recover CNS functions lost through destruction of nerve cells. A function is recovered only if some other nerves can take over the function. If an individual over the age of 2 recovers his language functions, then it is inferred that, following the stroke, language functions shifted from left-hemisphere to right-hemisphere control. This shift is possible only if the brain is not yet lateralized. I have seen reports that lateralization is complete as early as the age of 5 and as late as puberty. But if lateralization is complete, and some language function is lost with the injury, it is lost for good. The various impairments in language functions are called *aphasias*. Broca's aphasias are difficulties of various kinds in producing speech. Wernicke's aphasias are difficulties in comprehending speech.

In this chapter, we begin to track the development of individual humans which culminates in their becoming fully fledged language users, a wondrous and complex attainment. In order to make clear the developmental task a baby carries out in becoming able to produce a speech sound in her mother tongue, the language spoken to her, we need to look at the human anatomy for speech production and at the system used to classify speech sounds.

Human beings have a special anatomical link between the auditory (hearing) system and the speech production system. This connection is necessary so that human beings can learn to speak. Infants hear the speech they produce and at the same time get feedback from the movements of their vocal tracts: it is hearing one's speech and getting the muscular feedback at the same time that is necessary in learning to speak.

The Vocal Tract and the Production of Speech Sounds

The part of the body involved in the production of speech includes the lungs, trachea (windpipe), larynx (which contains the vocal cords), pharynx or throat, mouth (including tongue, teeth, and lips), and the nose. Altogether, these organs form a tube extending from the lungs to the lips (see figure 5.2). The upper part, above the larynx, is called the *vocal tract*. If we just breathe out, our breath makes no sound. Speech sounds come from constricting the larynx and vocal tract in various ways. The manner and place in the vocal tract where speech sounds are produced provides the basis for classifying them. The easiest way to observe how different speech sounds are produced is to do it for yourself.

First, put the tips of your fingers against your larynx (the adam's apple) and make the vowel sound of the *o* in hot or *a* in father (this sound is written as [a] in the International Phonetic Alphabet). You will feel your vocal cords vibrate. This is true whenever a speech sound that is voiced is uttered. All vowel sounds are voiced. We will consider the consonants in a moment. Now, instead of [a], make the sound [i], which is the vowel sound in *meet*. Observe how you have moved your lips, teeth, jaw, and tongue, particularly your tongue and lips. Try [æ], the sound of the *a* in b*a*t, and again you can observe that, in order to produce [æ], you have altered the shape of your vocal tract by moving your tongue, lips, and so on. The most important determinants of which vowel will be pronounced are the shape of the tongue, its height in the mouth, and the shape of the lips.

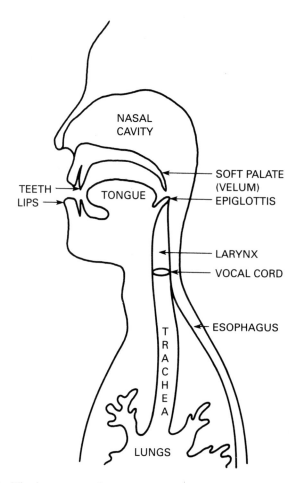

Figure 5.2 The human vocal organs

In addition to the pure vowel sounds, there are three diphthongs in American English: [ay], [aw], and [ɔy]. These are also vowels, but they are vowel sounds whose quality changes noticeably during production as the positions of the tongue, lips, and so on, are altered. This is easiest to hear in the [ɔy], the vowel sound in *boy* and *oyster*. The diphthong [ay] is the vowel sound in *bite*, and [aw] is the vowel sound in *brown*. The vowel sounds used in standard American spoken English are given in table 5.1.

When a person makes a vowel sound, the air from the lungs is not impeded in its path through the vocal tract and out of the mouth.

Table 5.1 The vowel sounds of American English (written in the phonetic alphabet, American variant)

Vowels			Diphthongs	
i	be*e*t, rec*ei*ve, mon*ey*	ʌ but, tough, oven	ay	b*i*te, d*ie*, *ai*sle
ɪ	b*i*t, cons*i*st, *i*njury	o boat, go, throw	aw	ab*ou*t, br*ow*n, c*ow*ard
e	ba*i*t, r*ay*, inv*ei*gh	ɔ bought, stalk, ball	ɔy	b*oy*, *oy*ster
ɛ	b*e*t, s*ay*s, *e*nd	a pot, car, honor		
æ	b*a*n, r*a*lly, *a*ctor	ə sof*a*, *a*lone, s*u*ppose		
u	boot, d*u*ty, m*o*ve	ɨ ros*e*s, buss*e*s, crutch*e*s		
ʊ	p*u*t, co*u*ld, foot			

When consonant sounds are made, the passage of air is impeded at various places in the vocal tract and in various ways: this is accomplished mostly by movements of the tongue, teeth, and lips. Consonant production can best be analyzed in terms of the place in the vocal tract and manner in which the sound is produced, and I want to provide a broad description of the consonants in these terms. But, first, there is a characteristic of consonants that applies to them all. Some consonants are *voiced* like the vowel sounds, which means that they are produced with enough constrictions of the vocal cords to cause them to vibrate. The *voiceless* consonants are produced with no constrictions of the vocal cords. The English phonemes /s/ and /z/, /t/ and /d/, /k/ and /g/, and /p/ and /b/ are four pairs in which the two consonants are produced in the same place in the vocal tract and in the same manner except that the first member of the pair is voiceless and the second is voiced. The shape of the vocal tract is the same for both members of a pair. Again, the reader can check this by placing finger tips on the larynx to feel the vocal cords vibrating; one can check to see if the first member of each pair is voiceless and the second voiced. Checking for voicing is somewhat difficult because it is hard to produce a consonant sound all by itself. When we think we are, we have usually appended [a], and the sound produced is [ta] or [da]. However, I think it is possible to produce /s/ and /z/ in isolation.

If you have tried out the feel of the voiced versus voiceless consonants with the pairs I suggested, you may have noticed that /t/, /d/,

/k/, /g/, /b/, and /p/ are all produced by blocking the flow of air from the lungs momentarily and then letting it out in a sudden burst. These consonants are called stop or plosive consonants. Although they have the same manner of articulation, they differ in their place of articulation. To produce /t/ and /d/, the airflow is blocked by placing the tip of the tongue against the inside of the gum of the upper, front teeth. For /k/ and /g/ the tongue is placed against the velum (soft palate). For /b/ and /p/ the lips are closed to block the air flow.

The pair /s/ and /z/ is composed of two fricatives. Fricatives are produced by constricting the stream of air from the lungs in the vocal tract. The fricatives /f/ and /v/, for example, are produced by placing the upper front teeth against the top of the lower lip and exhaling the air stream through this constricted space. The nasals like /m/, the sound with which *mother* begins, are produced by blocking the mouth and exhaling the stream of air through the nose. For /m/ the mouth is blocked at the lips. Table 5.2 lists the consonant sounds that are used to construct spoken English words (for further information on the articulation of English consonants, see Denes and Pinson, 1973; Fromkin and Rodman, 1978; Crabtree and Powers, 1991).

In the beginning, the human infant is like other primate infants, though with less body hair and less ability to fend for itself. Like other primates and less philogenetically evolved neonates, the human infant is born with a repertoire of behaviors, biologically adaptive for the species. Since the human infant will be completely dependent on the care-giving of others for survival, newborn babies have sucking, grasping, clinging, and reaching responses, which underlie feeding and proximity-seeking and maintaining behavior. More immediately relevant to language development is the very young infant's signaling repertoire: cries, cooing, smiling, and arm movements that are effective in eliciting care-giving and affectionate responses from the mother or mother surrogate. Infant cries and arm movements are observed from shortly after birth. Smiling and cooing (comfort sounds) appear within a few weeks or months.

The newborn's repertoire of survival behaviors is adaptive in just the way the innate repertoires of other animal species are and is assumed to have developed because of its survival value in the humans' environment. In the ecological niche occupied by the human species, language must be regarded as a biologically adaptive capacity. All human societies have language and no non-human species do. We want

Table 5.2 The consonants[a] of English

Manner of articulation	Place of articulation							
	1 Lips	2 Lip/teeth	3 Tongue/teeth	4 Tongue/ridge	5 Palate	6 Velum	7 Lips/velum	8 Glottis
Nasal	m hum			n Hun		ŋ hung		
Stop	p pit / b bit			t time / d dime		k come / g gum		ʔ button
Fricative		f fine / v vine	θ thigh / ð thy	s sip / z zip	š sure / ž azure			h help
Glide					y yelp		ʰw whale / w whelp	
Liquid				l lane / r rain[b]				
Affricate					č chunk / ǰ junk			

[a] Consonants are either voiced or voiceless. The nasals are all voiced. For the others, the consonant in the upper position is voiceless, e.g., p is voiceless, b is voiced.

[b] l and r are both voiced, both liquids, articulated at tongue/ridge. The difference in their sound is the result of the difference in the shape of the tongue as they are articulated.

to consider how the cries, cooing, smiling, and arm movements of newborn infants support language development. Perhaps the best way to consider the transformation from these behaviors to language is to watch it happen.

The Interaction of Infants with their Mothers

My co-workers and I have watched the transformation from an innate repertoire of signals to language use by means of a research project called "How the human infant becomes a language user." We presented our project to parents of first-born infants whose mothers would be the primary care-takers when the infants were about a month old. We described the project as an ethological, longitudinal study of infant-hood. We said we would like to come every other week when the mother would ordinarily be undressing, bathing, dressing, and feeding the baby and videotape the mother and baby during this sequence. We have made such a series of tapes for two girl and two boy babies (Jean, Carol, Allen, and Joel) starting when each baby was 10 weeks old, taping every other week until the babies were 19 months old, and making a final tape when the babies were 2 years old. Because we always taped the same events, we can compare the behaviors of each mother–infant dyad (pair) at various times, observing changes over time, and we can also compare the dyads with each other. This makes it possible to see what is common in the infants' histories as they become language users and what is peculiar to particular infants.

The reader may wonder why we began taping the infants when they were so young, clearly many months before they would utter a single word. Our answer is that a great deal that is learned in becoming a language user is learned in the preverbal stage. During the preverbal period, the human infant's innate signaling responses change, in part because of maturational changes in the infant. In addition, the infant's vocalizations are influenced by verbal and vocal communications directed to the infant. We will look at these changes.

In describing developments during the preverbal stage that underlie human communicative behavior, we will consider separately: perception of speech sounds, phonological development (learning to produce speech sounds), the development of gestures, and of conversational competencies. These kinds of developments are taking place simultaneously.

Perception of speech sounds is an innate capacity. What we and others (for example, Newsome, 1978; Richards, 1978; Shotter, 1978) have found is that mothers behave toward their infants as though the infants' arm and body movements and babbles, cries, and vegetative noises were intended by the infants to be meaningful and to communicate meaning. At 3 months, Joel is lying on the kitchen counter while his mother puts water in the sink to bathe him. Joel is waving his arms and his left hand touches the wall near a flower on the wallpaper. His mother says, "Oh, you want the flower."

Human infants are like other baby animals in having innate signals that are informative. As we pointed out in chapter 2, the signals are informative, but they are not intentional. None the less, mothers treat babies' acts and vocalizations as intentional, and as the babies become mature enough to absorb the information, they can learn from their mothers' responses what their particular acts and vocalizations are taken to mean. Joel can learn that if you extend your arm in the direction of an object, it is taken to mean that you want the object to be handed to you. Calling replaces part of the infant's crying behavior as he becomes mature enough to *intend* to gain proximity to or care from the mother. Bowlby (1969) puts the development of calling sometime during the second year. The fact that care-takers have responded to the baby's reflexive crying provides the experience that makes learning to call possible.

Perception of Speech Sounds

The first major study of infant speech perception (Eimas, 1985) used voice onset time (VOT) as variable. Eimas (1985) found that 1- and 4-month-old infants could discriminate /ba/ and /pa/ categorically as English-speaking adults do.

Both the consonants that begin the syllables /bah/ and /pah/ are stops. The speaker completely blocks the flow of air from the lungs through the vocal tract just before uttering the syllable. In /bah/ the vocal cords begin to vibrate simultaneously with the release of air to begin the utterance because /b/ is voiced. In /pah/ there is an interval between the release of air to begin the utterance and the onset of vocal cord vibration or voicing, called voice onset time (VOT). It is this interval that makes the hearer able to distinguish /bah/ and

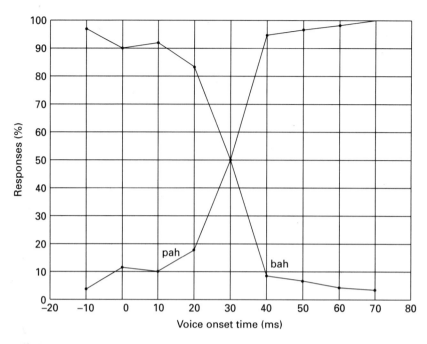

Figure 5.3 Categorical perception of [pah] and [bah]. Categorical perception is reflected in curves showing the relative proportions of responses when children were asked to identify a synthetic speech sound with a particular voice onset time as an instance of a voiced [bah] or a voiceless [pah] consonantal sound. Instead of a linear change in the percentages, the curves show that at voice onset times of less than 30 ms the children almost always identified the stimulus as [bah]; when voice onset time exceeded 30 ms, they tended to hear the sound as [pah]. The perceptual tendency shifted abruptly at 30 ms. The study, done by Catherine G. Wolf at Brown University, suggests that perceptual categories, rather than continuous gradations in the acoustic properties of the speech signal, shape the perception of speech (redrawn from P. D. Eimas, "Perceptions of speech in early infancy.' Copyright © 1985 by Scientific American Inc. All rights reserved)

/pah/, *ban* and *pan*, *bit* and *pit*, and so on. No single value of VOT defines the phoneme (speech sound). Hearers perceive a range of values of VOT as signaling the same phoneme. This characteristic is called categorical perception (see figure 5.3). It has also been shown that infants younger than 3 months can detect differences like that between /ba/ and /ga/ or *bun* and *gun*, a difference in place of articulation of the consonant and /*m*um/ and /*b*um/, where initial phonemes differ in manner of articulation (see Jusczyk, 1992, for a review of these findings).

There have been questions about whether categorical perception is innate, because it occurs in very young infants, or just rapidly acquired by infants from hearing their native language. Some contrasts are not heard by infants if they are not phonemic in their language (Eilers, 1980). On the other hand, Trehub (1976) found that, while English-speaking Canadian adults could not hear a contrast which is phonemic in Czech, infants of English-speaking Canadian parents, who had never heard any Eastern European languages, could hear the contrast as well as they could hear [ba] and [pa]. Subsequently, we tested 3–5-year-old preschoolers at the Tufts laboratory school who failed to hear the contrast. I had expected the preschoolers would *hear* the contrast, reasoning from the fact that persons moving from one speech community, for example French, to another, say American English, learn to speak American English like native speakers if they have not yet reached puberty. If they have, their native French accent will always color their speech in English. I conclude that prepubescent children *can learn to hear* and speak a new language like a native, while adults will always hear and speak through the filter of their native language.

A Reciprocal, Instinctive Model of Language Development

Developmental psycholinguists (people who study the development of human language and the differences between human language and animal signal systems) would agree that human beings have an innate predisposition to develop language: but language development does not happen without exposure to language, and the language developed is the one to which the infant–child is exposed. In researching how the human infant becomes a language user, I have found evidence that leads me to propose that not only is the human infant innately predisposed to acquire language but competent speakers (and perhaps mothers especially) are innately predisposed to use language in talking to very young children so as to *teach* them to use language (Holzman, 1984). It looks as though the behavior of the baby who is fostering her language development elicits language behavior from the mother that is appropriate to the stage of development of the infant's language skills. It also appears that mothers' linguistic behavior provides feedback that elicits responses from the infants that help them gain linguistic competence.

Babies utter non-cry vocalizations from the first day of life, but the young infant's repertoire of sounds is quite limited. For the most part, the sounds are produced when the baby opens its mouth, and lets air out with no oral obstruction and with enough tension on the vocal cords to cause them to vibrate and produce sound. The vocalization is not intended to have a particular sound like *dog* or *car*. Babies have to learn how to move their lips and tongues to make intentional sounds. Consonant–vowel combinations are produced inadvertently from time to time when the baby's mouth is closed and the mother shifts the baby's weight so that air is pushed out through the vocal tract. If the baby's mouth is closed, the air is obstructed and a consonant sound, [b] for example, is produced as the air is expelled through the baby's mouth. For the most part, young babies do not produce high vowels: the vowel sounds in *sea*, *bit*, *poor*, and *foot*, for example. In the early months the baby does not intend to produce a particular sound. If a vocalization sounds like *ma*, it is because *ma* does not require any elaborate movements in the baby's vocal apparatus. As the baby matures, he gains increasing control over his breathing and vocal apparatus and is able to produce a wide range of vowel sounds and vowel–consonant combinations.

When we look at the interaction between mothers and their prelinguistic infants we are struck by the mothers' vocal behavior – that mothers melodically vocalize to such an extent rather than verbalize. This behavior has been observed in numerous cultures, and appears to be universal. Whenever we come across a species-typical behavior, we look for biological–evolutionary explanations.

Exaggerated intonation and high pitch are effective in directing and holding the infant's attention. Cross-language comparisons of fundamental frequency characteristics, which determine pitch of the mother's and father's speech to adults and infants (Fernald et al., 1989), provide evidence for the generality of the occurrence of exaggerated intonation and high pitch in utterances to children. Fernald (1992) provides evidence for the generality of use of pitch contours for approval, prohibition, and comfort vocalizations by British, American,

German, French, and Italian mothers to their 1-year-old infants. These similarities may arise from cultural similarity of the speech communities rather than being evidence of a biological, species-specific phenomenon. However, as any person who has ever had a pet dog knows, its vocalizations convey a variety of signals: the menace of a deep growl, the pleading of a high whine, the call for attention of loud, sustained barking. The natural selection argument based on similarity of approval, prohibition, and comfort vocalizations by mothers of different speech communities to their infants who cry, coo, and babble is one of philogenetic continuity. We signal to our infants as they do us, as some mammals and the other primates do, until human infants' CNS maturation makes verbal communication possible.

Table 5.3 shows the distribution of more and less frequent conson-

Table 5.3 Relative frequency of English consonant-like sounds in the babbling of 11–12-month-old American infants

	More frequent consonants				*Less frequent consonants*		
Sound	A^a	*B*	*C*	*Sound*	A^a	*B*	*C*
h	31.77	21.0	18.3	v	1.03	1.0	0.0
d	20.58	30.0	13.5	l	0.96	1.0	1.6
b	9.79	5.0	10.0	θ	0.85	0.0	0.4
m	6.69	1.0	7.2	z	0.56	0.0	0.0
t	4.34	0.0	3.6	f	0.37	0.0	0.4
g	4.15	12.0	8.4	š	0.37	0.0	0.0
s	3.45	0.0	0.4	ð	0.34	0.0	0.8
w	3.39	17.0	8.4	ŋ	0.33	1.0	3.2
n	2.65	1.0	4.4	ž	0.10	0.0	0.0
k	2.12	1.0	6.3	r	0.10	0.0	0.0
j	1.77	9.0	11.6	č	0.00	0.0	0.0
p	1.63	0.0	1.6	ǰ	0.00	0.0	0.0
Total	92.33	97.0	93.7		5.01	3.0	6.4

[a] The A columns total less than 100% because the difference (2.66%) represents several sounds in Irwin's original tabulations that have no phonemic equivalent in American English phonology (e.g. [ʔçχ]).
Source: Locke (1983), reporting three investigations: (A) Irwin (1947); (B) Fisichelli (1950); (C) Pierce and Hanna (1974)

ants in the babbling of 11–12-month-old American infants. Among the 12 more frequent consonants are all six stops (d, b, t, g, k, and p), two of the three nasals (m and n), and one glide (w). Each of the voiced stops (d, b, g) is more frequent than its unvoiced cognate (t, p, k). The fricatives (/f/, /v/, /θ/, /ð/, /s/, /z/, /š/, /ž/), affricates (/č/ and /ǰ/), and liquids (r and l) are among the less frequent. I conclude that the more frequent are easier for infants to produce than the less frequent. Locke (1983) does not list the glottal stop. Perhaps none of his sources included it. I mention it because it is a frequently produced consonant in the prelinguistic period for Allen, Carol, Jean, and Joel.

The first evidence from the language development research involving Allen, Carol, Jean, and Joel for a reciprocal, instinctive model came from Goldner's findings (1981) on turn-taking between infants and their mothers. In the course of her work on my research project, Goldner transcribed all the turn-taking episodes on the tapes made nearest to the dates when the infants were 3, 6, 9, 12, 15, 18, and 24 months old. Goldner observed that the number of each mother's utterances over the two years that were vocalizations increased to a peak percentage and then steadily declined (figure 5.4). The 3-month and 9-month interaction episodes presented for Carol and her mother show the change in the mother's behavior. Vocalizing by the mother is a retrograde (moving backward) linguistic behavior, and yet increases during the baby's first 9 months to 1 year of life.

How would increased babbling by the mother foster language acquisition by her infant? The obvious possibility is that it fosters the infant's gaining control over her vocal tract and respiratory system so that she becomes able to intentionally produce speech sounds. Two teaching procedures can be observed in the mother's behavior: modeling and shaping. *Modeling* simply means producing a particular sound so that the infant can hear it and perhaps attempt it. *Shaping* is a procedure in which an infant vocalization is gradually altered by providing a model that changes by successive approximations to the desired behavior. The infant emits a babble and the mother responds with a babble, sometimes an imitation of the infant's, but a sound that is phonologically closer to English than the infant's babble. It is not that the mother necessarily intends to shape the infant's vocalizations: because she is an English speaker, she cannot help giving her babbles the phonological characteristics of English.

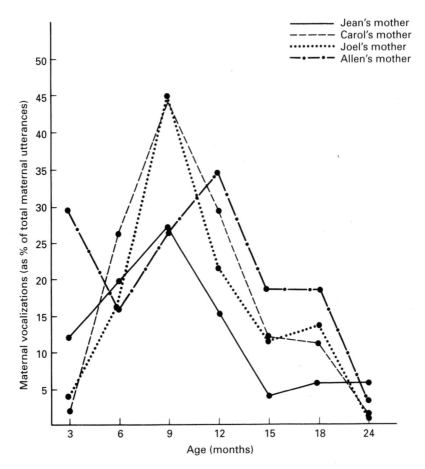

Figure 5.4 Mother vocalizations as percentage of vocalizations plus verbalizations (from Goldner, 1981)

Learning to Take a Conversational Turn

We observed, beginning with our earliest videotapes, the mothers' imposition of a conversational pattern on the infant's vocalizations. The mother does this by fitting her verbalizations and/or vocalizations in between those of her baby and constructing them so that they imply that her baby's vocalizations, vegetative noises (burps, wheezes, and so on), and actions are intended as contributions to the conversation. Snow (1977) has reported a similar finding. The effect of the mother's behavior is to provide the circumstances in which her infant can learn the first rules for participating in a conversation: only one person speaks at a time and both get a turn. Here is a turn-taking sequence with Carol and her mother when Carol was 3 months and 4 days old. Carol has been nursing; she stopped and looked into her mother's eyes. Mother is holding Carol's hand:

	CAROL	MOTHER
1	[ɛ̄] (*This has the sound of the* e *in* bed. *The flat line over the* ɛ *means that the pitch did not rise or fall*)	
2	[ʌ̀] (*The sound is that of* u *in* but. *The slanted line indicates falling pitch*)	
3		what
4	[â] (a *is the sound of* o *in* bother)	
5		yeah
6	[aw̄ aw̄] (w *is the sound of* w *in* witch)	
7		really
8	[ʌ̄wʌ]	
9		okay
10	[ah̄ ah̄ ah̄] (h *is the sound in* hat)	
11	burp	
12		fantastic

At 9 months, Carol is in the bath tub being washed by mother.

	CAROL	MOTHER
1	[aẁ] (*chews on washcloth*)	
2		It's nice, huh?
3	[m̀]	
4	[m̀]	
5	[hwh̄ wɛyɛh̄]	
6		[hɛ̀ʌɛ̄] [hm̄ hm̄]
7		[hm̄ hm̄]
8	[ʔɛm]	
9		[ʔoh̀]

10 [hya hya hya]

11   [hya hya hya]

Carol's vocalizations have been transcribed from the videotape in the notation of the International Phonetic Alphabet. If speech or vocalizations are transcribed using the IPA, then anyone who knows this system can read the transcription and figure out how the speech or vocalization sounded. IPA is used by linguists and anthropologists to communicate unambiguously about how speech samples sound. Speech in any language, as well as babble like Carol's, can be transcribed using the IPA. The portion of the IPA relevant to English transcription is reproduced in this chapter in tables 5.1 and 5.2. The square brackets surrounding Carol's vocalizations indicate that the transcription is phonetic, made on the basis of the sounds in Carol's vocalizations. When a transcription is enclosed by two slanted lines (/ /), rather than square brackets, the vocalization is a speech sound (including words and sentences) in the language being transcribed. This is called a phonemic transcription and can be made only if the transcriber knows that the sounds being produced are phonemes or meaning-relevant speech sounds. Since Carol does not yet have language, her vocalizations are not phonemic. The speaker must intend to be speaking words and the transcriber must understand which words the speaker is saying for a phonemic transcription to be made. The transcriptions would still be made in the phonetic symbols of the IPA, but within slanted lines to mean that these speech sounds are phonemes of the language being transcribed. Carol's mother's utterances have been transcribed *orthographically* (in the written English alphabet). The lines above Carol's and her mother's utterances give the pitch contours of their utterances. We pay attention only to whether pitch is rising, falling, or steady but not how fast or how much it rises or falls. If you compare the interaction between Carol and her mother at 3 months and 9 months, you will see the mother's shift from verbal to vocal.

Learning to Use the Pitch Contours and the Sounds of Speech

Mothers probably are not consciously aware of responding more frequently to babies' vocalizations with vocalizations of their own rather than with verbalizations. Unconsciously, they are led to vocalize because their babies evidence greater interest in their vocalizing, reflected in the infants' greater responsiveness to vocalizing. The mother's vocalizing is positively reinforced by the infant's response to it. If we assume that it is biologically adaptive for human beings to have language, then we can assume that the mother's increased vocalizing serves a biological function, the infant's acquiring the phonology of language. If we listen to the cooing or babbling of very young infants, we cannot tell what language their native language will be. If we listen a year or so later, we can hear the intonation (pitch contours) and phonetic structure (speech sounds) of the language they hear.

We have examined samples of the babies' babbles and mothers' vocal responses during the infants' first year. The following examples are for Allen. We find some true imitations in which the mother accurately produces both the infant's pitch and phonological form as

   1 ALLEN: [ʔah̄]   2 MOTHER: [ʔah̄]

Mothers also produce *stereotyped* baby noises in which the mother's response is not closely related to the infant's production. Processes of conventionalization appear to be at work. A mother will produce an "Anglicized" form of noises her baby is currently making. What often happens is that, after one or two close imitations, the mother slips into her stereotyped form, which may be produced in order to elicit more interaction by the baby.

ALLEN	MOTHER
1	[m̆]
2 [m̀]	
3	[m̄]
4	[m̆]
5 [m̀]	

[m̆] is a stereotyped utterance produced by Allen in the second year, together with an open-handed reach, a gestural–vocal communication indicating a desire to be given something out of his reach.

Here is another conventionalized response:

   1 ALLEN: [ag̑ʌ]   2 MOTHER: [gū]

In Western culture, babies are supposed to say "goo" so when Allen said "[agʌ]" the mother's imitation moved the vocalization in the direction of the cultural stereotype for baby talk.

At 12 months, and increasingly at 15 and 18 months, mothers imitate the pitch contour on a baby's vocalization but produce an English word closely related phonetically to the baby's production.

1	ALLEN:	[ɛ̂]		2	MOTHER:	yeah
1	CAROL:	[bo]		2	MOTHER:	boat, boat
1	JOEL:	[næ̀næ̀]		2	MOTHER:	no

We can interpret figure 5.4 in this way: the mother's vocalizations to her baby increase during the first months of the infant's life because the baby becomes more responsive to vocalizations in comparison to verbalizations. The mother's increased vocalizations are imitations of the infant's vocalizations, but include other vocalizations that are phonologically like English. It appears that this moves the infant's vocalizations in the direction of English phonology. Beginning at 12 months for three of the babies and 15 months for the fourth, the mother's vocalizations decline. Mothers are still responding imitatively to their babies' vocalizations, but selectively. If a baby's vocalization resembles an English word, the mother utters the word.

Here are examples of Carol's and Joel's interaction with their mothers at 18 months. Carol's mother puts Carol in the bath tub and says:

	CAROL	MOTHER
1		Hot today
2	[kò]	
3		Cold

Carol points to the video operator and says:

1	CAROL:	[t s ah]		2	MOTHER:	Joanne, right

Joel is sitting in the bath tub; he smiles at his mother, grinds his teeth, and says:

1	JOEL:	[t ih]		2	MOTHER:	teeth

A little later, Joel is just sitting in the tub, mother catches his eye and whispers:

JOEL		MOTHER
1		No (*whispered*)
2	(*laughs*)	
3		No (*whispered, but louder*)
4	[dɛh]	
5		Yes (*normal voice*)
6	[dɛh]	
7		Yes (*normal voice*)
8	(*laughs*)	

Mothers continue to vocalize non-imitatively to their babies but at low rates and in ways similar to the early months. Carol's mother says "Dubba, dubba, dubba" as she dries Carol at 15 months. Vocalizing has ceased having a teaching function for these mothers.

We started this discussion by pointing out that, before babies are verbal, they can learn the two basic rules of conversation: one person at a time and both get turns. The interactions between Carol and her mother presented to show the change in mother vocalization in the prelinguistic period are also examples of turn-taking in the prelinguistic period. In the course of the discussion we have seen that, in this small sample, mothers are probably unconsciously teaching their infants how to make babbles that sound like English words and conversations and the infants are learning English phonology. In the examples presented for Carol and Joel and their mothers at 18 months, we would be tempted to say Carol and Joel really know these words, but cannot pronounce them. I think this is the case.

Learning to Participate in a Ritualized Game

Even though the baby becomes a partner in turn-taking episodes with his mother (rather than simply having her fit her contributions around his so that a turn-taking pattern results), some of these episodes remain simply rituals. In many instances, including the games infants are taught to play, this is true. We have watched infants learning to participate in games like "peek-a-boo." The earliest example we have seen involved an infant, Sue, and her mother, whom we studied during Sue's first year.

When Sue was almost 5 months old, we first observed her mother, with Sue supine on the changing table and ready to be freshly diapered, throw a diaper over Sue's head and croon, "Where's the baby? Where's the baby?" She then removed the diaper and very brightly and enthusiastically called, "There's the baby!" Two weeks later, after her mother had carried out the routine through the two "Where's the baby?" utterances, Sue removed the diaper from her own face, and then her mother said, "There's the baby!" By the time Sue was 6 months old, Sue both covered her face with the diaper and removed it. In our observation at 6 months, the moment Sue's mother noticed she was pulling the diaper over her face, she quickly sang out, "Where's the baby? Where's the baby?" Sue pulled the diaper away from her face, and her mother said, "There's the baby!"

During our next observation, the mother was somewhat preoccupied as she diapered Sue. Sue pulled the diaper on and off her face with no response from her mother, who was jabbering about "baa, baa, black sheep." Again, Sue pulled the diaper on and off her face, with still no response from her mother, so this time Sue provided an elongated vocalization herself after pulling the diaper off her face. Even though Sue "knows" that "Where's the baby?" has a sequence – face covered, vocalization with rising pitch, face uncovered, vocalizations with level or falling pitch – she doesn't know what the actions or the vocalizations mean or signify. It's a little routine she has learned to do with her mother. Usually her mother is very interested in the game; her mother smiles, talks in a loving voice, and displays behaviors that are reinforcing to Sue at an age when she has strong attachment needs. So, going through the ritual is rewarding to Sue, even though she does not understand the question, "Where's the baby?" or that pulling the diaper away from her face provides the appropriate occasion for the response, "There's the baby." It is sound and action play, and the sounds do not have the meaning of words in the English language. Preverbal infants' linguistic abilities are just like those of the pets described in chapter 3. The fact that my friend's dog rolls over on its back with its feet in the air when my friend says, "Die for the Queen!" doesn't mean the dog understands the meaning of "Die for the Queen" in the English language. It is a sound signal to which the dog has been conditioned to give the appropriate behavior; such is the case with the prelinguistic or preverbal infant.

Gestures into Words

Infants are at the beginning of a developmental sequence that will culminate in their becoming language users. Therefore, their rituals and gestures, which are borderline linguistic behaviors, have significance because they are not part of the infant's repertoire of innate signaling behaviors but have been acquired in interaction with their mothers. We distinguish between rituals (including games like "peek-a-boo") and imitations, on the one hand, and gestures, on the other, on the basis of the function of the behaviors for the person engaging in them. Gestures have an instrumental function; rituals and imitation have a social play or practice function. The clearest example of a gesture by the infants we have observed is the requesting or directive gesture. It has also been observed in infants by Bates et al. (1975), Carter (1975), Menn (1976), and Masur (1978) among others. It consists of an open-handed reach accompanied by a vocalization with rising pitch contour. For Allen, the vocalization we observed was [m̂m]; for Carol, [ẑIs]; for Jean, [âh]; for Joel, [d̂æ]. Since we observed for only half an hour every other week, it is quite possible that the babies used requesting gestures other than the ones we observed.

The evolution of the gesture is from innate arm-extending movement to visually directed behavior. Not all reaches culminate in the infant's securing the object for which she is reaching. When an infant reaches unsuccessfully and at the same time vocalizes in the presence of her mother in an attention-attracting manner so that the mother (a) looks at her infant, (b) looks in the direction of her reach, and (c) offers her or points to a possible object and says for example, "Do you want this?," circumstances are right for the gestures to be learned. It is learned by conditioning as are the animals' learned signals described in chapter 3. The instrumental function of the requesting or directive behavior is to get someone to do something for you by indicating that you want it done. If the mother offers her infant what the infant wants, the requesting behavior is positively reinforced and is learned so that the infant will use that gesture appropriately. We have discussed the fact that infant vocalizations are moved in the direction of English words in their mothers' responses to them, and sometimes there is good evidence that vocalizations are the infant's intended approximations of English words. In the early stage, when infants become capable of using a vocalization with rising pitch together with an open-handed reach to produce a requesting gesture, it is not of much significance whether the vocalization is a word or just a consistent sound. Whichever it is, it has no meaning for the infant except as part of his requesting gesture. We will consider this the borderline period between prelinguistic and linguistic periods in the development of language.

Carol accompanied her reach with the vocalizations [z͡Is]. It looks as though [z͡Is] is Carol's reproduction of the last word in her mother's question, "Do you want this?" Allen used [m͡m] and Jean [a͡h] in the same way that Carol used [z͡Is], but we were not tempted to call these words because they do not sound like words. It is plausible that Joel's [d͡æ] is his rendering of *that*, analogous to Carol's rendering of *this*. We do not have evidence from the videotape that this is the case for Joel; Joel's mother has not asked Joel if he wants that – at least not on the videotapes. But Joel has used [d͡æ] three times in his request gestures, and never another word or vocalization, so the criteria described in chapter 6 for status as a word are met by [d͡æ]. We have put the beginning of the linguistic period earlier than some theorists would. These theorists would date the beginning of the linguistic period from the time the child uses words for *reference*, to name an object to which the child is calling attention.

Words in Ritual

One reason for deciding to date the linguistic period from the first three occurrences of the first word is that it is sometimes difficult to judge whether a child is actually naming an object as opposed to participating in a little ritual.

We have an example of Joel's imitating the word *kitty*, combined with a pointing gesture at 12 months. Joel's mother had, since Joel was 10 months old, engaged in pointing at objects and naming them for Joel. To a child who has not cracked the sound–meaning code, pointing plus uttering a word is learned as a ritual. Here is an example of an exchange between Joel and his mother in their backyard:

JOEL: (*points to a bear in a picture book*) [ki ki]
MOTHER: That's not a kitty. That's a bear.
JOEL: (*points to a kitty in book*) [ki]
MOTHER: Kitty. Uh huh. Gee that kitty just comes out all over the place.
JOEL: (*points to a grasshopper*)
MOTHER: That's a grasshopper. He's drinking from the kitty's water.
JOEL: [ki] (*points to a boat*)
MOTHER: Kitty, there's a kitty (*points to kitty*)
JOEL: [ki] (*points to kitty*)
MOTHER: Kitty. Uh huh.

JOEL:	(*takes blocks with pictures out of toy box, points to kitty on a block*)
MOTHER:	Where's the kitty cat? There's the kitty cat. That's right. Where's the kitty cat again? Where's the kitty cat?
JOEL:	(*points to chicken*)
MOTHER:	That's a chicken. Where's the kitty cat?
JOEL:	(*points to bunny*)
MOTHER:	Bunny. That's a bunny. Where's the kitty cat? Show me the kitty cat?
JOEL:	(*points to snail*) [ki]
MOTHER:	Kitty? That's not a kitty. That's a snail.

Joel has learned the word combined with a pointing gesture as an imitation of his mother. He has the word plus gesture as a social ritual, and again by the criteria described in chapter 6, [ki] is counted as a word.

At this point, these infants are making the transition to language use; they are learning to articulate the sounds of their language and to enjoy imitative rituals involving words. Further, they have learned to use rising pitch in their request vocalizations. This can be added to the two conversational rules: one at a time, and each gets a turn. Rising intonation (pitch contour) on the end of an utterance indicates that there is more to come; the discourse has not been concluded. In a conversation, if a speaker ends an utterance with rising intonation, this indicates that the speaker wants to pass the turn to another participant. In the case of the infant's request gesture, the turn is being passed on to fulfill the baby's request.

The prelinguistic period comes gradually to an end as the infant begins to incorporate an approximation of an English word into request gestures and/or social games and rituals. The infant learns first words in a social interaction with another human being, and the infant learns, as part of learning the word, the appropriate intonation for the word in that kind of social interaction. In other words, the infant is not learning the word; rather, the infant is learning to *use* the word in a particular social interaction.

Further Reading

Boysson-Bardies, B. and Vihman, M. (1991). "Adaptation to language: evidence from babbling and first words in four languages," *Language*, 67: 297–319.

A cross-linguistic study providing evidence that babies adapt their vocalizations to the vowel and consonant sounds in the ambient language. Infants babble in their mother tongue before they speak it.

Goodman, J. C. and Nusbaum, H. C. (eds) (1994) *The Development of Speech Perception: the Transition from Speech Sounds to Spoken Words* (Cambridge, Mass.: MIT Press).

Halle, P. and Boysson-Bardies, B. (1994) "Emergence of an early receptive lexicon: infants' recognition of words," *Infant Behavior and Development*, 17: 119–29.

Infants pay attention longer to words that have been found in early productive lexicons than to words rare in use in France. Evidence for a receptive lexicon in 1-year-olds, just emerging at 11 months.

Jusczyk, P. W., Hirsch-Pasek, K., Kemler-Nelson, D. G., Kennedy, L. J., et al. (1992) "Perception of acoustic correlates of major phrasal units by young infants," *Cognitive Psychology*, 24: 252–93.

The pattern holds across both subject phrases and predicate phrases and across samples of both child- and adult-directed speech.

Keller, H. (1961) *The Story of My Life* (New York: Dell reprint).

Liberman, A. M. and Mattingly, I. G. (1989) "A specialization for speech perception," *Science*, 243: 489–94.

Liberman and Mattingly promote the view that the specifically phonetic aspects of speech perception are the articulatory gestures of which all linguistic utterances are ultimately composed and stand apart from voice quality and affective tone, for example, which they propose are like non-speech sounds in their perceptual primitives. Perception of gestures is controlled by "a phonetic module," a specialization for speech that has its own modes of signal analysis and its own primitives so that phonetic perception is immediate. No cognitive translation from patterns of pitch, loudness and timbre is required.

Locke, J. L. (1993) *The Child's Path to Spoken Language* (Cambridge, Mass.: Harvard University Press).

Locke is interested in the communicative process in the infant to spoken language.

Mandler, J. M. (1992) "How to build a baby: II. Conceptual primitives," *Psychological Review*, 99: 587–604.

Describes a mechanism of perceptual analysis by which infants derive meaning from perceptual activity. Infants use this mechanism to redescribe perceptual information into image-schematic format. Redescription into image-schematic format simplifies perceptual information and makes it potentially accessible for purposes of concept formation and thought. In addition to enabling preverbal thought, image-schemas provide a foundation for language acquisition by creating an interface between the continuous processes of perception and the discrete nature of language.

Petitto, L. A. and Marentette, P. F. (1991) "Babbling in the manual mode: evidence for the ontogeny of language," *Science*, 251: 1493–96.

Deaf infants acquiring ASL make not fully formed signs analogous to hearing infants early vocal babbling.

Tomasello, M. (1992) "The social bases of language acquisition," *Social Development*, 1: 67–87.

Language is composed of conventional symbols shaped by their social-communicative functions. Children acquire these symbols in the context of culturally constituted event structures. In the acquisition process, children rely on cultural learning skills (i.e. imitative learning).

6

The One-word Period

The one-word period marks the transition from behavior that is continuous with the signaling behavior of other animal species to behavior that, as far as we know, is unique to the human species: the communicative and productive use of syntactic language. In chapter 5, we looked at developments in the prelinguistic infant's behavior related to the infant's becoming a language user. We noted that infants learn the first rules for participating in a conversation: one at a time, both get a turn. They learn to imitate, or learn by rote, what to them are just sounds but are actually English words. They also learn to employ what starts out as an instrumental act as a gesture. That is, Joel, Jean, Carol, and Allen acquired a request or a directive gesture based on reaching for an object (the instrumental act) and, at the same time, making a noise to get their mothers' attention. In this chapter we will consider the shift from action to discourse in carrying out interpersonal functions and the evolution of sounds and gestures into words. These developments take place in the course of the infant language learner's daily life, and for Allen, Carol, Jean, and Joel, it was primarily in interaction with their mothers. These infants became language users, as do most human beings, as part of their everyday experience.

The one-word period has fuzzy boundaries. Changes in the language behavior of human infants tend to be local and gradual. It does not happen that one day an infant cannot produce any words and a week later she has a vocabulary of 20 words, or even just 10. Vocabulary increases slowly early in the one-word period as we track it with the bi-weekly videos made in Allen, Carol, Jean, and Joel's homes as their mothers carry out the undressing, bathing, and dressing routines with their infants. The number of times the infants utter a word is highly variable. Carol spoke her first word, *Mommy*, on videotape at 1,0(1); Jean, *Daddy* at 8(8); Allen, *Allen* at 10(28); and Joel, *cup*, at 1,0(8).[1]

In the beginning, it is sometimes difficult to tell if the infant's speech sounds are words. When I was little, my mother used to say about my bad behavior, "The first time, it's an accident; the second, a coincidence; but the third time, it's a habit." I have adopted this criterion for "word." It doesn't have to sound like the adult version; it doesn't have to "mean" in a conventional way, but it does have to have sufficient consistency of sound and use to be interpretable as associated with a particular occasion, context, or referent. It has to have at least the status of what Terrace (1985) has called a "paired associate" or be an imitation of another's word, typically the mother's. The little child who holds out his hand and says "Thank you" as he looks at the cookie in his mother's hand, and also says "Thank you" as he gives his mother the toy he has been holding, associates "Thank you" with giving and receiving objects. "Thank you" is a paired associate with the action, give–receive.

We can identify vocalizations as imitations or paired associates (Terrace, 1985) because we are looking at infants in relation to the context in which they vocalize. We have heard the mother's utterance that the child is imitating. We see the referent with which the child's utterance is paired.

We included as words imitations by the child of its mother, words that occurred as parts of rituals and words used gesturally as described in chapter 5. In these cases, the words do not have referential meaning, that is, words are not being used by the infant to refer to objects or other aspects of the world; rather, they are used on occasions that have become associated for the child with a particular verbal behavior on her part. The game of "peek-a-boo," widely played by infants and caregivers, provides the occasion for the one who has been hiding her face to show it and for the other to say "peek-a-boo." "Hello," "goodbye," and other greetings are also verbalizations that have only occasion meaning rather than referential meaning. Parents usually understand that a child's word is a word when the child has a consistent meaning for it or occasion for its use, even if it does not sound the conventional way. Little children sometimes have difficulty pronouncing some speech sounds, and we make allowance for this. When Carol was saying [zIs], reaching for something out of reach and looking at her mother, and this was the only circumstance in which she used [zIs], [zIs] was a signal or gesture rather than an abstract word. When Joel went through the ritual with his mother of pointing at a picture, a bug, or an animal and saying [ki] (described in chapter 5), and this was his only use of [ki], the use was not referential. The occasion I feel least comfortable about calling word use is imitation, the most primitive speech act. The child imitates a word his mother has said. It may not even be a word from the sentence she has just said but from a sentence said several sentences earlier. The child may simply be imitating the sound.

The one-word period, as we have defined it, has an early stage (A) in which words are used only as imitations or paired associates, a more advanced stage (B) when the word is used in carrying out more than one speech act, and a final stage (C) when the child has experienced the nominal insight (Dore, 1978) that everything has a name. Because development is local and gradual, especially in the early weeks of the one-word period, the stages are not always synchronous for words. One word may be at stage B when another is just an imitation or paired associate. After the child has the insight that everything has a name, new words are acquired immediately as abstract symbols.

Little children are not able to think about their thoughts and beliefs, so it is impossible to get meaningful answers from them to questions such as "Do you remember before you could really talk what you thought when your mother said 'Where's the baby?', or you said 'kitty' and pointed at a grasshopper or 'this' and held out your hand for your duck?" One source of information about preverbal memories is Helen Keller's autobiography, *The Story of My Life* (1961).

Helen Keller was almost 7 years old when Annie Sullivan came to Helen's home in Alabama to teach her. In Helen Keller's book, events are recounted by Helen and, in addition, are reported in extracts from the letters of Annie Sullivan to Mrs Sophia C. Hopkins, who had been a matron at Perkins Institution and "like a mother" to Annie Sullivan when she had been a pupil there. The book is fascinating as a human document. In addition, the early chapters are relevant to the question of what it is like to be without language. It must be remembered that Helen Keller was without sight and hearing so that her experience of the world came from touch, taste, and smell only. She was cut off from the world in a way that infants are not. Despite her terrible disabilities, she was, according to Annie Sullivan, a large, strong, and ruddy child "as unrestricted in her movement as a young colt. She had none of these nervous habits that are so noticeable and so distressing in blind children" (Keller, 1961: 260).

What I found surprising is that Helen Keller had a substantial repertoire of gestures that she used to communicate with her family and others before Annie Sullivan came. For example, she played with a little girl, Martha Washington, the child of the Keller's cook. Helen tells how she liked to hunt for guinea fowl eggs, found in the long grass of out-of-the-way places. "I could not tell Martha Washington when I wanted to go egg hunting, but I would double my hands and put them on the ground, which meant something round in the grass, and Martha always understood" (Keller, 1961: 25). Helen had a large stock of such gestures, which, as she describes them, were like the early one-word period gestures, specific to one function, of Allen, Carol, Jean, and Joel. When Annie Sullivan arrived at Helen Keller's home, she was met by Helen.

> [Helen] felt my face and dress and my bag, which she took out of my hand and tried to open. It did not open easily, and she felt carefully to see if there was a key hole. Finding that there was she turned to me making the sign of turning a key and pointing to the bag. Her mother interfered at this point and showed Helen by signs that she must not touch the bag. (Keller, 1961: 259)

Helen considered her signs to be gestures rather than words. Even though they made it possible for Helen to communicate with family and friends and to be communicated with, Helen reports that her use of gestures never led to her gaining the understanding that "everything has a name."

The preverbal gestural repertoires of Allen, Carol, Jean, and Joel were much more limited than that of Helen Keller, but their gestures functioned in the same way as Helen's – to get someone to do something. Helen Keller does not report having gestures that were just for social play purposes, which Allen, Carol, Jean, and Joel had. When Annie Sullivan first spelled d-o-l-l and other words into one of Helen's hands, at the same time giving Helen the doll or other object in her other hand, Helen learned to finger spell and associate spellings with objects without understanding that the spelling was the object's name. Helen Keller later wrote:

The morning after my teacher came she gave me a doll – when I had played with it a little while, Miss Sullivan slowly spelled into my hand the word, "d-o-l-l." I was at once interested in this finger play and tried to imitate it. When I finally succeeded in making the letters correctly I was flushed with childish pride and pleasure. I did not know that I was spelling a word or even that words existed. I was simply making my fingers go in monkey-like imitation. In the days that followed I learned to spell in this incomprehending way a great many words, among them pin, hat, cup, and a few verbs like sit, stand, and walk. (Keller, 1961: 33)

Helen Keller had a large repertoire of gestures that she understood and produced before Annie Sullivan came to teach her. But having words as names is very different. It depends on understanding that words have referential meaning. The understanding that words name objects came to Helen Keller in a dramatic moment,

One day, while I was playing with my new doll, Miss Sullivan put my big rag doll in my lap also, spelled "d-o-l-l" and tried to get me to understand that "d-o-l-l" applied to them both. Earlier in the day we had a tussle over the words "m-u-g" and "w-a-t-e-r." Miss Sullivan had tried to impress on me that "m-u-g" is *mug* and "w-a-t-e-r" is *water*, but I persisted in confounding the two . . . She brought me my hat and I knew I was going out into the warm sunshine, and this thought, if a wordless sensation can be called a thought, made me hop and skip with pleasure. We walked down to the well house . . . Someone was drawing water and my teacher placed my hand under the spout. As the cool stream gushed over one hand she spelled into the other hand, water, first slowly and then rapidly. I stood still, my whole attention fixed upon the motions of her fingers. Suddenly I felt a misty consciousness as of something forgotten – a thrill of returning thought; and somehow the mystery of language was revealed to me. I knew then that "w-a-t-e-r" meant the cool something that was flowing over my hand. That living word awakened my soul, gave it light, hope, joy, set it free! (Keller, 1961: 34)

Annie Sullivan described what happened next.

A new light came in to her face. She spelled *water* several times. Then she dropped on the ground and asked for *its* name and pointed to the pump and the trellis, and suddenly turning around she asked for my name. I spelled *teacher* . . . All the way back to the house she was highly excited and learned the name of every object she touched so that in a few hours she had added 30 new words to her vocabulary. (Keller, 1961: 274)

As far as I can tell from what Helen Keller and Annie Sullivan have written, Helen's gestures remained like the words of Allen, Carol, Jean, and Joel at the beginning of the one-word stage. Each gesture was used by Helen for just one function until she had the insight that "everything has a name." Helen did not experience the intermediate stage in which a word is used for more than one function but still does not have the abstract status of a name or what we, technically, call a common noun. I think the reason for this is that her blindness and deafness deprived her of the experiences that foster the development of occasion meaning for words. Helen couldn't play "peek-a-boo." She was not taught to greet people with "Hi" and "Bye-bye." She could not imitate the words of her mother, and she would not have known if her mother imitated her. She was deprived of social play and ritual experience with language.

Along with other investigators of child language (Greenfield and Smith, 1976; Dore, 1978; Bates et al., 1988, for example), we have found that the one-word period is lengthy. For our children, it lasted from 4 to 6 months. I do not want to sound precise because the beginnings and endings have fuzzy boundaries. For the greater part of the one-word period, the single words were used for more than one function.

The transition from stage A, in which a word is used by a child for one kind of speech act or function, to stage B occurs when the word can be used in more than one type of speech act. For example, on the 12-month tape Allen produced /dædi/, *Daddy*, three times, imitating his mother. On the next tape at $12\frac{1}{2}$ months, Allen, hearing his father downstairs in the house, said "/dædi/ Daddy." In this instance he was *reporting Daddy* as associated with the vocalization and other sounds from downstairs. *Imitations* and *reports* are different speech acts. So, Allen's stage A, "Daddy," lasted, at most for two weeks.

Infants do not communicate to parents that they have an insightful experience, that everything has a name, or that they have cracked the sound–meaning code. Even children as old as 3 or 4 years appear unable to think about their use of language in the way Helen Keller reports doing at 7 years. For infants between 1 and 2 years of age, cracking the sound–meaning code is an unconscious process. A rapid increase in vocabulary or verbalization at 17–18 months was observed by Dore (1978) and Nelson (1973) and attributed by them to the infant's unconscious realization that objects have names. When the infant understands, unconsciously, that the speech sounds she hears are symbols standing for objects like tables, actions like jumping, and qualities like hot, the infant has cracked the code and can use words to communicate, think, and remember. We may say that, for the infant, words now have meaning as words in the English language.

To summarize what has been said thus far about the course of development of language use by the human infant: the newborn has an innate repertoire of signals, including smiling, cries, and babbling. Like animals in contact with human beings, the human infant in inter-action with others develops new communicative behaviors. In the kind of environment in which the infants of our research live as firstborns and with their mothers as principal care-takers, infants learn English phonology, first rules of conversation, and requesting gestures before they are really verbal. First words are learned as components of ges-tures and rituals, *not* as abstract symbols. Then, slowly or suddenly, the child gains the insight that everything has a name, and words become abstract symbols for the child rather than utterances tied to particular gestures or occasions.

The Primitive Speech Act

In chapters 4 and 5, I sketched the idea of speech acts and the com-plementarity of speech-act analysis and linguistic analysis in an under-standing of human language behavior.

During the one-word period infants manage to convey a variety of messages using the same word. Until the 1970s, the most widely held idea concerning the status of the one-word utterances of infants was that the one-word utterance stood for a sentence. This led to calling one-word utterances *holophrases*, meaning one-word sentences. John Dore (1978) proposed that the one-word utterances of infants should be conceptualized, not as holophrases, but as primitive speech acts. Dore pointed out that this both avoided the problems of trying to figure out what the sentence might be that the holophrases repres-ented and also took account of the intonational and gestural com-ponents of the one-word communication. This was important because it was the contrasts in the intonational and gestural accompaniments of one-word utterances that had encouraged the idea that one-word utterances mean more than the meaning of the single word. Dore saw that the single words were being used to carry out different functions and that contrasting intonation and gestures distinguished functions. For example, the infant, Dory, points to her mother's neck-lace and says "/bidz/," *beads*, labeling or referring to the necklace. Later, after Dory has been allowed to play with the necklace and her mother takes it back, Dory says "/bidz/," requesting that the necklace be returned to her.

We have discussed how Allen, Carol, Jean, and Joel learned to put final rising intonation on a vocalization or word while making a reach-ing gesture in order to ask for something, thereby performing what Dore (1978) termed a primitive speech act. Dore called the rising intonation plus reach the primitive force of the speech act. The word that the infant speaks (with the rising intonation) is the rudimentary referring expression, all the language there is in the primitive speech act. One-word requests like Carol's /zIs/, *this*, can be interpreted only by looking at what Carol seems to be reaching for and checking with her. And this is what her mother did. When Allen reached for his turtle-shaped bar of soap and said "/turtl/," he was using a prim-itive referring expression to ask for the soap.

It seems plausible that the requesting speech act developed initially from a failure on the infant's part to reach a desired object. He con-tinued holding out his hand, which didn't reach, in the direction of the object and made a vocal noise which attracted his mother's atten-tion. She looked in the direction of the reach, offered the object the infant seemed to want, and maybe a second or third if the first wasn't satisfactory. If the routine was successful, the infant's vocalization plus reach, the primitive speech act, would be conditioned in just the way behaviors of pets and experimental animals have been. Securing the desired but unreachable object would provide the positive re-inforcement to condition the reach plus vocalization.

I regard primitive speech acts as continuous with the signaling beha-vior of animals in contact with people, described in chapter 3. Distin-guishing utterer's meaning and meaning of the sentence in the language makes it possible to analyze the function of the speech act separately from its formal characteristics as an expression in the English language.

There would be no point in applying such an analysis to the signaling behavior of animals in the wild because each signal conveys particular information; the sending of the information is involuntary, its effect on the animals who receive it is involuntary. All is the result of innate coordinations that were biologically adaptive in the animals' environment of biological adaptation. The situation is different when we consider animals in contact with human beings and when we consider infants. Both become conditioned to respond to and to produce *learned* signaling behavior.

There are differences of opinion regarding the relationship of the function of a speech act (what the speaker means by an utterance) and the formal properties of the utterance as a sentence in the English language. Searle initially (1969) proposed that the relationship is quite direct, that the formal characteristics determine what function can be expressed. In my research (Holzman, 1973, 1974), I have found many instances in which the speaker uses an utterance in a way that is quite indirectly related to formal characteristics of the utterance. As we have seen, it is possible for pets and trained animals to understand what their trainer means by an utterance without any understanding of the utterance as a sentence in the English language. I think the same is true of infants; they understand what their mothers mean by an utterance before they understand utterances as a sentence in the English language. And they understand on the same basis that they are understood, by means of the intonation and gestures that go along with utterances. Mothers' speech to their infants is characterized by short and frequently repeated utterances that focus on the here and now so that what is happening to the infant is glossed over and over in the mother's speech in utterances short enough to have clear signal value. I feel reasonably confident that this is the case, not only on the basis of my own work but also because there is general agreement among child language specialists that infants respond to *prosodic* features of utterances (stress and pitch patterns) before they understand actual words or sentences. This is not unlike the response of pets.

In addition to the *communicative* functions of primitive speech acts, two other functions, observable in data for Allen, Carol, Jean, and Joel, are *actions for self*, not communicative in their intent. The first, *labeling* and categorizing as a basis for thinking, is seen by Lempert and Kinsbourne (1985) as having its origin in selective orienting to a percept by naming it. A large proportion of our thinking is mediated by words. When we were mulling over verbal thinking and mental-pictures thinking in class, the only problem which we solved using pictures rather than words was "How many windows are there in your house?" We all spontaneously took a walk through our houses, room by room, and counted the windows. Names for objects, actions, feelings, and so on are indispensable for filing their referents in our long-term memories so the referents can be retrieved from memory using their labels, the names we have attached.

The other action for self we can observe in our research data is *practice*. The infant repeats a word at least twice for it to count as practice, and often five or more times. Frequently, the infant's pronunciation of the word changes as she repeats the word, suggesting that the infant is working on pronunciation. Lempert and Kinsbourne (1985) hypothesize that the early naming, which they identify as action for self, is seen as communicative because the infant voices the name, the mother hears it and interprets it as meant for her ears.

We have coded the infant's vocal and verbal productions as communicative or not using direction of gaze and interactive involvement with mother as criteria. We code each utterance or action of infant and mother which appears on a videotape as either communicative or for self. The codings for self are (a) non-interactional and (b) self-guiding. Self-guides are mainly codings of the mother. She is talking to herself about her agenda, what she is doing. She is not trying for eye contact with her infant and her intonation shifts from the ear-catching dynamics of her infant-directed utterances to much less vibrant, and longer utterances. Communicative utterances are (a) to initiate an interaction; (b) to continue an interaction; (c) to continue but change the topic; and (d) to communicate with a third person. Fathers sometimes come on the scene and infants sometimes try to initiate communication with the video operator. (During taping the video operator does not speak to infant or mother.) Coding applies to both infants and mothers.

In any ordinary conversation between two people, topics get discussed. Conversational utterances of mother and infant are for the most part focused on the immediate context of the conversation rather than an interesting movie or the federal deficit. The talk is mostly about balls, soap, and other objects and activities associated with the baby's bath because the central event in all the tapes is the daily bath. The participants' contributions reflect the mother's fluency and the infant's lack of fluency. In addition to ordinary conversational contributions, there are mother utterances which teach and infant utterances which are for self: for "thinking" or practice. I do not mean that the mother consciously intends to teach or the infant to practice. In both cases I regard the behavior as instinctive in the contemporary formulation of instinctive (Bowlby, 1969; Holzman, 1984).

Over the course of the one-word period, infants develop from being signalers – like other animals – to being communicators, a capability unique to the human species as far as reliable research indicates. The one-word period has its fuzzy ending as infants become able to communicate using multi-word utterances, structured according to an early grammar (Brown, 1973). The use of syntactically structured utterances is, again, unique to human beings. As a result of these linguistic developments, speech acts are no longer primitive – limited to one word.

In the one-word period, it is possible to investigate whether speech arises from an innate need to communicate, with what is learned by the infant being the terms of reference of the speech community (Terrace, 1985), or whether pointing and speaking emerge as a component of action-for-self (Lempert and Kinsbourne, 1985). According to Lempert and Kinsbourne, pointing with naming reflects the infant's focus of attention, and is a component of the infant's self-orienting, and is not for the purpose of communicating.

Table 6.1 presents a sample of data on proportions of communicative and non-communicative utterances for Carol and Jean during the one-word period. The data indicate that early utterances of a word by Jean and Carol may be either communicative or for self. At 11 months and 5 days during videotaping Jean said one word, "Daddy," 27 times, and only 22 percent of the time was she actually talking to her mother. Most of the time, she was saying "Daddy" to herself. When Carol was 13 months old (1,1(2)), she said "Daddy" once and "bath" twice, all three times to her mother. When Jean was 16 months old (1,4(1)), she spoke five words a total of 14 times: 79 percent of the time it was to her mother. At the same age Carol spoke five words 24 times and only a third of the time was it to her mother; except for this occasion, at least half of Carol's utterances were for her mother.

Jean is more variable. I think her utterances become less frequent

Table 6.1 Communicative and non-communicative utterances

Age	C/(C + non-C)	No. types	No. tokens
Carol			
1,1(2)	100	2	3
1,1(26)	100	1	5
1,2(9)	0	0	0
1,2(19)	100	1	1
1,3(16)	60	2	5
1,4(0)	33	5	24
1,4(14)	67	5	30
1,5(0)	93	5	15
1,5(13)	52	12	44
1,6(2)	96	13	49
1,6(17)	85	20	81
1,7(2)	98	12	39
Jean			
11(5)	22	1	27
11(26)	0	1	2
1,0(9)	36	1	31
1,1(14)	79	5	14
1,1(19)	100	4	10
1,2(3)	100	2	8
1,2(10)	42	6	12
1,4(1)	79	5	14
1,4(12)	85	4	34
1,14(26)	45	4	33
1,5(9)	70	3	10
1,5(22)	58	3	12
1,6(6)	77	8	31
1,6(20)	75	4	8
1,7(7)	67	2	3

C = communicative; types = words; tokens = utterances.

than Carol's later in the one-word period because the two mothers have very different interactive styles with their language-developing daughters. Carol's mother always takes her cue from Carol and follows Carol's lead, while Jean's mother introduces her own topics, not necessarily ones which will elicit a response from Jean. Late in the one-word period, Jean's mother asked Jean, "Who's coming to dinner?" Jean responded, "Awdwy." "Yes," says Jean's mother, "Audrey and Stuart. Stuart is Audrey's husband."

Communicative and non-communicative utterances are aggregates of specific speech acts. The non-communicative examples we have described are practice and solitary play. Lempert and Kinsbourne's (1985) self-orienting function may be an aspect of either. Practice is intentional and may be directed not only at mastering the phonology of a word but also at understanding its reference for storing in long-term memory. Researchers are currently studying childhood memory; why, for example, it is so hard for adults to recall events from their early years. Most adults have only fragmentary impressions from their first $3\frac{1}{2}$ years, although 2-year-old children remember some events that occurred months earlier. Psychologists interested in "childhood amnesia" are investigating the role of language for storage and retrieval of information in long-term memory (*New York Times*, April 6, 1993). Imagine a filing cabinet with many photographs stored in it and think about finding particular pictures which have been filed away in folders with labels and without labels. When children become able to attach names to mental representations they have the basis for a memory filing system with names or labels on the folders. The labels make finding particular pictures much easier.

Word Inventories and Phonological Constraints

Jean and Carol produced far more words during their one-word periods than did Joel and Allen. We have frequently heard that, on average, girls are more verbal than boys. Our research bears this out. This developmental difference attenuates during childhood and disappears at puberty, which takes place, on average, two years earlier for girls than boys. Thus one source of the early difference in verbal productivity appears to be biological, the more rapid maturational course in human females than in human males. Another source appears to be psychological. Among our four subjects, Allen's word production suggests that he has higher standards for the phonological accuracy of his words than do Carol, and Jean, and probably Joel.

Table 6.2 shows a history for each child of words attempted and first understood by the mother as pronounced by her child. For example, the second word for Jean was shower, which Jean pronounced /awo/ (*a* pronounced as in c*a*r or like *o* in p*o*t). Carol's first is *Mommy*, pronounced /mʌmi/ (the *u* in b*u*t and the *e* in b*e*t). Joel's first is cup, pronounced /k ʌ/ and Allen's Adam, /ʔæda/ (with ʔ pronounced as *tt* in bu*tt*on, æ as the *a* in b*a*n). Looking at the word histories, we can ask if the words attempted suggest that any of the children's attempts were phonologically constrained, whether a child produced words containing only speech sounds he was confident he could produce accurately. This possibility is suggested by the research of Scollen (1976) who found that subjects practiced pronunciation, saying the word over until satisfied with pronunciation or avoided using words, presumably because they were unable to produce a particular speech sound (Donahue, 1986).

Table 6.2 shows that in addition to single consonants, words attempted include ones with consonant clusters, the final *tl* in bo*tt*le (Jean), the initial *spl* in spl*ash* (Carol), the initial *cl* in cl*ean* (Joel), and the medial *nd* in wi*nd*ow (Allen). The only correct pronunciations are Carol's *nt* in /pænti/ *pa*nty and *nk* in d*ri*nk. She managed these clusters but not the *dr* in drink. Consonant clusters appear late in all the histories. Jean is most daring, producing eight, none correct, and Allen is least daring, attempting only one cluster, *nd* in wi*nd*ow, incorrectly. The only consonants Allen attempts are stops (d, b, t, k, p), nasals (m, n), and a liquid (r). Carol and Adam's percentage of words pronounced correctly is twice as high as Jean's and Joel's. Donahue's research (1986) suggests that they might have produced more words with consonants they found difficult to produce if they had been more daring.

Enduring Early Words

The analysis of this development during the one-word period is based primarily on Jean and Carol because Allen and Joel are not as talkative as Carol and Jean and do not provide enough data for valid and reliable analysis. We began by selecting histories of words occurring during four or more of the taping sessions for each child. The data

Table 6.2 Words attempted by child and understood by mother

Jean	Carol	Joel	Allen
that/dæt/	hi	cup/kʌ/	Adam/ʔæda/
daddy	daddy	this/dl/	mommy
more/mo/	mommy	that/dæt/	baby
shower/awo/	no/næ/	yeah/ʔejhʔ/	out
ball/ʔʌbaʔ/	sock/dak/	no	more/mɔ/
this/dis/	yes/ye/	hi	no
off/ɔf/	tub/dub/	daddy	mine
up	soap/tsip/	hot/haʔ/	ducky
hi	Joanne/tsh/	clean/kin/	happy/ʔæpi/
no	juice/du/	box/baʔ/	window/dʌbdo/
ducky	fish/pls/	towel/kawa/	
bottle/bado/	shoe	flower/fawi/	
water/wado/	tush	yucki/yʌgi/	
tickle/tigo/	splash/spæ/		
peek-a-boo/pibo/	push		
cake/kik/	mommy's		

Table 6.2 Cont'd

book /bek/
back /bak/
fish /pls/
Audrey /adi/
apple /abo/
basket /beget/
burp /bʌwʌp/
sleeping /dipln/
nightgown /naygaw/

daddy's
doodies
panty
house
down
button /bʌten/
drink /bink/
pink
this /zis/

Total attempted	26	25	13	10
Total correct	5	13	3	6
Percent correct	20	54	25	60
Consonant clusters				
Attempted	9(tl, kl, dr, pl, sk, rp, sl, tg)	4(sp, nt, dr, nk)	3(cl, x = ks, fl)	1(nd)
Correct	0	2	0	0

Table 6.3 History of words occurring during four or more taping sessions

Word	Tapes	Occurrences	Age range	Tapes/total
Carol				
no	9	57	1,2(9)–1,7(2)	0.69
hi	7	30	1,0(29)–1,7(2)	0.54
this	7	10	1,1(12)–1,7(2)	0.54
bye	5	26	1,4(0)–1,7(2)	0.38
yeah	5	20	1,2(19)–1,7(2)	0.38
Daddy	5	18	1,1(12)–1,7(2)	0.38
Mommy	9	24	1,1(26)–1,7(2)	0.69
Joanne	4	28	1,4(14)–1,7(2)	0.31
baby	5	10	1,3(16)–1,6(17)	0.38
diaper	4	9	1,5(13)–1,7(2)	0.31
brush	5	12	1,4(14)–1,7(2)	0.38
soap	4	11	1,5(13)–1,7(2)	0.31
tub	5	29	1,3(16)–1,5(13)	0.38
bath	4	20	1,4(0)–1,6(17)	0.31

Total words = 14
Earliest age to latest age = 1,0(29)–1,7(2)
Carol = 1,0(29), first word occurring on four or more tapes

Word	Tapes	Occurrences	Age range	Tapes/total
Jean				
no	9	28	1,1(19)–1,6(20)	0.53
hi	8	31	1,1(14)–1,7(7)	0.47
that	5	13	0,10(18)–1,5(9)	0.29
more	7	44	1,4(26)–1,6(20)	0.41
up	5	8	1,2(10)–1,6(20)	0.29
Daddy	8	65	0,11(5)–1,7(7)	0.47
Mommy	11	40	0,11(26)–1,6(20)	0.55
fish	4	7	1,4(1)–1,7(7)	0.24
peek-a-boo	4	34	1,3(14)–1,5(9)	0.24
shower	7	61	1,1(14)–1,7(7)	0.41

Total words = 10
Earliest age to latest age = 0,10(18)–1,7(7)
Jean = 0,10(18), first word occurring on four or more tapes

for Carol and Jean are shown in table 6.3. If we ask which are the most used words, we get the same words: "no" and "Mommy" for both girls using as our measure the percentage of tapes in which the words appear to total tapes for each child. For Carol, both percentages are 69; for Jean, 53 and 55. If we look at the number of times the child says the word (occurrences), "no" is used by Carol many more times, 57, than "hi," her second most used word. "Daddy," by this measure, is Jean's most used word, 65 times, "shower" (61 times) is the second most used.

It can be seen in table 6.3 that the earliest words that endure in Jean's and Carol's one-word vocabularies are "that," "more," "Daddy," and "Mommy" for Jean, and "hi," "this," and "Daddy" for Carol, all words appearing on the first, second or third tapes. Earliest words are similar for the two infants. "That," "more," and "this" are used to make requests. Early on, Carol uses both "this" and "that" in her requests. Because her mother responds with "This?" or "This one?" Carol adopts "this" to request objects. Her earliest use of "This?" (tape 2) is to request a name. Carol is having her bath and playing with a tub in which three dolls can be placed:

MOTHER: rub a dub dub one man in a tub (*as she puts one of the dolls in the tub*)
CAROL: /zIs/ This? (*gazing at tub doll*)
MOTHER: This is a man.

Later as Carol is being dressed in her room after her bath:

CAROL: This?
MOTHER: This is curtains (*gazing at window where curtain is flapping in a breeze*)

Carol's /zIs/ looks like a request for a name, but since she does not incorporate man and curtains in her spoken vocabulary (at least during videotaping) we have counted /zIs/ as Carol's part of a social ritual rather than a real request for a name.

The majority of both Carol's and Jean's enduring words are heard on at least one of the last two tapes in these samples. Of Carol's words occurring on four or more tapes, only "tub" drops out. Of Jean's, "that" and "peek-a-boo" do not occur on at least one of the last two tapes. Carol's "tub" and Jean's "peek-a-boo" are specific to games played by infant and mother.

Beginning with Kathryn Nelson (1973), researchers have categorized early words according to their use. Nelson categorized words in the first 50-word vocabularies of her subjects as being used for social play or referentially. We have looked at the words occurring on four or more tapes to separate names of people, non-animate entities, and words that have occasion meaning, i.e. "hi" and "bye" are greetings, "no," "this," "that," "more," and "up," are directives, telling mother what to do, or, as in the case of "no," what not to do. "Daddy," "Mommy," and "baby" are the names used by Carol and Jean for themselves and their parents. Joanne is the name of the person taping Carol and her mother. None of the other three children took much note of the person doing the taping. Joanne's behavior was not different from that of the others, circumspect and non-intrusive, but Carol was intrigued by Joanne. I do not know why. The last group of words are for the most part object names. "Bath" and "shower" refer to the same activity. Jean just calls a bath a shower.

If we look at the words that endure and are most used by Carol and Jean, they do not suggest a contrast between referential and social play uses as differentiating Carol's and Jean's motivation for acquiring and continuing to use them. Both Carol and Jean acquired many words that after a few appearances disappeared. Words acquired later may have been retained but we do not have the data to be able to tell.

Infant–mother Dialogue and Development of the Infant's Language

We consider Terrace's proposition (1985) that the development from paired associates (conditioned coordinations of word and referent) to words as names (abstract symbols that refer, but are not tied to a particular occasion, context, or speech act) as the necessary precondition for the development of syntactic language. Helen Keller has described the difference between her use of gesture to indicate what she wanted, to hunt eggs, have a purse opened, and so on, and her realization that "everything has a name." She wrote that this understanding "set her free." Becoming abstract sets words free. As a paired associate, a word is bound to the circumstance in which it was learned. As a name, abstract symbol, a word can be used in a variety of speech acts and can participate in all the syntactic operations appropriate to its syntactic category. Dory (Holzman, 1974) used "beads" in two primitive speech acts: with rising inflection to ask for the necklace, with flat or falling inflection to indicate the necklace's presence. At this point she might be capable of acquiring combinatorial speech, "Want beads," or "Give me the beads" to make her request and "beads here" or "the beads are on the table" to report the location of the necklace, for example.

We will now look at ideas and data on infant–mother dialogue and the progress of infants from one word at a time to combinatorial speech. Terrace (1985) has proposed that the instinct to refer, communicate, is an aspect of the human innate endowment. What is acquired by humans is knowledge of the terms of reference in their speech community. Lempert and Kinsbourne (1985) view labeling as action for the self, an aspect of orienting to objects of interest. Our data indicate that early in the one-word period, children do both, but non-communicative utterances in the presence of the mother become scarce as the one-word period draws to a close. Even though a child's utterances may be for self and not to communicate with the mother, the child has only one way to acquire words, by hearing them used; *to refer*: "Here's the ball," mother says, handing the ball to the child; *to request*: "Give me the ball," mother says, holding out her hand for the ball the child holds; *to greet* the child: "Hi," or indicate that she is departing: "Bye-bye, Carol." These are all utterances of the mother meant to communicate to her child. In addition, parents notice, sometimes to their dismay, that very young children understand, from hearing their elders, the occasions which call forth "Damn it," for example, and use the expletive in appropriate situations themselves. "Damn it" was not meant as a communication to the child, but, as an element in the child's verbal environment, it is available to be acquired if the child is so motivated and its occasion for use is understandable. Parents model labeling, action for self, when they self-guide their activities in their child's presence even when their language use is not so colorful that they remember the child picking it up.

Getting from One-word Utterances to Multi-word Utterances: Where the One-word Period Ends

We examined evidence in chapter 5 that the prelinguistic infant is acquiring knowledge necessary for language use even though she is not yet able to speak. During the one-word period, there is evidence

Table 6.4 Distribution of mothers' responses, "says again" and frames, early and late in infants' one-word period

	Allen			Carol			Jean			Joel		
	Says again	Frame	Total	Says again	Frame	Total	Says again	Frame	Total	Says again	Frame	Total
Early	14	0	14	11	13	24	24	26	50	18	2	20
Late	24	44	68	20	50	70	24	72	96	67	49	116
Chi square	$P < 0.001$			$P = $ n.s.			$P < 0.01$			$P < 0.01$		

of infant linguistic development. Even though infants do not combine words into multi-word utterances, their mothers' responses to their utterances indicate that mothers are getting feedback from the infants indicative of increasing ability to understand their mother's multi-word utterances.

We took as data to test this idea the first four mother utterances following her infant's word in our samples of infant–mother interaction from each taping during the one-word period. We selected the first four mother utterances (if there were as many as four) because the infant is more likely to be attending to what her mother is saying if she has just said a word. Sometimes mothers engage in long monologues. These may be of little interest to the child.

We categorize mother utterances as (a) teaching responses, (b) conversational, and (c) utterances not related to the topic of the verbal interaction. Previously (Holzman, 1984), we had looked at the numbers of mother's conversational as opposed to teaching responses in her first two utterances following an infant one-word utterance when the infants were 18 and 24 months old. We found an increase in conversational as opposed to teaching responses, but 24 months is after the end of the one-word period for Allen, Carol, Jean, and Joel, even though many of their utterances are still one word.

Now we are looking at just the one-word period for evidence of infant language development in mother responses. In order to tighten up the analysis, we concentrated on two of the four mother teaching utterances. The four are (a) "Says again," (b) frames, (c) positive feedback, and (d) requests clarification. We used "Says again" and frames because they both include the child's word. "Says again" means the mother's utterance is just the word her child has said but perhaps with different intonation. Frames are mother utterances that include the child's word but put it in a syntactic frame. "Says again" confirms the child's usage and provides a model of the word's adult phonology. Frames provided syntactic and semantic information for use of the one word. The distributions of "Says again" and frames among the first four mother utterances following her child's utterance of a word are given in table 6.4.

Totals increase markedly from early to late, primarily because infant utterance of words increases very slowly during the first part of the one-word period.[2] The pattern of response of the boys' mothers is very different from that of the girls'. Early on, boys' mothers do no framing (Allen) or almost no framing (Joel), while Carol's and Jean's mothers have almost equal numbers of "Says again" and frames. Both the girls' mothers produce many responses like the following:

JEAN: Daddy
MOTHER: Daddy
          Do you hear Daddy?

CAROL: ball
MOTHER: ball
          yes
          Where's the ball?

Both Jean's and Carol's mothers say their child's word, thereby affirming their understanding of the child and modeling the adult pronunciation of the word. The boys' mothers do this also, but the girls' mothers in addition provide frames from which the child can acquire information about how to use the word and correct syntax. The fact that the boys' mothers' framing increases dramatically late in the one-word period suggests that the girls' mothers regard their daughters' comprehension as linguistically advanced earlier than the boys' mothers do their sons'. This hypothesis gets further support from the decline in the ratio of "Says again" to frames late for the girls. Where early, there were approximately equal numbers of "Says again" and frames, late Carol has 2.5 as many frames as "Says again" and Jean, 3.0. For example:

```
 1  CAROL:   toe
 2  CAROL:   toe? (points to other foot with sock on)
 3  MOTHER:  Where is your other toe?
 4  MOTHER:  Must be inside here (i.e. in the sock)
 5  MOTHER:  huh?
 6  CAROL:   toe
 7  MOTHER:  Yeah
 8  CAROL:   knee?
 9  MOTHER:  This one's the knee.
10  MOTHER:  Right.
```

There are no mother "Says again" responses in this dialogue, but there are two frames, (3) and (9), two conversational responses continuing the child's topic but not using the child's word, (4) and (5), and two positive feedback, (7) and (10).

How do children move from one word at a time to multi-word utterances? In our research, it has been in dialogue with mother. What I will report comes from Carol and Jean because they and their mothers produced enough dialogue during taping sessions to provide reliable data. To set the stage, instances from Carol's four tapes that take her from 1,0(29) to 1,2(9) are given on p. 102.

We see that most of these early dialogues are initiated by the child. What this means is that mother is on the alert for vocal or verbal behavior by her child that provides her with the opportunity to respond, and that Carol's mother's responses are useful for language and world knowledge acquisition.

From the beginning of the one-word period, mothers respond to their children on the basis of the meaning they impute to their children's utterances. Even an utterance like Carol's at 1,0(29), a vocalization with unclear intent, is responded to as if the mother knew Carol was attempting, unsuccessfully, to say yes. So mother models the correct pronunciation. If Carol is not attempting yes, her mother's "yes" will not be attended to by Carol. Children acquire only linguistic information that they are interested in having. Some linguistic knowledge is innate. The type and amount are still subject to debate. What must be acquired (cannot be innate) is the terms of reference, the actual words which name objects, actions, qualities, and so on, in a speech community. These are not rule governed, but are rote learned by hearing the word and connecting it to its referent, a trial-and-error process which is amazingly error free.

The paths taken by Carol and Jean from one word at a time to multi-word utterances are similar. The transitional form is the vertical construction (see also Veneziano et al., 1990). Sometimes the child herself produces it, sometimes in concert with her mother. Basically, a vertical construction is composed of words produced one at a time, sequentially with separate intonation contours rather than being under a single contour as are the words of a phrase, "a ball," or a sentence, "That's mine." These latter are horizontal constructions. We have categorized vertical constructions from most primitive to most advanced:

Carol	Speech act	Mother	Speech act
1,0(29)			
1 (a) /zIs/ this?	Question	(b) This is a wash cloth	Answer
2 (a) [ʔIsIs]	Vocalization, intent unclear	(b) Yes	Shapes to a word
3		(a) These are good	Report
(b) /gʌ/ good	Imitation	(c) Good	Says again
		(d) Right	Positive feedback
1,1(12)			
1 (a) /dɛ/ that?	Question	(b) What is that?	Question
		(c) That's Joanne	Answer
		(d) That's Joanne who's taking pictures	Expanded answer
2 (a) /dɛ/ that?	Question	(b) This is a man	Report
3 (a) [dæ, dæ, dæ]	Vocal practice		Answer
(b) /dæ/ dad	Naming	(c) Where is dad?	Question
		(d) Dad's working	Answer
4 (a) /dIs/ this?	Question	(b) This is curtains	Answer
1,1(26)			
1 (a) /mʌ bok/ my boat	Report	(b) Is this your boat?	Question, verify
2		(a) No	Prohibit act
(b) Shakes head no, agrees			
1,2(9)			
1 (a) /næ næ/ no no	Report	(b) No no	Agree, shape
		(c) Right	Positive feedback
		(d) That's a no no	Frame

(5) VIL: Imitation of last word said by mother for second word
     in vertical construction. Mother's word is a repetition of child's
     word.
     CHILD: door
     MOTHER: yeah, that's a door.
     CHILD: door

(5) VI: Vertical imitation, not last word.
     CHILD: baby
     MOTHER: baby pictures
     CHILD: baby

(5) VRM: Vertical repetition with mother utterance not contain-
     ing the child's word interposed
     CHILD: shampoo
     MOTHER: yeah
     CHILD: shampoo

(5) VR: Vertical repetition
     CHILD: Daddy
     CHILD: Daddy

(4) VMI: Vertical construction imitating mother where mother's
     word is not same as child's first word.
     CHILD: baby
     MOTHER: do babies take baths?
     CHILD: bath

(3) VM?: Vertical construction with child's second word answer-
     ing mother's intervening question
     CHILD: gramma
     MOTHER: where's gramma?
     CHILD: down

(3) VMS: Vertical construction with mother's intervening
     statement
     CHILD: bye
     MOTHER: yes, that went bye, right.
     CHILD: bug

(3)   VC: Vertical construction
      CHILD: ball
      CHILD: bye

(2)   HC: Horizontal construction
      CHILD: my shoe

(1)   HS: Horizontal construction, sentence
      CHILD: this didn't work

The most advanced construction is the sentence, numbered 1. The other constructions are ordered in terms of decreases in competence to those numbered 5, the most primitive. The constructions numbered 5 are all vertical constructions in which the child produces the same word as he has just produced or imitates a word the mother has just produced. In all the more advanced constructions, the child produces at least two different words in his constructions.

It can be seen from table 6.5 that the majority of both girls' constructions during the one-word period are from the most primitive group. Even late in the one-word period when their utterances are significantly more numerous than early, the group of vertical imitations and repetitions comprise more than 50 percent of their constructions. Jean's second most important category is horizontal constructions. She produces just two of these early and 19 late. After the taping at 1,7(7), which we picked for the fuzzy end of Jean's one-word period, her production of multi-word utterances accelerated so that in the subsequent 10 tapings ending at 2 years, she produced 75 horizontal constructions and an additional 20 sentences. She produced no sentences during the one-word period.

Carol's second largest category in the one-word period was vertical constructions, 24 produced, five early, 19 late. She produced only three horizontal constructions, and Jean only four vertical constructions, one of which was produced early. Data for Jean seem paradoxical: a higher percentage than Carol of most primitive and a higher percentage of most advanced. Is this because Jean is more holistic, imitative as a language acquirer and Carol more analytic? Bates et al. (1988) present much data consistent with there being important individual differences in the way infants acquire language, differences based on the relative importance of such factors as social motivation and verbal memory leading to "high rote style" and exceptional "analysis for understanding and excellent receptive vocabulary" leading to "high analytic style." According to Bates et al. (1988), these two different styles are unrelated to general intelligence – if there is such a thing.

We turn now to the development of children's combining words to form multi-word utterances. Our data are all from taping a scenario in which the mother and child are together so that it is always possible for them to be communicating with each other, but frequently they are not – even when they are audibly talking or vocalizing. We have said that infants may be using words to self-orient and think and mothers may also as they go over the agendas guiding their behavior. Both mother and infant are conceptualizing, reflecting. When an individual puts different words together in order to conceptualize, she is relating the words to each other meaningfully so that the words are organized, not an arbitrary sequence. Veneziano et al. (1990) posit that the infant is engaged in separate activities: *chaining*, uttering one word after another, and *relating*, organizing the meaning of the sequence. Veneziano et al. propose that the beginning of grammar depends on coordinating chaining and relating. Our findings regarding the emergence of two-word sequences show aspects of the mother's contribution to the process. We have said that mother's repetition of her child's word is affirmative for the child and provides an adult phonological model and that the child's repetition may be for practicing pronunciation or for play or thinking. When the mother follows her child's word with a verbal contribution, it may enhance the child's ability to organize the meaning of two different words. When Carol was 1,2(19), the following dialogue took place:

1 MOTHER: Would you like a cup?
2 MOTHER: Would you like to pour some water?
3 CHILD: /du/ juice
4 MOTHER: It's no juice here
5 MOTHER: Let's just pour this water

At this point Carol's attention slips away. She vocalizes for herself. Finally (11 units later) Carol vocalizing to herself, mother talking to Carol:

Table 6.5 Frequency of vertical construction types: Carol and Jean

Tape no.	VIL (5)	VI (5)	VRM (5)	VR (5)	Total (5)	VMI (4)	VM? (3)	VMS (3)	VC (3)	HC (2)	HS (1)	Total	% (5) of total constructions
Carol													
225		3			3							3	100
226	3	3	1	4	11	1						12	92
227	1	1		3	5	1			3			9	56
228	1	1		3	5	1		2	2			9	56
229				5	5		1	3	5	1		15	33
230			1	10	11			1	4			16	69
231	1			11	12	1	6		7	2		28	43
232				6	6		2	3	3			14	43
Total	6	8	2	42	58	3	9	9	24	3		106	55

Table 6.5 Cont'd

Jean											
319			3	8	11					11	100
320		3		1	1					1	100
321			2	8	10					10	100
322			3	1	7		1	1	1	9	78
323				1	1					2	50
324		2	2	2	6		1			6	100
325	1			5	6				1	8	75
327	1	2	2	1	6					6	100
328		2	1	2	5		1		2	9	56
329		2	2	2	6	1	2		1	11	55
330			2	1	3	1			4	8	38
331			2	6	8		1	1	1	11	73
332		1	2	4	7		2		4	13	54
333	1	3	1	1	6	1	1	1	4	12	50
334		1	1	1	3	1	2	1	1	8	38
335			1	9	10		1		2	15	67
Total	3	16	24	53	96	4	12	4	21	140	69

After your bath but not right now. No juice here now. I think we'll put that cup away because I don't think it's a good idea to drink that [bath] water.

We can infer that Carol is calling the water juice and intends to drink it. She is not too intent on this since her attention lapses. She doesn't make a fuss. But since her mother decides to put the cup away, we sense that she doesn't trust Carol not to fill the cup from the tub and drink. Mother provides words that Carol might combine with juice to produce a vertical construction. She wants to drink the water poured into the cup and pretend it's juice.

Maybe she is not cognitively developed enough to think water is pretend juice so that she might say juice/cup, two words in her vocabulary. As yet she does not produce any verbs, so pour/juice is unlikely. From the words used by her mother, only the ones she can produce will become part of a construction. At 1,1(12), Carol produces with her mother's interlocution:

CAROL: baby
MOTHER: Do babies take baths?
CAROL: bath

At 1,5(20) Carol uses "bye" as a sort of verb.

CAROL: bug
          bye
          bye
MOTHER: Yes
          That bug went bye
          Right
CAROL: bug

Mother expands Carol's construction, affirming its meaning:

CAROL: brush
          bye

As mother puts her brush away, providing evidence for the meaning to Carol of vertical constructions involving nouns she knows and "bye."

At 18 months, mother puts Carol in the bath tub. She is worrying a bit about the water temperature.

MOTHER: Is the water too hot?
CAROL: cold

Thus, before Carol uses true verbs, she produces an adjective. We cannot say what she understood cold to mean because she is too young to understand questions like, "What does cold mean?" It will probably be several years before such a question will make sense to Carol.

At 1,6(17), Carol holds out a toy fish for her mother to wind up so it will swim in her bath. It was moving and has stopped.

CAROL: Mommy
       turn
       more

She has used a true verb in a construction that suggests that Carol understands that turning the key causes the fish to move. She uses "more" to mean "again." She utters two horizontal constructions with verbs which we have classified as prefabricated routines – not spontaneously created for the occasion but previously rote learned from mother's utterances and frequently used. The first is "taking pictures," the second is "have tinkle." Mother frequently says "Joanne's taking pictures" to explain Joanne's video camera to Carol. Mother also asks Carol "Do you have a tinkle," her way of suggesting that Carol, newly toilet trained, might want to use her potty. We call these prefabs until there is evidence that the child has analyzed the construction so that she is aware that it consists of separate words usable in combination with other words. In their study of the meaning of mean lengths of utterance at 20 months, Bates et al. (1988) suggest that their 20-month-old children who produced utterances longer than one word primarily produced what I have called prefabs.

Jean has been put in the bath tub. She looks around and does not see her toy duck in the tub.

JEAN: ducky (*six repetitions*)
MOTHER: Where do you want the ducky?
JEAN: shower (*Jean's word for bath, bath tub*)

The mother's question provides a clue to Jean concerning an appropriate second word for her vertical construction. Jean is more developed in her language use than is Carol, evidenced by the verbs in her vocabulary (Bates et al., 1988). Jean then produces, with no intervening speech by her mother, three vertical constructions using the verb, *wash*:

JEAN: wash (*seven repetitions*)
        soap

She is sitting in her bath and wants to be given the soap to wash her duck.

JEAN: soap
        wash

She is using the soap to wash ducky. Mommy, sitting on the floor next to the tub, rests her arm on the side of the tub.

JEAN: wash
        Mommy

Jean's constructions with wash indicate that wash is a flexible symbol, capable of being used by Jean with a noun as object, *wash Mommy*, or as a subject, *soap wash*.
    At 17 months, Jean uses another verb, *open*:

JEAN: open
        door

This is a report to her mother about what she is doing. During this taping Jean says, "Me get it": "get it" is probably a prefab, but the horizontal construction, *me get it*, is Jean's. Competent speakers might say "I'll get it." The use of "me" as subject of the sentence is confined, in middle-class, native English-speaking homes, to language-developing children.
    At 1,5(9), Jean responds to her mother's question, "What is that?" which had followed Jean saying "that" twice with "that towel." Again, early on, developing English speakers leave out functors like "is" and "a" (Brown, 1973).
    At 1,5(26), Jean produces three vertical constructions:

JEAN: bottle (*3 times*)
in there

She is telling her mother where she knows her bottle is. "In there" is a prefab and not a horizontal construction.

JEAN: Daddy (*2 times*)
MOTHER: Where's Daddy?
JEAN: at work

"At work" is another prefab.

JEAN: Mommy
MOTHER: whatee?
JEAN: book (*2 times*)

Jean wants her mother to read to her.

Even though Jean used "me" as subject of "me get it," beginning 1,5(26) she uses "my" in vertical constructions:

JEAN: my
Daddy

At 18 months:

JEAN: my
pee you

JEAN: my
book

She appears to realize that "my" denotes possession and in her next utterances in each instance she names the object she possesses. I do not understand why these phrases are not produced as horizontal constructions. It may be that in these early productions, there is not the automatic construction that fluent speakers produce as they speak without having to think about constructing utterances. For the beginning speaker, English is like a foreign language. If you tried to communicate in France or Italy with native speakers and you were just beginning to learn the language, production of utterances would not proceed automatically, effortlessly either. Since our data are small samples, one half-hour of interaction bi-weekly around one sequence of events, horizontal constructions, put together without having to be thought out, could have become so when our camera was not there to record it happening.

As the one-word period comes to its fuzzy ending, Carol and Jean (but not the boys) produce some horizontal constructions. All four children produce vertical constructions, with and without interlocutions by their mothers. When a person becomes able to communicate in utterances longer than one word, communication improves. "More bottle" is more enlightening to hearer, less dependent on hearer's reading the context, than just "more" or just "bottle." The infant's use of "more bottle" marks an advance in his mental and articulatory capacities. The two-word utterance is harder to plan and to say than a one-word utterance. A central issue debated by linguists and child language theorists concerns the extent to which early multi-word utterances are influenced by syntactic constraints, responsible in English, for example, for phrase structure rules. We will return to this issue in chapter 7 (see also Wijner, 1990).

To conclude the presentations of material on the vertical and horizontal constructions of Carol and Jean, I have constructed a table for each girl (tables 6.6 and 6.7) of their non-imitative, non-repetitive constructions. The tables indicate the speech acts and their meaning, based on observing the acts taking place on videotape.

It can be seen that the most frequent speech acts of both are reports (rep) to their mothers about what is going on – even though the mother is right there – or directives (dir) to mother, requests that mother do something. These are Carol's only observed speech acts. In addition to directives and reports, Jean asks one question, Mommy/boo, meaning, *Mommy, where is my book?* We infer this from mother's response, "Your book is downstairs" and Jean's then going downstairs. In addition, Jean produces two greetings, "Hi, Linda" and "Hi, how are you."

Human Beings without Syntactic Language

What can happen to prevent a human being from acquiring syntactic language? Putting aside serious damage to areas of the brain essential

Table 6.6 Speech-act analysis: Carol's constructions

Speech act	Constructions	Meaning
Vertical constructions		
Dir	comb/no	don't comb my hair
Rep	bug/bye	bug going down the drain
Dir	mommy/towel	mommy hold towel
Rep	ball/mine	my ball
Rep	ball/bye	ball floating toward drain
Rep	tubby/bath	after mom, "yes, it is a bath tub"
Dir	bath/no	not ready to get out of bath
Dir	no no/bath	mom has said, "Now's time to get out"
Rep	doody/bye	diaper thrown in wastebasket
Rep	toy/bag	toys are in bag
Rep	bag/toy	mom: want to take your toys out of the bag?
Rep	camera/Joanne	camera is used by Joanne
Rep	fish/gramma	topic comment after Mom says "Oh gramma's fish, gramma brought you that fish"
Dir	ball/out	afterwards Mom says "No, that doesn't come out"
Rep	gramma/down	afterwards Mom says, "Right, gramma's downstairs"
Rep	car/key	names object
Rep	hamper/cover	hamper needs cover
Rep	tinkle/mommy	calling mom's attention to potty
Rep	Joanne/this	Joanne doing/using this
Rep	money/down	money's downstairs
Dir	shampoo/hair	topic comment: shampoo mommy put in hair
Dir	shampoo/back	(I want to put) shampoo back
Dir	toe/pigs	toe = pigs, to play this little piggy
Rep	Joanne/out	Joanne has left the room
Rep	Joanne/picture	Joanne's taking pictures
Rep	apple/pie	names object
Horizontal constructions		
Rep	taking pictures	Joanne is taping child and mother
Dir	no bye	child doesn't want the water let out of tub
Rep	have tinkle	child needs to urinate
Rep	my shoe	child states possession

Dir = directive; Rep = report.

Table 6.7 Speech-act analysis: Jean's constructions

Speech act	Constructions	Meaning
Vertical constructions		
Dir	fish/shower	child wants the fish in the tub
Dir	fish/peek-a-boo	child wants mother to play peek-a-boo with the toy fish
Dir	peek-a-boo/no	child wants to stop playing peek-a-boo
Rep	fish/shower	child wants to play with fish in shower
Dir	bottle/here	child wants to put water in bottle
Rep	door/open	child opens the door
Question	mommy/book	child asks mother where her book is
Dir	bottle/more	child wants more bottles
Horizontal constructions		
Rep	the ducky	this is the ducky
Rep	big cup	this is the big cup
Rep	open door	I am opening the door
Dir	me get it	I want to get it
Dir	in there	put the brush in there
Greeting	hi Linda	sees Linda
Rep	bottle in here	I put my bottle on the shelf
Rep	my daddy	possession
Dir	more boy	find the other child
Rep	my peeyou	I made a bowel movement
Rep	my book	possession
Dir	more bottle	I want another bottle
Dir	please turn	wind up toy
Dir	ride the horsie	I want to ride the horse
Greeting	hi how are you	I am responding to seeing someone like mother does

Dir = directive; Rep = report.

to language, it is lack of language experience during the critical period for language development. The critical period ends at puberty. Just as songbirds who do not develop their song before mating never do, so also human beings if they have not developed syntactic language before puberty do not. There are two such cases for which there is evidence. The first is that of a pubescent boy, Victor, captured in the woods near Aveyron in southern France in 1798 (Shattuck, 1980).

His story and the attempt of Dr Itard to teach him French is movingly recounted by Shattuck. He learned to recognize *lait* (milk), for example, and to associate the word with its referent, but he did not become able to create phrases or sentences and eventually Dr Itard gave up. The year 1798 was a long time ago, and nothing is known about Victor's life before his capture. In order to survive on his own, it is surmised that he had to have been, perhaps, 4 years old when he was abandoned. He had a scar on his throat that could have been caused by a knife wound made to end his life. Why would anyone have wanted him dead? Could he have been mentally retarded? Such questions make it impossible to use Victor's history as definitive evidence for the critical period hypothesis. In November 1970, Genie, a 13-year-old girl who weighed only 59 pounds and was only 54 inches tall, was admitted to the Children's Hospital in Los Angeles, California. She was incontinent, could not chew solid food and could barely swallow. She understood a few words: red, blue, green, brown, mother, walk, go, and a few others. Her productive vocabulary was confined to stop it, no more, and several shorter negatives. She was the child of a psychotic father and an almost blind, abused mother. Genie had spent her life tied to a potty chair in a small, dark room. Her father and brothers barked at her rather than speaking to her. When her mother fled with her, seeking help for herself from a social agency, the agency sent Genie to Children's Hospital (Rymer, 1993). Genie received a great deal of attention, improved substantially physically, and went to live with a foster family, at the same time receiving concentrated attention and tuition from a graduate student in linguistics at UCLA, Susan Curtiss, who was doing her dissertation on Genie. At professional meetings during the 1970s, Susan Curtiss presented papers about Genie's language and cognitive development which boded well. Genie had been given Piaget's (non-verbal) tests of cognitive development and had been found to be at the concrete operational stage, developmentally like a 7-year-old. This meant she certainly had more than enough cognitive capacity for language development. But the sad fact is that Genie, now a woman in her thirties, like Victor, never acquired syntactic language.

Notes

1 The numbers represent the infant's age in years, months and (in brackets) days.

2   By happenstance, each child had an even number of tapings so that "early" is made up of the first half of the tapes and "late" by the second half.

Further Reading

Bates, E., Bretherton, I. and Snyder, L. (1988) *From First Words to Grammar* (Cambridge: Cambridge University Press).

Harris, M. (1992) *Language Experience and Early Language Development: From Input to Uptake* (Hove, England: Lawrence Erlbaum).

> Harris relates early vocabulary to maternal speech using studies of infants and mothers interacting in a laboratory room filled with toys.

Rymer, R. (1991) "A silent childhood," *New Yorker*, April 13 and 21.

> The sad story of Genie's treatment by professionals in the medical academic community at UCLA.

Shattuck, R. (1980) *The Forbidden Experiment: the Story of the Wild Boy of Aveyron* (New York: Washington Square Press).

> An absorbing account in its historical, philosophical context of the work of Dr Itard with Victor, the wild boy of Aveyron.

Terrace, H. (1985) "In the beginning was the name," *American Psychologist*, 40: 1011–28.

> The difference between the apes' one-word behavior and that of the young human clearly described. The necessary foundation to syntactic language is abstract names for objects, actions, and so on. Only human beings are able to accomplish this abstraction.

7

The Linguistic System and Early Language Development

Within a period of 3–4 years human beings, who start out in life able only to cry and coo, become language users. In the late 1960s and 1970s I used to see full-page advertisements in magazines featuring a picture of an exotic and winsome 4-year-old captioned, "She speaks fluent Mandarin [for example]. Why can't you?" These were advertisements for foreign language schools that specialized in preparing Americans to speak a variety of foreign languages fluently. The advertisement was compelling. Certainly, an adult American could learn to do anything a 4-year-old child could do – and it shouldn't take very long. This ad hasn't appeared for quite a long time. Perhaps it has been banned under the law that prohibits false and misleading advertising. It was certainly misleading. Children are able to learn to speak a language without consulting grammars or dictionaries. They become fluent in their mother tongue, like the little speaker of Mandarin, by the time they are about 4 years old – and some do it considerably earlier. Furthermore, children who move from their native country to another country, where a different language is spoken, will become fluent in the new language in less than a year, unless they have social or emotional problems standing in the way. They learn the language from playing with other children and having it used as the language of instruction in school. The child will learn to speak the new language without an accent. For an adult, learning a new language is much more problematic, and the evidence is that any human being who has not yet learned to speak any language before puberty will never learn one.

In this chapter I want to consider current ideas about human language development. To begin, I must say that there is a lack of consensus among those who study the topic in explaining the stunning fact that, with very few exceptions, 4-year-old children are masters of the complex behavior that is human language use. It is as though, at the age of 4, all human beings could play the cello like Yo Yo Ma, or the piano like Peter Serkin. We are all geniuses at learning to use our native language. This chapter is about what developmental psycholinguists (the people who study the development of the ability of human beings to use language) understand as language learning – what has to be thought about and explained.

In chapter 5, I described various capabilities, clearly important for language use, that infants display before they utter a single word having referential meaning; for example, being able to take your turn in an interaction, even if you only vocalize or perform a communicative gesture.

One school of psycholinguists takes human communication as the behavior to be explained and includes among variables conventions which have developed in cultures to foster social cohesion and order and which are not the same in all societies or even across social classes in a particular society. Japanese native speakers, for example, have an elaborate system of politeness markers determining how children address their elders, how employers and employees speak to each other, and so on. Speech communities have pragmatic conventions to indicate old information. For example, if I say, "I saw him last week," the hearer must have previous information identifying "him." Perhaps the hearer has just asked, "Have you seen President Clinton lately?" Psycholinguists (for example, Bates and MacWhinney, 1987, 1989; Bates et al., 1988), who take communication as language use in real time in its social, cultural, and functional context, have a much more complex phenomenon to analyze than the psycholinguists, like Steven Pinker (1984, 1989), who treat language acquisition as separable from social and cultural context and as a domain apart from the general cognitive domain.

What I have observed in my research on children's language acquisition in their natural environment is that all aspects of communicative competence are acquired in parallel. Children acquire language as it is used with them. It is a gradual process, begun when they are babies. Some aspects of language use are more readily acquired than others, like the first rules of conversation, and are acquired earlier than other aspects of language use. In general, comprehension precedes production because the hearer can use the context in which the utterance occurs to help understand a message, while a speaker gets credit only for what is in her utterance. The reason why it is so hard for little children to communicate by telephone is that there is no context, except tone of voice, no action, only words. Since language is acquired in real time and context as it is being used in communicating with the (usually) young child acquiring her native tongue, the true account must include acquisition of all aspects relevant to actual language use in its cultural, social context.

What is acquired in the prelinguistic period that can be inferred from the infant's behavior – becoming able to produce a particular speech sound at will, to gesture meaningfully and interact, without words, with mother in a conversational manner – is physiological–acoustic and sociocultural knowledge. Not everyone agrees that the one-word period is a linguistic stage. Bickerton (1990) calls the period "protolanguage." We would say then that the acquisitions of the prelinguistic and maybe the one-word period are productive for the infant in advance of more narrowly linguistic and cognitively demanding aspects of becoming a language user. These earliest productive behaviors are rote learned, by imitating a model. They begin the infant's socialization to language use in his specific culture. Speech sounds differ across cultures as do the conventions for social interaction.

On the basis of this summary, I conclude that communicative performance, using language, is the behavior to be explained, the position of Bates and co-workers. At the same time, I believe that it is possible to analyze aspects of language use separately and that doing so makes them easier to understand. To the extent that I have been able to do so, I treat aspects of communication with language as discrete topics, so in this chapter I will consider the acquisition of the basic linguistic system: the rules for word and word-string construction (in English, sentence construction).

Integral to the differing visions of what is to be explained, there is controversy about the extent to which the knowledge necessary for becoming a language user is innate and the extent to which it is learned. Becoming a walker, someone able to move around on two legs by taking steps alternately with right and left foot, is an innate capacity in the human being. All of the developments, beginning with being able to hold up one's head and culminating in being able to get up on one's feet and balance one's body, will take place without assistance or teaching if the infant is permitted its own time-table. This has been demonstrated in Loczy, a home for 0–3-year-old orphans in Budapest, Hungary, where it was a principle of founder Dr Emmi Pickler's theory of child development that children should not be treated as objects, but should be self-motivated and should undertake and complete actions on their own volition in order to become competent human beings. Some infant care activities, like bathing and feeding, had to be carried out by a care-giver, although the care-giver would always propose the activity to the infant before carrying it out. But motor activities – sitting, crawling, grabbing toys, and so on – were totally the responsibility of the infants. Careful records of the ages at which these infants achieved motor milestones (Gessell, 1940) conform to average ages at which they are achieved in the research of Gessell and to norms for Hungarian infants and children. Walking is an innate human behavior whose emergence depends on maturational constraints. It cannot even be necessary to see walking modeled by other human beings since blind children, who have not seen anyone walk, do so.

A First Account of Early Language Acquisition

One of the two pre-eminent positions regarding language development (Pinker) is that the knowledge and capacity required for language use is for the most part innate in *Homo sapiens* and domain specific or modular, separate from other cognitive knowledge and behavior (Markman, 1992). The second position (Bates) is that language is simply one aspect of cognitive capacity and knowledge, not a separable, specific domain, much of the knowledge coming from learning rather than being innate.

When I was beginning to study language acquisition in the 1960s, how the infant separates the speech sound stream into words, the basic meaning unit of language, was the subject of much discussion. William James, arguably America's greatest psychologist, had believed that, for the newborn, the world is a "blooming, buzzing confusion." Visual sensations turn into perception of objects as the infant acquires visual experience in the world. Auditory sensations, arising because someone is speaking, gradually turn into perception of speech sounds through experience, hearing people talk. Today, research (for example,

Bower, 1966; Eimas, 1985) has provided evidence that physical object perception and speech sound perception are innate capacities rather than precipitates of experience. No matter how distorted the retinal image because of the orientation of the object in space, a shirt flapping in the breeze is still seen as a shirt. A speech sound is heard as the same sound over acoustic segments varying in duration, and in beginning temporal relations and energies (Eimas, 1985). Although I cannot prove it, I think it would be impossible to acquire language if the physical object and speech sound were not innate categories. Experience is not so uniform for humans that necessarily it will yield identical perceptual precipitates for everybody. Here, then, are two prerequisites for language use which have been found to be innate.

Psycholinguists, like Pinker, who take the nativist, domain-specific view of language, tend to concentrate on acquisition of syntax and other linguistic rule-governed aspects of language and to believe that these are what makes humans able to produce sentences that they have never heard and thus could not be imitating. All one needs is to know the rules and the capacity to acquire these is innate and domain specific. What is it about language that makes it appear to be innate like walking, rather than learned like playing hopscotch? First, all human beings with few and understandable exceptions (CNS damage, other injuries) walk and talk. Our closest living relatives, chimpanzees, have behaviors which are precursors to human walking and talking so that we can see signs of the evolutionary trail: innate behavior has to have evolved. Hopscotch is a game whose rules one has to learn in order to play and the rules have to be explained. "You stand here, throw your pebble into the first square," and so on. The rules for talking grammatically are much more complicated than those for playing hopscotch, and they are not explained to young children. Yet by the age of 4, children speak, following grammatical rules, and are not aware that they are doing so, a compelling reason to believe that the capacity to acquire grammar is innate (like walking). Further, the experience that very young children have with language use is highly variable. Some children are talked to extensively, some very little. Topics, vocabulary used also vary greatly, yet children converge on the same grammar, that of their speech community. Their minds abstract the grammatical rules without conscious thought. These facts make the "language acquisition device" (LAD) and universal grammar (Chomsky, 1965) influential, reasonable ideas.

"Language acquisition device" is simply a label for the innate component of human capacity to acquire the linguistic rule-governed aspects of language: phonological rules, how the speech sounds of the language are rule governed; syntax, how to combine words to form grammatical sentences; morphology, how to transform words of one syntactic category into another: nouns into verbs, e.g. nation becomes nationalize. Love, which is both a noun and a verb, becomes lovable as an adjective. Morphological rules also express "agreement" among parts of a sentence: for example, subject and verb, *the girl dances, the girls dance.* When a person has acquired these kinds of rules, she possesses competence, defined as the unconscious knowledge of the grammatical rules of her language.

The child develops language gradually, but it seems miraculous that it happens at all because it depends on the child acquiring rules on the basis of the limited, particular speech he hears and attends to. Any human being could become a speaker of English, Chinese, or Arabic if that were his native language. The LAD is innately endowed with universal grammar (UG). UG is analogous to a set of blueprints corresponding to each of the possible human language types. From the phrases and sentences spoken to him, the infant unconsciously deduces which of the blueprints the speech sample "fits" and discards the other blueprints. He is then guided in his acquisition of language by the constraints imposed by the blueprint which the speech sample he hears fits.

The fit of language to blueprint is not perfect so there will be exceptions to grammatical rules and exceptions must be learned. They do not fit the blueprint. Elements of language that correspond to the blueprint are acquired rapidly and without error. Elements that do not conform are called "marked" and are acquired with more difficulty. Young children acquiring English as their native language do not make word order mistakes (Brown, 1973; Pinker, 1984).

English is an SVO – subject, verb, object – language. You know who did what to whom because in an ordinary sentence the agent, who did it, the subject S comes first; what S did, the verb, V, is second, and the object, O, who subject did it to, is last. The world's languages are SVO, VSO, SOV, VOS and free order. Notice that there are no OVS or OSV languages (see table 7.1).

The most common violation of SVO order in English is in forming questions. The declarative sentence is the unmarked form, the question,

Table 7.1 Distribution of the world's language types

Type	Example(s)	% of world's languages
Subject *verb object*	English	35
Verb subject object	Irish, Arabic, Welsh	19
Subject *object verb*	Russian, Turkish	44
Verb object subject	Quiche (Mayan), Malagsy (Madagascar)	2
Free order[a]	Diurbal (Australian aboriginal)	extremely rare

[a] Free-order languages do not have constituent structures within the word-string corresponding to the sentence.
Sources: Crabtree and Powers (1991); Kenneth Hale, personal communication

the marked form. English is an SVO language, but to turn a declarative sentence into a yes/no question the first auxiliary to the verb is placed before the subject, violating the SVO order.

You can come
S   aux   V

Can you come?
aux   S   V

Should she have won the prize?
aux   S   aux   V   O

Being able to ask well-formed questions is a late development in the child's acquisition of basic English grammar. Early on, children use question intonation, "You're coming?" rather than word order, "Are you coming?", to signal a question.

In addition to yes/no questions, English and other languages have "wh" questions employing *who, what, when, where, why,* and *how* placed before the question:

Who are you calling?
What were they doing?
When did she slip on the ice?
Where did that cake come from?
Why did your mother bake it?
How did she get someone to deliver it?

A large part of what the child is doing as she begins to acquire her language is unconsciously determining from what is said to her what the morphemes (words and grammatical markers) in the lexicon are and what their properties are. The child also has to learn that "hit" is a verb that requires a subject and an object. "The rock hit the wall," that "give" requires a subject, object, and an indirect object, "Mary gave the diamond to her mother," and that "diamond" is a noun that requires an article. In this way, the child acquires the core grammar of her language and begins to acquire the marked elements, the constructions that do not fit the blueprint.

Starting from the nativist position, Steven Pinker (1984) has constructed a theory of child language development consistent with what we know from observation and empirical research regarding the acquisition of English. Most importantly:

1   Language develops gradually in the child.
2   There is rapid and error-free development of word order in sentences.

What is acquired is syntactic rules which are abstract. Noun, verb, noun is the correct order for a declarative sentence. It is necessary for the theory to explain how the child initially figures out which of the words he hears are nouns, which verbs, since, from the beginning, children's multi-word constructions follow the word order – more accurately, constituent structure order – for English sentences. (Pinker's work has been devoted to the acquisition of English.) Pinker proposes that when speaking to children, the nouns parents use refer to people and physical objects, and the verbs to actions like *eat* and *jump*, and states like *want* and *see*, which make the verb easy to interpret.

1   "Do you see the doggy?" said the father as the neighbor's dog came up the walk.
2   "Do you want a cookie?" said as he holds one out for the young child to take.

Parents don't use, with their young children, nouns like *sincerity* and *trust*, or verbs like *elapse* and *mitigate*. The use of concrete referents for nouns and easily interpretable verbs makes it possible for the child to unconsciously categorize words as nouns or verbs and to construct utterances that conform to the most important grammatical marker in English, word order.

Pinker's model is a competence model and his concern is with whether the language young children hear makes it possible for them to categorize words as nouns, verbs, and other syntactic categories. Because the nouns and verbs used in parent talk to children refer to objects, people, and actions the child is observing, she can fit them into appropriate syntactic categories. Pinker calls this "semantic bootstrapping." The categories themselves are innately given in the universal grammar blueprint. Pinker is not concerned with individual differences in the paths to competence. Differences in paths of language development reflect differences in children's psychological makeup and communicative goals, factors important in a performance model of language development.

Frequently friends, including scientists working on the theoretical laws of their own disciplines, have wanted to discuss with me their theories concerning human language. The theory most often suggested to me is that the language system is learned by imitation or by rote with no understanding of what is being learned, which is also the case when something is learned through conditioning. As we have seen, this is how some elements of human language are learned. The relationship between the sound and the meaning of most words is arbitrary. There is no rule or principle that can be used to explain why we call the four-legged seats with backs that we sit on *chairs* instead of *elephants* or *beds* or *spoons*. The formation of some complex words is rule governed so that if one knows the meanings of the component words one can figure out the meaning of the complex word. If one knows *bath* and *tub* or *type* and *write*, then *bathtub* or *typewrite* can be figured out. But there still remains the fact that the meanings of the component words (*bath, tub, type,* and *write*) are not rule governed. This aspect of human language, the relationship between the sounds of words and their meanings, is rote learned. But as soon as the language learner starts to learn that the objects we sit on are actually called *chairs*, there are rules to be learned. As is the case with many rules having to do with human concepts, the rules are not hard and fast. The category of *chairs* has fuzzy boundaries. In general, chairs are to sit on, but stools and sofas are not chairs. The language learner must learn the general rules that govern language, but also that there are exceptions and irregularities.

The young child, ready to start school, has learned 8,000 words in the normal, day-to-day experiences of life. Little children learn words from having the words used in interaction with them. A mother says to her child, "See the doggy," or "Pet the doggy," or "Stay away from the doggy; he might bite," as a dog comes on the scene. The mother does not say, "Now, I am going to tell you what a doggie is; it has fur, four legs, and a tail." Little children do not learn meanings of the words they know by having the words defined for them. Instead, they *induce* the meanings of words or the range of objects a word refers to on the basis of hearing the word used in their life experience. This explains why farm children will learn *horse, cow, pig*, and *chicken* at an age when city children have not yet realized that horses, cows, pigs, and chickens are not the same kind of animal as *dogs* (unless they have picture books of farm animals and parents who name the pictures for them).

"The experience of children" does not provide a satisfying explanation for their being able to acquire their relatively large vocabularies. Young children appear to be specially able to acquire the knowledge for competent language use. A child frequently does not have to use a word in order to check its meaning. The child unconsciously induces the meaning as he hears the word and watches what is going on as it is used. Words referring to salient, concrete objects, vivid, perceptual qualities, and events can be learned readily. The noun *dog*, the adjective *hot*, and the verb *jump* are easy to learn because what they refer to are interesting (or painful) or contrast vividly with other words. The noun, *idea*, the adjective, *mean*, and the verb, *wait*, are harder to learn because what they refer to are abstract. It takes more experience with the use of these words to induce the range of their meanings.

Since the 8,000-word vocabularies acquired by children before starting first grade were learned through life experience, what they refer to should be important or interesting enough to catch the child's attention so that the word can be associated with its referent. It's easy to understand children learning *candy, ice cream, naughty, stop*, and *hot*. But something like Helen Keller's reaction to her realization that "everything has a name" must contribute to children's vocabulary growth. Just the realization that things have names may be all that is required for words and their meanings to be learned by the language-prone human child. Children also induce the meanings of grammatical morphemes (the ending on words that indicate plural or past tense) and functors ("little" words such as *and, or, a, the, is, in,* and *on*), for example. Children acquire these meanings even though they are much less prominent for learning through experience than the meanings of *sun* and *jump*, which are words referring to an object and an activity that are visible and interesting. Furthermore, children begin acquiring the grammatical morphemes as soon as they begin to produce utterances more than one word in length. Allen, Carol, Jean, and Joel "sprinkle" grammatical morphemes in their early multi-word utterances in a non-systematic way. Sometimes "s" appears in an utterance where it is needed, as in "Joel's towel," said by Joel as he points to a towel. But, in the same construction and same context a few minutes later, Joel says, "Joel towel." The errors that young children make in forming plurals or the past tense provide evidence that they induce the rules for forming plurals and past tense rather than learning them by rote or imitation.

1   My foots are warm.
2   My feets are cold.
3   Tommy hurted hisself.

In sentences (1) and (2), the plural of foot is incorrect. The correct plural, *feet*, is irregular. The two sentences show that the speaker in each case used /s/ to form the plural. Sentence (1) assumes that the plural of foot is like that of all the words that have the regular plural ending. The speaker of the second sentence has learned that the plural of foot is irregular but has not quite mastered the irregular form. In sentence (3) the speaker is using the general rule for forming the past tense, written orthographically as "add *ed* to the present form." But *hurt* is an irregular verb and has the same form *hurt* in the present and past tenses. The speaker has formed the third person reflexive in sentence (3) by using the rule for first and second person reflexives: add "self" to the possessive pronoun, as in "myself," and "yourself." But the third person rule – add self to the accusative pronoun, yielding *himself* – is irregular.

Errors like those in sentences (1), (2), and (3) provide evidence that children induce the rules governing grammatical morphemes because it is unlikely that *hurted, hisself, foots,* and *feets* were learned by imitation. Most grown-ups do not use these incorrect forms, thereby providing them to be learned by imitation. However, imitation cannot be ruled out. The classic experiment of Jean Berko (1958), now Jean Berko Gleason, provided experimental evidence that rule induction rather than imitation is the way children learn the plural, past tense, and other grammatical morphemes. The subjects in her experiment were preschool children. The experiment consisted of eliciting grammatical morphemes from children. In eliciting plurals, Berko first pointed to the picture of an imaginary animal she called the "wug" and said to a child-subject in the research, "Here is a wug." Then she pointed to a second picture of two wugs and said, "Now there are two of them. There are two _____" (figure 7.1).

The child-subject had to supply the missing word, wug/z/. Berko (1958) found that 76 percent of her preschool children could supply the correct plural. They could not have learned the plural by imitation because there is no such animal as a wug. The children could not have heard anyone say, "Look at the wug/z/," as two of them walked by. Using the same technique, Berko elicited plurals for *bik*,

THIS IS A WUG.

NOW THERE IS ANOTHER ONE.
THERE ARE TWO OF THEM.
THERE ARE TWO _____.

Figure 7.1 Wug pictures (redrawn from J. Berko, "The child's learning of English morphology," *Word*, 14(1958). Reprinted with permission)

gutch, and *tass*, more nouns she invented. Children supplied the correct plurals: bik/s/, glutch/ɨz/, and tass/ɨz/.[1] When children erred, it was not by supplying the wrong form of the plural, but rather by not responding at all. Berko elicited the past tense for verbs she invented – bing/d/, rick/t/, spow/d/, and mott/ɨd/ – and found that 63, 73, 36, and 32 percent of her subjects could supply the grammatical morphemes for the past tense of these invented verbs. Again, when the children erred, it was not through supplying an incorrect morpheme. Errors were all failures to respond.

The rules for forming the plural and past tense in English reflect a more general phonological rule of English. If a word has a voiced ending, either a vowel sound or a voiced consonant, the grammatical morphemes added for the plural, past tense, or third person singular present tense will be voiced, for example, dove/z/, beg/d/, and row/z/. If the word has a voiceless ending, the added grammatical morphemes will be voiceless. If the word ends with either the voiced or voiceless version of the grammatical morphemes, add the mid-vowel /ɨ/ and the voiced version of the morpheme, for example, piece/ɨz/, pat/ɨd/, and buzz/ɨz/.

Here we have a grammatical rule of English for forming the past tense of regular English verbs. What makes them regular is that they are rule governed, "computed by a suffixation rule in a neural system for grammatical processing" (Pinker, 1991: 530). The rule is genetically determined, innate. But what about the irregular verbs, those whose past tenses are not formed according to the general rule: verbs like *break, broke*; *swim, swam*; *sleep, slept*; *run, ran*; *go, went*; *see, saw*; *bring, brought*; and a host of others? The language-acquiring child cannot be inducing a rule to account for these varied past tense forms.

Klima and Bellugi (1966), using data from the research of Brown published in 1973, have shown a progression in children's gaining control of the intricacies in the grammar of English. Klima and Bellugi (1966) called our attention to the fact that Roger Brown's subjects used the word *don't* correctly long before they used *do*. *Do* is an English auxiliary verb, a fact which does not have to be known in order for *don't* to be used appropriately and correctly, even by very young English speakers. In the same way that *don't* is learned just as a word at an early age rather than as the negative form of the auxiliary *do*, *went*, *swam*, *ate*, *stole*, and other irregular past tense verbs are learned early just as words, unrelated to a present tense form. These are called strong past tense verbs and because they are in frequent use they are early acquisitions in children's vocabularies. As children acquire verbs with the regular past tense form, they begin to "over-regularize," to say *goed* and *breaked* instead of *went* and *broke*. At this time children have acquired the rule for forming the past tense and follow it even with the exceptions where it doesn't apply.

Eventually, they learn the exceptions and no longer over-regularize. Their grammatical intuitions tell them that the rule-governed past tense *walked, skipped, baked, jumped, cried, cooked,* sound right. At this time, *breaked, stealed, swimmed, flyed, goed* no longer sound right to the child, even though the regular past tense rule is being appropriately applied. The child has learned by rote, by simply hearing the irregular forms used by the competent speakers who converse with her and memorizing them. Pinker (1991) presents an excellent account of this development which is typical of language development in general: part is innate; part is learned by example of the competent members of the child's speech community. Pinker provides evidence that regular and irregular pasts are computed in different subsystems of the mind. The developmental course of acquisition of the past tense suggests the existence of separate rule-governed and associative memory systems. Three neurological impairments selectively effect rule-governed and rote-learned pasts: agrammatic aphasia and specific language impairment interfere with the generation of rule-governed pasts and spare rote-learned pasts. Williams syndrome spares the rule-governed and interferes with the rote-learned pasts.

Although some aspects of word meaning and word sound correspondence are not rule governed and have to be learned by rote, sentence formation is rule governed, and if one knows the rules for forming sentences then one can produce sentences one has never heard. In accounting for adult ability to produce sentences they have never heard, it might be thought that the rules, grammar, and syntax of adult language were learned in school. But the remarkable fact is that the basic syntax of the language spoken in the speech community is mastered by children by the age of 4 years or so. The syntax of their language, those grammatical rules for forming sentences, are induced by children from the language spoken to them.

We have looked at the rules for forming plurals and past tenses in English and now I want to present some ideas about the rules for constructing English sentences that take into account their being acquired by young children. It must not be forgotten that rules for constructing sentences are being acquired by children in situations in which language use is a naturally occurring part of the child's interaction with others. If the child is acquiring the syntax of her language, it is because the child is interacting with competent speakers.

There is an old story that in bygone days a king raised two infants together, with no one speaking to them, to find out what the original language of human beings was. (There were members of religious fundamentalist sects as late as the nineteenth century who believed it was Hebrew.) Of course, the infants never learned any language. A twentieth-century study has been reported to have been carried out by the Russian psychologist, Alexander Luria, of twin boys of average intelligence who spent most of their time together with very little contact with anyone besides each other. At the age of 5 their speech was primitive and infrequent. They were subsequently placed in separate kindergarten groups. Within 3 months, their language use was on a par with that of the other children in the kindergarten. In order to play with the other children, the twins had to acquire true language. By true language, I mean language that has the vocabulary and syntactic rules of the speech community.

There are grammatical rules in languages that are not acquired by the age of 5. In English, we have a verb form called the subjunctive. It is used, for example, when the speaker wants to indicate that the message is hypothetical or contrary to the facts. When Patrick Henry said,

4 If this be treason, make the most of it

he used the present subjunctive, *be*, instead of the present indicative *is*. When a person says,

5 If I were you, I wouldn't eat that worm

he is using the past subjunctive forms *were* and *wouldn't*. I think (5) is regularly used by speakers of American English, but (4) has gone out of use since Patrick Henry's time; children no longer hear it and therefore do not acquire it. There are other syntactic rules in English that seem to be in the process of falling into disuse. The present subjunctive is just an example. Whatever the rule, if it is not used, it will not be acquired by young children.

Table 7.2 Sentences separated into noun phrase (NP) and verb phrase (VP)

S	
NP	*VP*
6 the mouse	ate the cheese
9 a man	chopped the wood
10 the spider	caught a fly
11 a child	drew the picture

The sentences of English and other languages are organized simultaneously into linear and hierarchical structures (see, for example, Lashley, 1950; Chomsky, 1965; Morgan and Newport, 1981). Linear organization means that there is a correct order for the words of a sentence (see table 7.2).

  6 The mouse ate the cheese
*7 Mouse the the cheese ate

(An asterix placed before a sentence signifies that it is ungrammatical.) Sentence (6) has the linear order for an English sentence; (7) does not. Hierarchical organization means that groups of words form separate parts, or constituent structures of sentences.

  8 The mouse which lives in my drawer eats cheese

"The mouse which lives in my drawer" forms the same constituent in sentence (8) as "the mouse" in (6). Grammatical sentences in any language can be divided into constituent structures that are shorter than the whole sentence.

    If we go word by word through sentence (6) and give the words the names of their syntactic categories, we have:

The	mouse	ate	the	cheese
article	noun	verb	article	noun

and we notice that the sequence, article – noun, occurs twice. We will leave (8) for the time being and cast about for some other sentences that have the same structure as (6).

9 A   man   chopped the   wood
   article noun   verb   article noun
10 The spider caught a fly
11 A child drew the picture

Many sequential human behaviors are hierarchically organized like sentence production and can be broken down into constituent structures. Close analogies to speech and sentence can be found in music. A melody is like a sentence. It is composed of musical phrases which are its constituent structures, and which have notes in a particular order like the words in a noun phrase or verb phrase. The behavior that intrigues cognitive developmental psychologists as analogous to the production of multi-word utterances by the very young child acquiring language is goal-directed action like putting together a nesting boxes toy (Greenfield, 1991), which is developing at about the same time. Greenfield found that, with three boxes, her subjects by 36 months did the nesting on the basis of sub-assembly. Either placing the smallest box into the next smallest and then placing this sub-assembly in the largest box or by putting the next to largest box in the largest (the sub-assembly) and then the smallest in the sub-assembly. Even though all the children in her study were shown the sub-assembly strategy as a model to imitate, no 11-month-old ever achieved the sub-assembly strategy over eight trials. The sub-assembly strategy is like hierarchical organization of sentences. Greenfield's finding of this parallel development in action and language use is intriguing. Psycholinguists who view language development as the product, primarily, of learning and as part of cognitive development find support for their position in such findings.

Simon (1969), as quoted by Bloom (1991), has pointed out that virtually all complex systems exhibit hierarchical organization. Bloom argues that it is the unique properties of language development that suggest that language is a domain separate from cognitive development. When he says "language," he is talking about narrowly linguistic phenomena like phonological representations, syntactic structure, inflectional morphology, and so on.

Sentences (6), (9), (10), (11) have the same constituent, syntactic structure even though their meanings are very different. In science we are always on the look-out for underlying regularities, and the regularity we are noticing is the basis for structural linguistics. Conventionally in linguistics, constituent structure is spelled out in *tree diagrams* or *rewrite rules*.

The letter S at the top of the tree diagram stands for sentence. S has two immediate constituents (parts into which the entire sentence can be separated) called the noun phrase (NP) and verb phrase (VP).

Sentence (6) has as NP, "the mouse"; sentence (9) has "a man" as NP; (10) has "the spider"; and (11) "a child." Sentence (6) has as VP "ate the cheese." Sentence (9) has as VP, "chopped the wood," (10) has "caught a fly"; and (11), "drew the picture." The NP, which is one of the two constituent structures into which the entire sentence can be separated functions as the subject of the sentence. The VP, which is the other part, is the predicate of the sentence (see figure 7.2).

The subject NP and/or the predicate VP can be very complicated, for example, they can contain other sentences, as does the subject NP of sentence (8).

NP and VP are the immediate constituents of S, but they each have constituents themselves. For sentence (6) the constituents of the NP, "the mouse," are two single words: an article (Art) and a noun (N). When the tree diagram gets to the place where the constituents are single words, the constituents are placed directly below their category names and are written as words, rather than indicated with "branches." The constituents of the VP, "ate the cheese," are a verb (V) and an NP, which in this case is also formed from an article and a noun. The

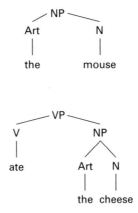

Figure 7.2 Tree diagrams for noun phrase (NP) and verb phrase (VP)

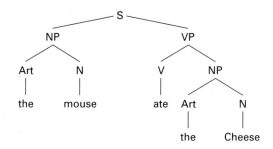

Figure 7.3 Tree diagram for "The mouse ate the cheese"

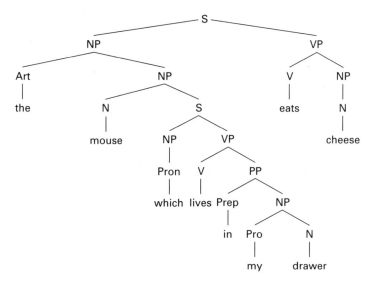

Figure 7.4 Tree diagram for "The mouse which lives in my drawer eats cheese"

tree diagram for sentence (6) is shown in figure 7.3. The tree diagram for sentence (8), "The mouse which lives in my drawer eats cheese," is shown in figure 7.4.

An alternative way to convey information about the constituent structure and hierarchical organization of sentences is by *rewrite rules*. Rewrite rules "rewrite" the symbols on the right-hand side of the symbol, →, which stands for "can be rewritten as" until the symbols stand for single words. Rewrite rules convey the same information as the tree diagram. Consider the sentence, "A dog stole the turkey" (figure 7.5). Each rewrite rule corresponds to one of the nodes and its branches of the tree diagram. The rewrite rules start with the rewriting of S into its immediate constituents, just the way one begins to make the tree diagram, and each rewrite rule corresponds to one of the nodes (the symbol to be rewritten) and its branches (what the symbol is rewritten as). Figure 7.6 gives the tree diagram for the following sentence:

12   Angie bathed the kitten in the fishbowl

Noun phrase, verb phrase, noun, article, and so on, are all syntactic categories. A syntactic category may contain other syntactic categories just as NP and VP do. The symbols that label the branches from

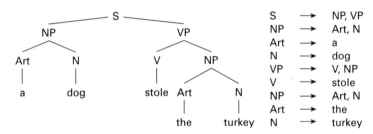

Figure 7.5 Tree diagram and corresponding rewrite rules for "A dog stole the turkey"

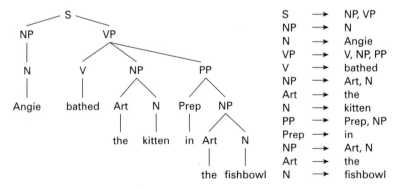

Figure 7.6 Tree diagram and rewrite rules for "Angie bathed the kitten in the fishbowl"

a node on a tree diagram designate syntactic categories; these are sub-categories contained in the syntactic category designated at the node.

All languages have syntactic categories, and the speakers of a language know the syntactic categories of their language, just as they know constituent structure. What is mind-boggling about this fact is that native speakers of a language, including children, have this knowledge without being taught and, in the case of children and some adults, without knowing that they have this syntactic knowledge. We know speakers have this knowledge because the results are observable. Whenever a speaker produces a grammatical sentence (that isn't memorized), the speaker is unconsciously using the constituent structure rules of the language to produce the sentence.

As described above, there is another way of observing speakers' knowledge of the syntactic categories and other aspects of their language's syntax, and that is to question their "grammatical intuitions." In this section on sentences, I have been relying on the readers' grammatical intuitions to bring them through the discussion to the conclusion that English sentences do have linear and hierarchical organization.

Thirty-seven years ago, Roger Brown published an experimental study (reprinted, Brown, 1970), which provides evidence that syntactic organization determines how utterances will be understood by children. Brown invented three nonsense words, *niss*, *sib*, and *latt*. He used these in connection with sets of pictures to see if the way he used the nonsense word as verb, mass noun, or count noun, in describing the pictures, would determine the meaning for the word induced by the children.

> The first picture shows a pair of hands performing a kneading sort of motion with a mass of red confetti-like material, which is piled into and overflowing a blue and white striped container that is round and low in shape. The important features of the picture are the kneading action, the red mass, and the blue and white round container. The motion would ordinarily be named with a verb (like *kneading*), the mass with a mass noun (like *confetti*), and the container with a particular [count] noun (like *container*) . . . Each of the remaining three pictures of this set exactly reproduce one of the three salient features of the first picture, either the motion, the mass, or the container. In order to represent the motion a second time, it was necessary also to show a mass and a container. However, the mass was here painted yellow so as not to duplicate the original, and the container was of a

different size, and shape, and color from the original. The other two sets of pictures involved different content but always an action, a mass substance, and a particular object. In one case, the first picture showed hands cutting a mass of cloth with a strange tool. In the third set, hands were shown emptying an odd container of a slushy sort of material. (Brown, 1970: 23)

The children were shown the first picture in conjunction with one of the nonsense words identifiable either as a verb, a mass noun, or a count noun. Then they were shown the remaining three pictures of the set and asked to point out again what had been named in the first picture.

If the nonsense word was to function as a verb, the experimenter would say, "Do you know what it means to sib? In this picture (the first picture described above) you can see sibbing. (Showing the other three pictures) "Now, show me another picture of sibbing." If the word were to function as a count noun, the experimenter asked, "Do you know what a sib is?" If the word were to function as a mass noun, the experimenter asked, "Have you ever seen any sib?"

Each of the preschool children in the experiment saw all three sets of pictures and heard each of the nonsense words: one used as a count noun, one as a mass noun and one as a verb. The results are presented in table 7.3.

This experiment is a beautiful demonstration that preschool children use syntactic information. Syntactic categories like verb, count noun, and mass noun are recognized by preschool children because of the set of grammatical operations in which they participate. Brown marked *sib*, or *niss*, or *latt* as a verb by putting the nonsense word

Table 7.3 Picture selection for words belonging to various parts of speech (syntactic categories)

Category depicted	Verbs	Count nouns	Mass nouns
Actions	10	1	0
Objects	4	11	3
Substances	1	2	12
No response	1	2	1

Source: Brown (1970)

in an infinitive construction when he asked, "Do you know what it means to sib (or to niss or to latt)?" Only verbs can be operated upon to produce infinitive constructions. He then said, "In this picture you can see sibbing (or nissing or latting)" thereby producing the present participle construction of the verb. Thus he carried out, in instructing his subjects, two syntactic operations on a nonsense word (for any particular subject only one of the three nonsense words was used as a verb) in which only a verb can participate.

The remaining two nonsense words were used in the syntactic construction, NP, in which only nouns can participate. When the nonsense word was used as a count noun, Brown said, "Do you know what a sib (or a niss or a latt) is?" He made *sib* the noun following the article *a* in the NP in the predicate of the sentence. When the nonsense word was used as a mass noun, Brown asked, "Have you ever seen any sib (or any niss or any latt)?" Again he made the nonsense word the noun in an NP. The nonsense words count as mass or count noun, depending on whether they follow *any* or *a*. Only count nouns can follow the indefinite article *a* and only mass nouns the quantifier *any*.

This experiment by Roger Brown provides evidence for the "psychological reality" of syntactic categories. The preschool children in this experiment interpreted the nonsense words as verbs, count nouns, or mass nouns, depending on the syntactic operations he carried out with the nonsense word. I doubt whether the children had ever heard the words *verb* and *noun*, much less knew what they are in the sense of being able to define them. But the children's grammatical or syntactic intuitions caused them to use the nonsense words as belonging to the syntactic category appropriate to the syntactic operations in which Brown made the nonsense word participate.

In recent years what Brown demonstrated is receiving attention under the rubric "syntactic bootstrapping" (for example, Gleitman, 1990), the analogue of Pinker's "semantic bootstrapping." The child's joint use of the two goes a long way in explaining how it is that human beings manage to develop their extensive lexicons (vocabularies) and understanding of the syntax of their language without consulting grammar books and dictionaries but simply through use. "Semantic bootstrapping" helps the language acquirer assign words to syntactic categories. Because the words are not semantically transparent, highly visible, like *boy* and *run*, but are abstract like *integrity* and *prove*, they are difficult to assign. "Syntactic bootstrapping" helps in assigning meaning to words based on their syntactic relations to other constituents of a sentence. If the word comes after a beginning noun phrase like *the boy*, *my mother*, *a spider* and ends the sentence, it must be an intransitive verb (doesn't take a direct object) a verb like *ran*, *jumped*, or *died*. If it is followed by a direct object NP like *a cake*, *some spaghetti*, or *a book*, it must be a transitive verb like *baked*, *ate*, or *read*.

I have said that by the time English-speaking children are about 4 years old, they have acquired the basic grammatical rules of English to the extent that these are reflected in the English spoken to them. It has been shown (Klima and Bellugi, 1966) that children's abilities to produce syntactically well-formed negative and interrogative sentences in English develop together. This is not surprising since control of the system of auxiliary verbs is necessary (but not sufficient) for syntactically correct negatives and interrogatives.

In the earliest stage of development questions are marked by intonation for yes/no questions and the *wh* words *what* and *where*. Negatives are marked by *no*, or *not*, either preceding or following the rest of the utterance.

13 No a boy bed
14 Wear mitten no
15 See hole?
16 What dat?
17 Where kitty go?

In the second stage children add the words *don't* and *can't* to their negative vocabulary, and they include negatives within utterances instead of placing them at the beginning or end of the utterance.

18 That no mummy
19 Don't bite me yet
20 I can't see you

Second-stage interrogatives include:

21 You can't fix it?
22 See my doggie?
23 Why you smiling?
24 Where my mitten is?

They tend to be longer than first-stage interrogatives, to include *why* as a *wh* word, but are not more developed structurally than the interrogatives of stage one.

In the third stage, children have mastered the auxiliary system. They produce sentences in which the positive verbal auxiliaries *can, do,* and *will* appear as well as the negatives, *can't* and *don't*.

25 Oh, did I caught it?
26 Will you help me?
27 What he can ride in?

On the basis of the examples provided by Klima and Bellugi (1966) we would say that mastery of the copula and irregularities in verb tense is not complete but that the glaring failures at stage three is to correctly form *wh* questions. All of Klima and Bellugi's (1966) examples are similar; the *wh* word is correctly preposed in the interrogative, but the subject NP and first auxiliary are not interchanged even though they are in the same children's yes/no questions. In the days of transformational grammar (Chomsky, 1965), the rules of transformational grammar provided the explanation. Two transformations are involved in producing *wh* questions as opposed to one for yes/no questions. Children's competence at the third stage makes one transformation possible but not two and transformational theory requires that if the transformation which prepose *wh* words is required, it is applied before that which interchanges subject NP and first auxiliary.

Research that postdates that of Klima and Bellugi (1966) with more subjects has found that the rule interchanging subjects and first auxiliary is applied to both kinds of questions at about the same time (Ingram and Tyack, 1979; Erreich, 1980; cited in Gleason, 1993). Scientific progress in understanding the development of language occurs, as in other fields, on the basis of better theory and better data. Here we see the role of better data in overturning a theory, in this case that the order of children's acquisition of grammatical rules depends on how many transformations of the simple declarative structure (the deep structure) are required to produce derived forms like yes/no and *wh* questions.

Today, there is no generally accepted theory explaining children's acquisition of their linguistic system even though universality of acquisition and stages in the process indicate an innately programmed capacity.

There are questions about the role of learning and cognition in the process still to be resolved. The wider questions about becoming a language user involving performance as well as competence will be considered in subsequent chapters of this book.

Note

1 /ɨ/ is the mid-vowel required to form the plural or the past tense when the singular noun or the present tense verb end with the voiced or voiceless consonant, the voiced version of which forms the plural or past tense marker.

Further Reading

Cairns, H., McDaniel, D., Hsu, J. and Rapp, M. (1994) "A longitudinal study of principles of control and pronomial reference in child English," *Language*, 70: 260–88.
Development of syntax in children 3, 10–4, 11.
Crain, S. (1991) "Language acquisition in the absence of experience," *Behavioral and Brain Sciences*, 14: 597–650.
Describes some recent findings on how learners acquire syntactic knowledge for which there is little, if any, decisive evidence from the environment.
Farrar, M. J., Friend, M. J. and Forbes, J. N. (1993) "Event knowledge and early language acquisition," *Journal of Child Language*, 20: 591–606.
Role of event knowledge in early language acquisition.
Fenson, L., Dale, P., Reznick, J., Bates, E., Thal, D. and Pethicta, S. (1994) "Variability in early communicative development," *Monographs of the Society for Research in Child Development*, no. 242.
Goodluck, H. (1991) *Language Acquisition* (Oxford: Blackwell).
Language acquisition from the linguistic, rather than the biopsychosocial perspective. An excellent introductory text.
Hall, D. (1994) "How mothers teach basic-level and situation-restricted count nouns," *Journal of Child Language*, 21: 391–414.
"Person" (man) before "passenger" basic level count noun is psychologically privileged.
Hampson, J. and Nelson, K. (1993) "The relation of maternal language to variation in rate and style of language acquisition," *Journal of Child Language*, 20: 313–42.
Determined whether the "motherese hypothesis" has been adequately tested

in previous studies. Results imply that earlier studies have been looking for the effectiveness of maternal input too late.

Naigles, L. (1990) "Children use syntax to learn verb meanings," *Journal of Child Language*, 17: 357–75.

Ninio, A. (1994) "Predicting the order of acquisition of three-word constructions by the complexity of their dependency structure," *First Language*, 14: 119–52.

An attempt to account for the order of acquisition of different three-word constructions by a child learning English as her first language.

Pinker, S. (1994) *The Language Instinct* (New York: Morrow).

A large-scale, accessible treatise, covering many aspects of language development, taking syntactic development as central, and packed with information.

8

The Communication Skills
of Young Children

If you heard the question

1 Did l'il tweetie faw down?

being asked in a tender, rather high-pitched voice, you wouldn't
have much trouble figuring out who was being asked if he or she
had fallen down. It would most likely be a very young child because this
question is being asked in the *baby talk register* of American English.
All languages have several registers, different sets of rules for using
the language, depending upon who is talking to whom and whether
the language is being used for talking or writing.

Young children become language users in the course of their everyday experience. They come to speak as, most importantly, their parents
do. Friends, a mother, father, and 4-year-old son, moved to Cambridge,
Massachusetts, from Philadelphia, Pennsylvania, where the father had
been a professor. We were invited to their house for dinner soon after
their move. The mother introduced me to the little boy. I can't remember what caused me to do this, but I asked him, "Where were you born?"
He answered promptly, confidently, "Ah was bone in Pennsylvania," in
a strong southern drawl. He was born in Pennsylvania, but his parents
had been born and had grown up in the South.

I didn't see the little boy again for six months or so, during which
time he had been going to nursery school in Cambridge and spending
a lot of time playing with other preschoolers. Now when he talked to
me, I heard no trace of the southern drawl, he sounded like the Cambridge kids he played with. Children don't want to be different from

their peers and unconsciously they adopt the speech pattern of their playmates, if they have not yet reached puberty. The pattern may be identified as a speech register if it has characteristics that make the conversation of children with their peers distinguishable from the conversation of children with adults, adults with other adults, and so on.[1] In this chapter, the baby talk register and the child's acquisition of the parental role register will be discussed.

The Baby Talk Register: Adult Talk to Very Young Children

The features of the baby talk register include speaking in short utterances, a good deal of repetition of utterances, and speaking at a higher than usual pitch with exagerrated intonation. Speaking more slowly and clearly than usual are sometimes baby talk register characteristics (Snow and Ferguson, 1977). Simplifying the pronunciation of words as in *l'il* for *little*, *tweetie* for *sweetie*, and *faw* for *fall* is probably less frequently a feature than others, in part at least because we have been taught that doing this interferes with young children's learning to pronounce words correctly. They will try to pronounce what they hear.

The features just mentioned do not exhaust the list that has been proposed for the baby talk register. There is no hard and fast list of features, but there is a short list of ways in which the features of the register make it a better means of communication with very young children than the adult register (Snow et al., 1986). Ferguson (1977) lists simplifying, clarifying, and expressive as the characteristics of the register that its special features foster. Short utterances are generally simpler than longer ones and easier for young children to understand and produce. Repetition of utterances clarifies them because, in the first place, the repetition provides further opportunity for the infant to hear, remember, and figure out what the verbalization means and what its structure is. Speaking extra slowly and clearly also enhances the child's chances of being able to understand the meaning and structure of the verbalization.

The adult's pronouncing *little* as *l'il* serves no purpose. The young child sometimes has difficulty pronouncing some speech sounds, particularly consonant clusters like the *tl* cluster in *little*, and simplifies in her own pronunciation. The child's problem is in articulating the sounds, not in hearing them, and the adult who adopts a babyish pronunciation of words is simply misinforming the infant language learner. Perhaps the unconscious motivation for babyish pronunciation is the expressive characteristic of the register. The adult is expressing tenderness and the feeling that the infant should be responded to in a special way. Use of higher than usual pitch and exaggerated intonation are motivated by the adult expressive purpose. These features capture and keep the baby's interest in what the speaker is saying. The speech of the mothers of Allen, Carol, Jean, and Joel to their infants displayed the features of the baby talk register discussed except for simplified pronunciation.

I have not yet mentioned another commonly suggested feature of the baby talk register: using *Mommy* and *Allen*, for example, in face-to-face discourse where, if adults were talking to each other, they would use the personal pronouns, *you, I, me, yours,* and *mine.* The reason suggested for using Mommy and the child's name instead of the pronouns is that the child doesn't have to shift from second to first person to answer his mother's questions.

2 Do you want a cookie?
3 I do.
4 Does Joel want a cookie?
5 Joel does.

It is assumed that 4 and 5 are "easier" than 2 and 3 because 4 and 5 do not necessitate a pronoun shift. Our findings suggest something else. We put all the utterances of the mothers of Allen, Carol, Jean, and Joel when the infants were 3, 6, 9, and 12 months old into the computer and got a rank order for the frequency of words spoken for each mother. We found that, at all data points, *you* was among the three most frequent words, *I* was among the top 10, and *Mommy* or *mother* was not spoken at all. When Allen was 12 months old, *Allen* was among his mother's top 10 words, but *Allen* was used to get his attention, not as a subject or object in sentences. It was not that these mothers were not using the baby talk register, for they were. The average length of their verbalizations to their infants was between three and four words at every data point and all four engaged in much repetition of utterances. Their speech was marked by exaggerated intonation; in addition to the use of higher than usual pitch, they sometimes whispered and growled. When the children were well into the one-word period, there were scattered instances of the use of *Mommy* and infant's name as sentence constituents. But they tended to follow the child's use of Mommy or his own name. Joel said *Mommy* holding a book out toward his mother. Joel's mother said,

6   You want Mommy to read it?

Joel's mother used the word *Mommy* because Joel had just used it, and she expanded Joel's utterance into a sentence. Her question provided a little lesson for Joel about how to put his request in "better" English, and at the same time her question acted as a check on their communication. She was asking Joel if by *Mommy* and the gesture of handing over the book he meant he wanted her to read it. She could have said, "You want me to read it?" and not repeated Joel's *Mommy*. I think that mothers' repetition of their infants' words in the one-word period serves a word-teaching function. I am not sure how conscious mothers (and others) are that they are adapting their speech so that it is comprehensible to their children and is providing language lessons. Cross (1977) has produced evidence that mothers' speech to children between the ages of 19 and 32 months is "finely tuned" to the rapidly changing psycholinguistic capabilities of the children. What that means is that there are highly significant differences in mothers' speech to children in this restricted age range that depend on the capacities of the children rather than their ages. I very much doubt whether mothers have the finely tuned adaptation of their speech to the rapidly changing capacities of their children under their voluntary or conscious control. The ability to adapt language use to the needs of the developing language user appears to be an aspect of the innate, linguistic capacity of the human species, like the vocalizing and word-teaching behaviors of mothers described in chapters 5 and 6.

Acquisition of Parental Register

The defining characteristics of a register are determined by the function of the role the person is playing when he speaks in the register. Children naturally experience their parents in the mother and father roles in relation to themselves. Teachers and other interested adults get the feel of children's perception of their parents in these roles seeing children playing the mother or father in the doll corner of the preschool class or as subjects in the interested adult's role-playing experiment. Preschoolers find it difficult, maybe impossible, to separate role from person. "Daddy" cannot be grandpa's child. He's "Daddy" and that's all. When my sons were in kindergarten and first grade their friends would come to the door and ask them and my husband to come out and play ball. If they asked "Is Tom or David here?" and I said "No," they frequently asked me, "Is your daddy home?" referring to my husband, Tom and David's father. In general, children younger than 7 years of age do not understand that a person can at the same time be their parent and the child of their grandparent (Watson and Amgott-Kwan, 1983). Nor are young children able to understand, unless it has happened to their own father, that a father could change his occupational role and still be a father. Young children identify father, mother, and themselves as unalterable combinations of kin, occupation, physical characteristics, and so on. I remember my 5-year-old asking me, "How much allowance will I get when I'm old as Daddy?" and another time, "What grade will I be in when I'm a hundred?" Reality was for him, for all time, the life we were living. He did not remember the time before his brother was born. He could not conceive of any real change occurring in his life and relationships.

Young children lack conscious ability to describe father or mother as "roles" that adults may occupy. On the basis of experience interacting with their parents, researchers have found that children are able to pretend to play the parental roles and talk like father or mother for a doll who is the parent in interaction with a doll who is a baby or young child. Anderson (1986) found in her research that 88 percent of fathers' directives to child were direct imperatives as compared to 46 percent of mothers' and 31 percent of child's to parent.

If children have interacted verbally with people in roles other than mother and father they will have unconsciously become aware of register variation and be able unconsciously to imitate the appropriate verbal style for some roles. Anderson (1986) found that 5-year-old children unconsciously know characteristics of the register appropriate to mother or father and young child interacting. Fathers have deep voices. Their sentences are shorter than mothers', and for the most part they use direct imperatives to guide their children's behavior. Unlike the mothers, fathers do not usually explain why they issue directives. "Don't run," rather than, "Better not run because the sidewalk's slippery." Mothers in Anderson's research were more talkative than fathers, more polite, and used more endearments (for example, *sweetie*) and baby talk (*night-night*, *doggie*) than fathers.

The parental role register reflects the social values of a society and these cannot be innate. However, young children "pick-up" socially determined language use variation along with acquiring more purely linguistic aspects of a language – like phonology, morphology, and syntax. For whatever reasons, children are better able to perform behaviors on the basis of just seeing or hearing them than are adults. Parents marvel that after they have read a story to their preschooler two or three times, the child corrects any deviation from the last time in the parent's recounting of the story. The young child's acquisition of register without conscious understanding of its relation to the functions of the related role contrasts with the adult's conscious understanding of the relation of register and the functions of role.

Fine Tuning as a Register

One of the many miraculous abilities of competent language users is their accuracy encoding their thoughts in language appropriate to the intended audience. Because we are generally on target – our speech is finely tuned to audience needs – we don't "talk down" to people, meaning we don't oversimplify our discourse. On the other hand, our language use is not abstruse. The physicist describing the evidence for black holes uses very different terminologies with the intelligent lay person, astrophysicist, or school child. A mother or father trying to explain procreation to a 12-year-old child or where babies come from to a 6-year-old gives radically different accounts. We unconsciously fine tune our language to the capacity of our intended audience.

Research that suggests an innate predisposition of humans to acquire a developing language use support register concerns the ability of 4-year-old boys, with no younger brothers or sisters, to adapt their language use to low-verbal (MLU 1.0–1.5) as opposed to high-verbal (MLU 1.8–4.0) 2-year-olds. The 2-year-old groups did not differ in age, cognitive ability, or maturity of their behavior, so what the 4-year-olds were responding to was just the difference in the linguistic performance of the 2-year-olds. The researcher, Elise Masur, had 10 4-year-old boys each explain to one high-verbal and one low-verbal 2-year-old boy how to play with a toy filling station with a ramp, an elevator, and a garage. The 4-year-olds explained the filling station to one of the 2-year-olds on one day and the other on another day. Five of the 4-year-olds explained the toy to his high-verbal 2-year-old first and the other five explained first to the low-verbal 2-year-old. Masur computed the mean length of utterance (MLU) for the 4-year-old boys on their first 10 verbalizations to the 2-year-old boys. She has reported (Masur, 1978) that the MLUs of the 4-year-old boys were significantly higher to the high-verbal 2-year-olds than to the low-verbal 2-year-olds, except to the five low-verbal 2-year-olds who did not speak at all. When the 2-year-olds did not speak, the MLUs of the 4-year-olds were like those to the high-verbal 2-year-olds. These results show that people as young as 4 years of age have the capacity to adapt their speech to the capacity of the listener as revealed by the listener's MLU. If the listener does not speak, then the clue to his psycholinguistic capacity was lacking, and the speaker did not adjust his speech.

Masur calculated MLUs on the first 10 utterances rather than on the utterances of the entire session because, as the 2-year-olds began to manipulate the filling station and the cars, short utterances predominated for both the 4-year-olds and 2-year-olds. Their talk was mostly in direct response to each other, checking and clarifying what should be done with the toy. "This way?" was said by a 2-year-old as he placed a car on the ramp. "Okay," responded the 4-year-old.

Masur's findings are important because mother's fine tuning of their speech to their own infants is one thing, but 4-year-old boys with no younger siblings fine tuning *their* speech to 2-year-olds they have just met is quite another. Arguments that seem plausible about implications of adults' cognitive development in their adapting to their infants are not so plausible with 4-year-old boys. It seems more likely that the ability of human beings, even as young as 4 years of age, to adapt their speech to the psycholinguistic capacity of very young children is part of our innate linguistic endowment rather than something learned through experience, a speech register rather than the ability to take the perspective of another.

Egocentrism and Perspective-taking

Psycholinguists who believe that adaptation of one's speech to the needs of a beginning language user is learned through experience would argue that each person's experiences as a beginning language user provide the experience necessary to be able to adapt speech to other beginning language users; in other words, any human being who has become a language user has been through the beginning language user experience and therefore is able to take the perspective of the beginning language user. However, it has been widely assumed by psychologists that perspective-taking is a cognitive skill that does not develop in the human being until the person is about 7 years of age. Before this, human beings are not aware that other people may have perspectives that are different from their own. This is what is meant by egocentrism. This is the theory of Jean Piaget (1962), and it has dominated cognitive developmental psychology since the 1960s, until recently. The finding that 4-year-olds vary their speech to high-verbal and low-verbal 2-year-olds would be difficult for Piaget's theory to explain, even if the onset of the ability to take the perspective of another were moved down to 4 years, because a person could not have been both a high-verbal and low-verbal 2-year-old.

Most of the studies of communication that have been done using young children as subjects have found that they are poor communicators, and very often poor communication has been attributed to the lack of ability on the part of the sender of a message to take the perspective of the message receiver into account. The sender does not take into account what information the receiver needs.

Referential Communication

One of the types of communication between children that has been studied is *referential communication*. If one child can see an object hidden from the view of the second child, how do they communicate so that the second child finds out what the object is that the first child sees? A common way to investigate the problem is to seat the children facing each other at a table with a barrier between them so that they cannot see each other or the other's side of the table. The object, usually a picture of an object, to be communicated, is placed on the table in front of the child who is designated the speaker, and the speaker describes the object for the listener who cannot see it. On the basis of the speaker's description, feedback from the listener, if there is any, and speaker's responses to the listener's feedback, if there are any, the listener decides what the object is. Obviously, this can be so easy that there is no communication problem. If the picture is of a familiar object, such as a dog, a candy cane, or a horse, the task is so easy that nothing can be learned about communication. Research has been concerned with discovering how communication is accomplished when it is difficult. Over the course of many experiments, we have come to see that being unable to take the perspective of another may not be the only reason, and may not be the reason at all, why communication fails. I have just said that it would be easy for one child to communicate the subject of a picture to another, if the picture were of a dog or a candy cane, because the object is a familiar one and has a name known to all. The referential communication task usually involves communicating the identity of one of several objects in a picture that are difficult to distinguish or which do not have names.

The listeners have a page before them on their side of the barrier like figure 8.1. Half of the speakers in this experiment (Carrier and

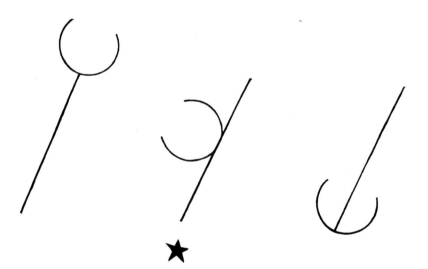

Figure 8.1   Line with half-circle figures from Carrier–Leet experiment (1972)

Leet, 1972) have a page just like figure 8.1 except that the middle drawing of the line with the half circle has a gold star pasted under it to indicate to the speaker that this is the target drawing that she is supposed to identify for the listener. The other half of the speakers have a page before them that has only the middle drawing of the line with half circle on it. Having speakers who can see exactly what information the listeners have (speakers who have all three drawings on their pages) and speakers who have only the target drawing permits the experimenter to test whether knowing exactly how things look from the listener's perspective improves communication.

When there are a small number of alternatives side by side, as in figure 8.1, and the speakers have the same page as the listeners, they can identify the target for the listeners by saying, "It's the middle one." The second graders in this experiment who had pages just like the listeners for the 11 different targets rarely used position to identify the target drawing. Typically, speakers described the drawings as objects as much as possible. One speaker whose page had only the target drawing on it described it successfully to his listener: "It's half a ball going up." Another successful pair with a speaker who had all three drawings had a listener (Petie) who consistently took the initiative and described the pictures as objects.

PETIE: Is it shaped like a devil's fork for one thing?
CYRUS: No.
PETIE: Is it shaped like an arrow?
CYRUS: No.
PETIE: Okay, I got it.

What impressed Carrier and Leet (1972) about the children's performance on this referential communication task was that they did not see the task the same way the researchers did. Carrier and Leet expected the children to have a serious task-oriented attitude. The children tended to treat the task as a guessing game, which they enjoyed and wanted to prolong, so speakers sometimes gave "hints" rather than adequate information. This can be seen in the exchange between Maria (speaker) and Carol (listener) on the target shown in figure 8.2. Maria (speaker) had only the target drawing, the sets of dots on the left, on her page.

Figure 8.2   Dot figures from Carrier–Leet experiment (1972) (Maria's page had only the drawing on the left, the target drawing)

MARIA: It's black.
CAROL: I have plenty of black things here.
MARIA: (*silence*)
CAROL: If I was on that side, I couldn't think of anything to say either.
MARIA: If I tell her what I'm thinking of she'll probably know it (*said to experimenter*).
MARIA: Four dots.
CAROL: They all have four dots.
MARIA: They're black and first it goes up and then comes back down and stays some more.

Carrier and Leet (1972) found that their subject's ambiguous and egocentric responses were more frequent on the difficult trials, like figure 8.2. Here is the interchange between Michele and Munchie, a pair with a speaker (Michele) who had all three drawings of figure 8.2 on her page.

MICHELE: It's left. (*Michele is identifying the target drawing by its position on the page.*)
MUNCHIE: My left or your left?
MICHELE: I don't know. Over there (*pointing*).
EXPERIMENTER: Try to use words.
MICHELE: It's on the side close to Maria's mother.
MUNCHIE: That's my right.
MICHELE: No, it's left.
MUNCHIE: It's my right.
MICHELE: Tough luck.

Michele and Munchie's problem arose, not because Michele initially failed to take Munchie's perspective, but because right and left are cognitively difficult. Munchie knew that people facing each other have their right and left sides opposite each other. She did not know that her question was just going to confuse Michele because the relationship between target and side of the page is independent of Michele's and her position *vis-à-vis* each other. The target was on the left side of the page for both girls. This is not a problem caused by the failure to realize that there is another perspective than one's own. Michele's and Munchie's communication about the target broke down because of cognitive overload. Neither understood the problem of coordinating their perspectives and their pages. Research has shown that even 4- and 5-year-olds are capable of taking the perspective of another if the communication task is cognitively simple. Maratsos (1973), for example, found that 4- and 5-year-olds understood that a blindfolded person needed information that a sighted person did not.

Role-taking

An elegant demonstration that cognitive complexity rather than lack of ability to take another's perspective caused failure on a role-taking task has been made by Shatz (1978). Her subjects were 4- and 5-year-olds. She showed each of them a picture of a child who was either the same age as the subject or was a 2-year-old and asked the subject to pick a present for the child from a group of four toys. Two of the four toys, a pull toy and a set of stacking toys, would be appropriate for a 2-year-old; two toys, a magnetic board with letters and numbers and a set of sewing cards, would be appropriate for a preschooler like the subject. Then subjects were invited to pick out a toy for themselves. Shatz's results are shown in tables 8.1 and 8.2.

Table 8.1 shows that only 10 of the 58 subjects chose a toy that was

Table 8.1 Preschoolers' selection of a given type toy: four-toy experiment

	Toys appropriate for	
Intended recipient	*2-year-old*	*Preschooler*
2-year-old	21	8
Preschooler	2	27

$n = 58$
Source: Shatz (1978)

Table 8.2 Subjects' selection of same or different toy for self: four-toy experiment

	Toys for self	
Intended recipient	Different	Same as for other
2-year-old	24	5
Preschooler	17	12

$n = 58$
Source: Shatz (1978)

Table 8.3 Toy selection for a 2-year-old with added toys for a school-age child

	Toys appropriate for		
Age of subject	2-year-old	Preschooler	School-age
4-year-old	3	8	1
5-year-old	8	4	0
Total	11	12	1

Source: Shatz (1978)

not appropriate for the intended recipient, the child whose picture Shatz had shown them. Table 8.2 shows that subjects were unlikely to pick for themselves the same toy as they had picked for a 2-year-old. Only 5 of 29 subjects did so, showing that, when they picked a toy for a 2-year-old, it was not on the basis of their own preferences.

Shatz then made her task more difficult by adding two more toys: a teething ring and a rattle, appropriate for a baby, or an activity puzzle book and a game called Racko appropriate for a school-age child. This time the task was the same for all subjects: select a toy for a 2-year-old child. It was more difficult than before because there were *six* toys appropriate to *three* ages from which to chose rather than *four* toys appropriate to *two* ages. Tables 8.3 and 8.4 show the results when the added toys were for a school-age child or for a baby. If you compare tables 8.1 and 8.3 you can see that adding the two extra toys confused preschoolers. Even though only one preschooler picked a toy appropriate for a school-age child to give to a 2-year-old,

Table 8.4 Toy selection for a 2-year-old with added toys for an infant

Age of subject	Toys appropriate for		
	2-year-old	*Preschooler*	*Infant*
4-year-old	3	5	4
5-year-old	6	3	3
Total	9	8	7

Source: Shatz (1978)

half the preschoolers picked a toy for a preschooler to give to the 2-year-old (table 8.3). When the preschoolers had only four toys to chose from, over two and a half times as many picked an appropriate toy as an inappropriate one (table 8.1). When the added toys were appropriate for an infant, toys for 2-year-olds, preschoolers, and infants were picked almost equally often (table 8.4).

What we can see from Shatz's experiment is that a task that preschoolers can do can be made so difficult by adding items to it that preschoolers can no longer do the task, even though it is the same task. This is because of cognitive overload. You can probably multiply 45 by 11 in your head, but not 4,932 by 673. They are both multiplication problems, but multiplying a four-digit number by a three-digit number entails remembering so many numbers, if you do it in your head, that it may not be possible to do all the multiplication – a failure caused by cognitive overload, not by a failure to understand how to multiply.

Experimental work that caused people to conclude that preschoolers' communication fails because they are unable to take another's perspective may have been too difficult for preschoolers because of cognitive overload. When children do fail in a task, like Munchie and Michele, for example, they sometimes resort to quite immature tactics. Possibly they are responding to a feeling of frustration. Have you ever seen an adult kick a door when his key wouldn't unlock it?

The Child's Developing Theory of the Mind

When I discussed animals as signalers and human beings as communicators (chapter 4), I stressed that being able to think about one's intentions – thought, beliefs, feelings – and those of others (secondary consciousness) is crucial to communication and the social relations among human beings. Taking the perspective of another and lying are possible human behaviors both dependent on secondary consciousness. Over the past dozen or so years a lively theoretical and research interest has emerged concerning the development of the child's "theory of the mind" as the child's emerging secondary consciousness is being called.[2] Pretense and deceit (misinforming, engendering false beliefs) are important research topics because they provide evidence of the child's ability to separate reality and representations of reality in her mind, to know what is real and what is pretend, deceptive, or misleading. If a 5-year-old is shown a candy box and asked what is in the box, she will probably say candy. When the box is opened, and she sees it actually has a pencil in it, she may be disappointed or think it's a good trick. If she's asked what another child would think if shown the closed box, she will say candy. If the same little experiment is carried out with a 3-year-old, she will say candy when shown the box. After she is shown that it has a pencil in it, if she is asked what another child shown the closed box would think was in it, she will respond, "Pencil." If asked to recall what she originally thought was in the box, she will again say, "Pencil." She cannot conceive that she or other children could hold a false belief (cited in Leslie, 1987; Perner et al., 1987). It looks as though we have not moved very far along the evolutionary path beyond the animals who are unable to engender false beliefs in others of their species by transmitting signals that carry misinformation. As adults, we are aware that humans can hold false beliefs, but understanding of basic components of "the mind" develops over time in children the way language use does.

Both language use and the behaviors of children indicating theory of mind development are mixtures of acquired understanding ("rules"), and imitative or scripted behaviors (Nelson and Seidman, 1984; Lillard, 1993). Lillard (1993) points out that the sociodramatic play of young children seems to involve representing the mental representations of other children – meta-representation.

1ST CHILD:　　(*to 2nd Child who is coming into a part of the preschool classroom called the beauty parlor*) Hello, Mrs Jones, did you come to get your hair done?

2ND CHILD: I need my hair cut and set.

1ST CHILD: Sit right here, and I'll cut your hair. (*She picks up a stick which she holds against 2nd Child's head*) Snip, snip, snip. (*She moves the stick around 2nd Child's head.*)

Is the first child representing the stick to herself and second child as a scissors? Or is she just acting on the stick as if it were a scissors?

We have become wary of attributing sophisticated grammatical knowledge to beginning language users, MLU 1.5 or less. Utterances like, "Let me see," and "Where did you get that?" are usually imitations of adult productions rather than creations of the child. In the same way, parental register use and pretend play (for example, Anderson, 1986; Leslie, 1987) are at least in part products of imitation or scripts rather than of separation in the child's thinking of mental representations of reality and reality. For this reason, I will concentrate on engendering false beliefs as a marker of developing theory of mind. Chandler et al. (1989) present data supporting early onset of glimmerings of the understanding that people act in accordance with what they believe about reality rather than reality itself and can be influenced to hold false beliefs.

The controversy between early (2-year-old) and late (4-year-old) onset focuses on what behaviors constitute evidence that a child understands that reality and representations of reality may differ. Some experiments that require a child to absorb information about deceptive behavior from a narrative account or require a child to explain why the described behavior was deceptive may underestimate the child's understanding that the conscious intent of a behavior was to misinform someone. Withholding information as a means of deceiving another is not regarded as a reliable measure of deceptive intent because it can be challenged as being non-intentional. Only behavior which is transparently intended to deceive qualifies as a measure of the child's understanding that (a) reality and beliefs about reality may differ; (b) actions are based on beliefs about reality; and (c) beliefs about reality can intentionally be manipulated.

Chandler et al. (1989) devised a game in which players hide a treasure with the help of a puppet whose feet leave inky prints on the gameboard (see figure 8.3). The object of the game is to deceive another player about where the treasure (a small bag of fake jewels

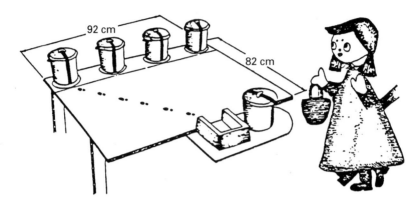

Figure 8.3 Hide and seek materials (reproduced from Chandler et al., 1988)

and gold) is hidden. The experimenter, E1, kept track of deceptive behavior of the child hiding the treasure to mislead a second experimenter, E2, about the hiding place. The children were taught the game by being finders. With the child outside the experiment room with one of the two experimenters, E2, the other, E1, would put the treasure in one of the containers on the game board and leave the container clearly out of place. E2 and the child would then be brought in to find the treasure. After this "lesson" the child had two practice turns hiding the treasure.

Then the puppet was produced and it was shown that all the puppet's movements on the game board left a trail of inky footprints. A sponge was used to clean up the prints and was then placed on a corner of the gameboard. As in the first phase of the experiment, the child was made the finder and sent out of the room with E2, while E1 used the puppet to hide the treasure. The puppet left a clear set of prints leading to the container where the treasure was hidden. When the child came back in the room he was told to look carefully at the board and then to decide where the treasure was hidden.

Then the child was told it was his turn to help the puppet hide the treasure. E2 was again asked to leave the room. The child was told to help the puppet hide the treasure so E2 couldn't find it. At the end of this and all remaining trials children were asked why, for example, it was a good idea for the puppet to erase his tracks, if he had done so.

In the next step, if on the previous trial the child had erased the puppet's footprints, he was dissuaded from doing this. Either independently or with help, the child devised the strategy of setting inky footprint trails to empty containers.

Chandler has ordered deceptive strategies in terms of confidence he has that their use indicates intention to deceive:

1   Wiping out the puppet's tracks.
2   Openly lying, suggesting to E2 that she search in containers the child knows are empty.
3   Purposely laying inky footprint trails to containers the child knows are empty.

Chandler's analysis of deceptive strategies of the children shows no effect of age. The deceptive strategies of the youngest ($2\frac{1}{2}$ years) were as sophisticated as those of the oldest ($4\frac{1}{2}$ years). By this measure, $2\frac{1}{2}$-year-olds carry out the behavior like $4\frac{1}{2}$-year-olds.

Playing devil's advocate, consider the experimental procedure if children do not spontaneously produce a particular deceptive strategy, then teach it. One might conclude that $2\frac{1}{2}$-year-olds imitate or learn these behaviors rather than spontaneously producing them. Did they equally give evidence that they understood they were using deceptive strategies? Could they explain why erasing footprints or laying false trails led E2 to look in an empty container? With ability to explain as the criterion, the older children ($4–4\frac{1}{2}$-year-olds) did significantly better than $2\frac{1}{2}–3\frac{1}{2}$-year-olds. The argument against this finding as evidence is that it relies on the child's being able to say why he laid false trails or erased footprints rather than just his ability to carry out the behaviors. We are caught in a dilemma. Using behavior as criterion may overestimate children's secondary consciousness. Using declarative knowledge, the ability to explain their behavior, may underestimate children's secondary consciousness.

Notes

1   Speech registers get identified and described when sociolinguists find that they reveal interesting social facts about the group using the register or defined by it.
2   Woodruff and Premack (1979) succeeded in teaching deceptive pointing to two of four chimpanzees, but only after an intense five-month effort.

They argued that their success was evidence that chimps have a primitive theory of mind. This does not seem persuasive evidence. Chimps can be taught to form paired associates – a token and a banana – and more elaborate chained responses as well by positive reinforcement. These associates were interpreted as "sentences" by Premack and Premack (1972). Neither of these chimp behaviors develop spontaneously as they do in children, nor are they followed by more mature linguistic and meta-representational behavior as they are in children. Natural acquisition of language and of a "theory of mind" seem to be human characteristics.

Further Reading

Dobrich, W. and Scarborough, H. S. (1992) "Phonological characteristics of words young children try to say," *Journal of Child Language*, 19: 597–616.
    Examines the possible persistence of phonological selectional constraints on young children's lexical choices. Results suggest that selectional constraints persist only briefly in the course of language acquisition.
Fernald, A. and Morikawa, H. (1993) "Common themes and cultural variation in Japanese and American mothers' speech to infants," *Child Development*, 64: 637–56.
    The baby talk register in Japanese and American English.
Flavell, J., Green, F. and Flavell, E. (1995) "Young children's knowledge about thinking," *Monographs of the Society for Research in Child Development*, 60.
    Children's understanding of the activity of the mind from age 3 to age 8.
Wellman, H. (1990) *The Child's Theory of Mind* (Cambridge, Mass.: MIT Press).
    The young child's secondary consciousness.
Wellman, H. and Hichling, A. (1994) "The mind's 'I': children's conception of the mind as an active agent," *Child Development*, 65: 1564–80.
    An attempt to describe a possible child construction of secondary consciousness.
Wimmer, H. and Weichbold, V. (1994) "Children's theory of mind: Fodor's heuristics examined," *Cognition*, 53: 45–57.
    Young children are not able to formulate a theory of mind before age 4 – confirms previous studies.

9
Semantic Development

By the time people in the US graduate from high school, become adults, they have acquired vocabularies, words they recognize and can potentially use and understand, of between 60 and 120,000 words (Pinker, 1994), although in their day-to-day experience many fewer actually get used. How do we acquire our impressively large vocabularies? Not by looking words up in a dictionary. Early on, children acquire words exclusively on the basis of their day-to-day experience. That rectangular object your mother uses when she is bathing you that tastes awful is *soap*. The white spilly stuff you drink is *milk*. The thing that's hard to get over your head and your arms is a *shirt* or an *undershirt*. When your mother put the glass of milk on the table she said, "Careful, don't spill your milk," and then when you accidentally hit the glass and it tipped over, she said, "Oh, oh, the milk spilled." The language used talking to young children glosses their experience and provides the world–word match. I overheard a 3-year-old boy say to a friend, "You don't know what never mind means? Well, if you start to say something and you don't want to say it, you could say 'never mind.'"

Children acquire names for objects like *soap*, substances like *milk*, verbs like *spill*, grammatical morphemes like /d/, spill "ed", to mark the past tense of a verb, and words, *hi, bye,* and idioms, *nevermind, look out,* that do not refer to objects, but have occasion meaning – there are appropriate occasions for their use. When children attend school their everyday experience is radically altered and their acquisition of words begins to be influenced by the school culture. Vocabulary acquisition may depend on the child's problem-solving strategies for figuring out word meanings as well as simply observing the word–world match and acquiring the basic syntactically governed noun and verb inflections:[1] noun plural forms, and verb tense markers.

Jeremy Anglin (1993) has carried out research to estimate the size of the vocabularies of first, third, and fifth graders and the proportions of what he calls "previously known words," and of words that show evidence of children's having figured out their meaning, what he calls "morphological problem-solving." Anglin classified words as root words, idioms, inflected words, derived words, and literal compounds. Root words are singular nouns, present-tense verbs (except third-person singular), adjectives and articles. Idioms are phrases like *beat around the bush, in hot water, keep your shirt on*. Root words and idioms are learned as sound–concept associations by observation or rote. Anglin proposed that inflected and derived words and literal compounds could be figured out on the basis of morphological problem-solving. Derived words include *silliness, readmission, magnetize, foundationless*, and *separately*.

Literal compounds include *live born, western saddle, milk cow, low level*. Anglin's estimates of the average first-, third-, and fifth-grade vocabularies and the proportions that show evidence of problem-solving and no such evidence can be seen in table 9.1.

Anglin's methods yield a conservative estimate of vocabulary size (Miller and Wakefield, 1993). Forty percent of first-grade vocabulary shows evidence of morphological problem-solving, suggesting an active cognitive stance in relatively early word learning. By fifth grade, 50 percent of vocabulary shows evidence of morphological problem-solving, a 20 percent increase. Children's immersion for the preceding four years in the school culture of learning could account for the increase. The almost four-fold increase in vocabulary is certainly the result of schooling, learning to read, and reading to learn. Even before children go to school and begin to increase their vocabularies from their reading, they have been learning the meanings of words from the way they are used in sentences.

They can do this because the meanings of the other words in the sentence are already known to them. They no longer, upon hearing a word or sentence, look around to see what is going on in order to figure out the meaning of what is being said. Instead they guess at the meaning of the new word from the context of the rest of the sentence or discourse and begin to use language to learn language. A child, hearing:

Table 9.1 Anglin's estimates of vocabulary size of first, third and fifth graders

Word type[a]	Grade 1		Grade 3		Grade 5	
	No. of words	Estimate	No. of words	Estimate	No. of words	Estimate
Root words	5.19	3,092	7.69	4,582	12.64	7,532
Inflected words	4.62	2,753	6.94	4,135	9.39	5,595
Derived words	3.01	1,794	9.36	5,577	27.00	16,088
Literal compounds	4.38	2,610	7.47	4,451	13.95	8,312
Idioms	0.25	149	1.12	667	4.14	2,467
Total	17.45	10,398	32.58	19,412	67.12	39,994

[a] Anglin's experiment and method of estimating word type means are described in Anglin (1993).
Source: Anglin (1993)

1 He was a *mean* boy to pull the dog's tail, might think *mean* meant *rash* or even *dumb*. After all, the dog might bite.
2 It was a *mean* night out. That raw, cold wind froze my nose and ears.

Hearing (2) would make *rash* and *dumb* unlikely. Cause physical pain would be a possible definition for (1) and (2).

3 "I think you're *mean*," Jody said to her mother when she told Jody that she couldn't go to the party if she didn't clean up her room.

Sentence (3) alters the possible definition derived from (1) and (2), making it broader; *meaning* causes pain, physical or mental. I am claiming that, in learning verbal concepts (word meanings), the learner unconsciously forms an hypothesis about word meaning from the sentence heard. The next sentence heard that contains the word provides positive or negative evidence about the hypothesis. If the evidence is negative, the learner changes the hypothesis.

Werner and Kaplan (1950) conducted an experimental investigation of the processes underlying the acquisition of word meanings from sentence contexts, like the example of *mean*. They, however, used invented nonsense words, and their sentences were constructed so that the six sentences for a nonsense word provided increasingly definite clues to the meaning of the word. They studied the acquisition of 12 nonsense words by five groups of 25 children each: 9, 10, 11, 12, and 13-year-olds. One of their nonsense words is as follows:

Protema (to finish, complete)
1 To protema a job, you must have patience.
2 If a job is hard, Harry does not protema it.
3 Philip asked John to help him protema his homework.
4 John cannot protema the problem because he does not understand it.
5 You should try to protema your homework when it is only half done.
6 The painter could not protema the room because his brush broke.

Werner and Kaplan (1950) found that older children, as compared to younger children, were much better at figuring out the meanings of the nonsense words. The younger children were hampered by their difficulty in separating word meaning from sentence meaning. This may happen whenever the word learner does not hear the word in a variety of sentences. In my own case, I was surprised when I recently looked up *arcane* in the dictionary to find that it means "secret." My definition based on the sentence(s) in which I had heard or read it had to do with savage rites of primitive people of long ago. *Arcane* must have been an adjective modifying rites in a sentence about primitive customs. The sentence context became part of my definition of *arcane* and I did not read other sentences that would have caused me to eliminate from my definition the sentence context of primitive rites.

Most of the word meanings that we know have been acquired through our life experience, including reading, rather than through looking words up in the dictionary. Therefore, it is always possible that some words will have different meanings for people because of different life experiences. Where it is really important to have a shared meaning for a word, parents of young children tend to check and make sure. Roger Brown (1973) has reported that the parents of Adam, Eve, and Sarah did not correct their children's grammar, but did correct them when they mispronounced words or said things that were not true. We can tolerate immature syntax as long as we can understand the child, but we want to be sure that meanings come through clear and true.

In addition to being organized syntactically, language is semantically (pertaining to the meaning of the words) organized in the minds of its speakers, and this organization involves both language and thought. The evidence at this time is that syntactic organization, for the most part, is independent of other cognitive systems. It has been pointed out by Vygotsky (1962) that there can be thought without language and language without thought. All the thought processes of the prelinguistic infant are thoughts without language. Piaget's theory (1962) is that prelinguistic infants think by acting on objects that they see, hear, and feel. There is language without thought whenever language is used ritualistically or in play without the words used having meaning for the user. Joel's game with his mother at 12 months of pointing and saying "kitty" is an example of language without thought. When the child begins to use words meaningfully, the semantic development of language begins. By the time children are 5 years old, relations have been established in the child's mind between words, as well as between language and experience of the world. Semantic organization refers to the relations established among words. Semantic organization of language has been studied in various ways, a few that relate to development of language in children will now be discussed.

Word Associations: their Development in North Americans and Japanese

One kind of semantic organization in the human mind can be observed by finding out which words are closely related so that thinking of one word reminds a person of another. When you read the word *apple*, what word comes to mind? For me, it is *orange*. Louis Moran (1973) did a study in which he compared the word associations of Japanese and North American preschool children and adults. He defined four types of associations to classify the responses of his subjects to the 60 words he used as stimuli.

1   *Functional*: the association is between two physical referents (physical objects) used together.

Stimulus	*Response*
table	chair
bat	ball
fork	knife

2   *Iconic*: ascribes a quality to a referent

Stimulus	*Response*
apple	red
brave	eagle

3   *Enactive*: action on referent

Stimulus	*Response*
apple	eat
rip	pants

4   *Logical*: abstract relation between referents

Stimulus	*Response*
table	furniture
strong	weak

For (4) table is a member of the superordinate class, *furniture*, and *strong* and *weak* are adjectives with opposite meaning.

Moran's (1973) instruction was to say the first word that comes to mind when you hear each of the words on his list of 60. He found that both the Japanese and the American children gave primarily enactive responses. Japanese adults gave primarily iconic responses; 65 percent of North American adults' responses were logical and another 20 percent were functional.

Moran's findings suggest that preschoolers' semantic organization of language is similar for Japanese and North Americans. The great difference between the two adult populations suggests that culture, including schooling, plays a large part in determining the semantic organization of language in adults. In my seminar on language and thought, we speculated that, if we tested college students who were (a) art, music, and literature majors and compared them to (b) science majors, we would find a difference like that between Japanese and North Americans. When we repeated Moran's experiment with the two groups, we were disappointed to find that the responses of both groups were primarily what Moran called logical. We had thought that having artistic temperaments would cause art, music, and literature majors to have some word associations that were more like those of the adult Japanese than the adult North American. We concluded that the influence of culture and schooling prevailed over possible artistic associations of the art, music, and literature majors.

Moran's adult North American responses and our experiment indicate that the most accessible or perhaps acceptable semantic organization of language for English-speaking North American adults is an abstract organization in which words are related to other words rather than to experience.[2]

Naming and Categories

The categories in Moran's research are the result of his thinking about the responses of his four groups of experimental subjects responding to his direction to say the first word that comes to mind. This is a very different method for finding out young children's basis for forming categories of objects and naming the category than that of Ellen Markman and her collegues (Markman, 1992). Markman's stimuli are objects or pictures of objects so that their names will be nouns like *dog*, *cat*, or *animal* rather than verbs like *run*, *crawl*, or *move*. She has been interested in children's use of taxonomic (based on common characteristics) versus thematic (causal, temporal, connections between objects) relations among objects. Children over the age of 7 group objects taxonomically. Cars, bikes, and scooters go together because they are vehicles; sharks, salmon, and flounder because they are fish. Younger children may put a dog and a bone together because dogs eat bones, or a foot and a shoe because people put shoes on their feet.

This kind of research finding is not new. Entwistle (1969) found that syntagmatic (like thematic) association gave way to paradigmatic (like taxonomic) at about the age of 7. Age 7 does not mark a sudden watershed change, and Markman and Hutchinson (1984) carried out research to investigate variables which influence young children to use taxonomic instead of thematic relations as the basis for categorization. Two-year-old children presented with pictures of two different dogs and a picture of dog food select a dog and dogfood, which are thematically related, as being the same kind of thing. If one of the dogs was called a *dax* in this research and the children were told to find another *dax* they were likely to select the second dog rather than the dog food. If an object is given a name, children are constrained to look for a categorical rather than thematic relation between objects. Markman suggests that this is an abstract constraint not based on knowing the meaning of the word. (Dax does not mean anything.) It might be, though, that the children were translating *dax* into *dog* and this explains the constraint.

In a further experiment with $4\frac{1}{2}$–$5\frac{1}{2}$-year-olds, unfamiliar objects as well as unfamiliar names were used so that the unfamiliar names could not be translated into familiar names for familiar objects like *dax* into *dog*. Two examples of taxonomically and thematically related object training pictures are shown in figure 9.1. The figures on the left present objects as potential category members, the figures on the right as thematically related. Figure 9.1b shows an object (3) attached to another (1), figure 9.1d an object (2) on top of another (3).

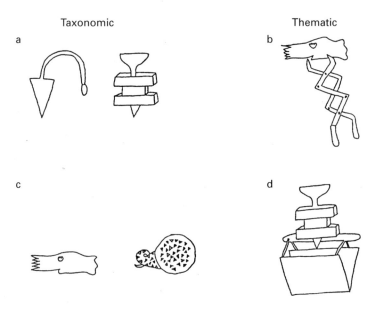

Figure 9.1 Examples of unfamiliar objects presented thematically and taxonomically: (a, c) sample taxonomic training pictures in experiment 4; (b, d) sample thematic training pictures in experiment 4 (reproduced from Markman and Hutchinson, 1984)

In the test presentation, the first object would be shown to the child who would then be shown (2) and (3) and asked to find another, in the no name condition, or another *dax* or *wot*, for example, in the name condition. As in the previous experiments, labeling object (1) resulted in more taxonomic than thematic choices for these unfamiliar figures, evidence for an abstract constraint rather than translation. *Abstract constraint* is a daunting term, but it means that ideas in children's minds are influencing the way they organize their experience with the world. We have said that physical objects and speech sounds are innate categories. Secondary consciousness and our capacity for acquiring language are innate. However, much about the language we use is the result of learning, interaction with parents, teachers, peers, from which children learn how to communicate meaningfully, (Halliday, 1975).

Input can be the source of great misunderstanding. During one college year I was the built-in sitter for a family with an 8-year-old son and a 5-year-old daughter. I found Susie's misunderstandings thought-provoking, and I remembered some as I thought about semantic development and naming. One Sunday morning Susie told me, "We're going to have bacon-'n'-eggs *with* bacon for breakfast." I didn't investigate at the time, but it looks like *bacon-'n'-eggs* are fried eggs. Another day, Susie's mother told me that Susie had come home from kindergarten and described the paintings she had seen in art appreciation: one description sounded like Gainsborough's *Blue Boy*, another like *Pinky*, a third like a Picasso clown. Susie's mother asked, "What were their names?" "They are all called Masterpiece," said Susie. Whoever was showing these pictures to the kindergarteners wasn't pitching her communication accurately. She was talking over the heads of her audience – what I said our language instinct largely prevented us from doing. "Masterpiece" is a category designation that kindergarteners lack the cultural experience to understand.

All vertebrates have the innate capacity to form categories (see chapter 4). Memory would not be useful if some kinds of things were not connected in memory. For developmental psycholinguists investigating the ways in which the developing child categorizes her experience, organizing the contents of her mind, provides a window through which to look at the child's reality. We know that from early on it's going to be full of objects, people, speech sounds, environmental features, and noises. Some will get named and put into categories. Naming in the young child's experience is mostly a matter of being told the name that goes with the object or event that she and an adult are looking at. Assigning an object, for example, to a category is subject to constraints inhering in the child's mind on the possible meanings of words, like the innate category, physical object, which gives rise to what Markman (1989) calls the whole object constraint.

Categories depend on what is important to the child and salient (noticeable). My 3-year-old son said to me, "You and my red truck and Skinny Bunny (a rubber toy) don't have a penis." We three made up a category. We lacked an important and salient feature. Tommy hadn't noticed that our female dog, an unkempt Airedale, belonged to the group. What a young child will label or name, and why may depend on its shape, for example (Gentner, 1978), or its function (Nelson, 1973).

Ways to Organize the Contents of the Mind

The enactive responses of the young children described by Moran (1973) derive from their day-to-day experiences. Other investigators (such as Anglin, 1977; Holzman, 1981) have proposed that the earliest concepts that children have for words are just memories of instances in which a word has been linked to a specific referent object, event, or experience. If one asks a young child what a dog is, the child will respond by telling an instance of personal experience with a dog associated in his memory with the word, *dog*.

After a number of encounters with dogs, the separate memories will coalesce to form an average or prototypical image in the child's memory. The prototypical image develops before the scientific analytical concept. The analytical concept is associated with *awareness* of both similarities and differences; the prototypical image with *lack of attention* to differences. An important difference between the two is that the prototypical image is the result of automatic, effortless mental processing, while the analytical concept is the result of purposeful, deliberate mental processing. One implication of this difference is that, from an early age, everyone will have verbal concepts, information including names, for prototypical images. Anglin (1977) found that American preschool children identified pictures of unfamiliar species such as the wombat, an Australian marsupial that resembles a bear, as an animal, while refusing to identify a picture of a familiar butterfly as animal; it was not the right shape. Anglin's subjects had a verbal concept, the word *animal*, for four-legged furry creatures that looked like their mental image, their prototype.

An analytical concept is based on analysis of the attributes that are necessary for a particular animal, like *dog*, to be classified in a given category like *mammal*, and this is what makes the analytical concept purposeful and deliberate. Before they go to school, children are not likely to have analytical concepts for organizing the contents of their minds, while adults and older children will. While it does not happen automatically, nevertheless a great deal of the work to organize language and thought in terms of analytical concepts is done in school.

I want to discuss prototypical mental images and analytical concepts as ways of organizing contents of the mind having to do with animals, and I know such discussions are easier with examples to think about. However, I do not want to present a prototypical image for *mammal* that seems to be the category Anglin's subjects thought of as animal. Just imagine the side view of an average size, four-footed, furry, nondescript animal and it will do. When a young child is asked whether a picture is an animal, as in Anglin's (1977) research, the child compares the picture with the prototypical mental image held in memory and decides. When an older child, who has been to school, is asked such a question by an experimenter, the older child responds differently. The typical concept formation experiment seems like school to a child, and she treats the question as if it were a question from a teacher. (The typical experiment is probably being carried out in the school the child attends.) Science instruction begins in the first year of school, and children learn to distinguish fish, birds, and mammals in a scientific way: in terms of features rather than shapes. At the same time they learn that all three are examples of the superordinate concept, animal (see table 9.2), and have features in common, such as mobility and use of oxygen, which distinguishes animal from the superordinate plant. Plants use carbon dioxide and cannot move themselves.

Human beings have wonderfully complex filing systems for the contents of their minds. Being able to organize and store in memory the same content as analytic concepts based on defining features, as prototypical mental images, or just as the memories of an instance of experience, are all three capacities of the adult and older child. Which

Table 9.2 The superordinates *animal* and *plant* and the analytic concepts for mammal, fish, and bird

| Features | Animal | | | | Plant[a] |
	Mammal	Fish	Bird	Others	
Number of legs	4	none	2	?	no
Wings	no	no	yes	?	no
Live birth	yes	no	no	?	no
Fur	yes	no	no	?	no
Teeth	yes	yes	no	?	no
Lungs	yes	no	yes	?	no
Oxygen utilizing	yes	yes	yes	yes	no
Mobile	yes	yes	yes	yes	no

[a] Plants have none of the listed features, which are defining or criterial features, of one or more of the animals (mammal, fish, bird).

method of organizing will be utilized at any time depends on the circumstances. I want to apply this analysis to preschool children's comprehension of spatial prepositions.

Preschool Children's Comprehension of Spatial Prepositions

I became interested in spatial prepositions because they are relational words. The nouns that children learn name objects or substances that have physical reality. Verbs do not name things, but the verbs children learn name physical activities for the most part. Verbs need a subject so that a mental image can be evoked. The word *jump* all by itself does not name anything that can be visualized, but *Daddy jump* or *doggie jump* creates an image. Spatial prepositions are like verbs in that they cannot create an image standing alone. They differ from some verbs, like *jump*, which are exciting or interesting. The only motivation for learning the meanings of spatial prepositions is to clarify and refine sentence meaning.

As a first look at preschool children's understanding of spatial prepositions, my students and I did a comprehension experiment to see if preschool children understood the words *on, next to, in, underneath,*

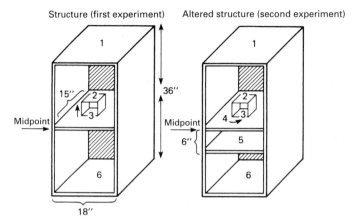

Figure 9.2 Cookie Monster structure

behind, over, outside of, below, between, in front of, above, beside, inside, under, and *out of* (Holzman, 1981). Comprehension was tested in the context of a game in which the child placed a Cookie Monster doll in locations which were the referents of the prepositions.

For the first experiment, child and experimenter sat next to each other facing the structure (figure 9.2). The first direction to the child was, "Put Cookie Monster *in* the red box"; the red box was sitting on and glued to the middle shelf of the structure which was colored blue. Children were asked to respond to the prepositions in the order in which I have listed them. The majority of the children were able to respond correctly to all the prepositions. The errors made by the other children were heavily concentrated. At least 20 percent of the 70 children who participated in the experiment made errors on *underneath, below, over,* and *under.* I attribute the errors to these children's not having featural abstractions for the prepositions but, instead, having concepts for the prepositions that are mental images, coalescences of their memories of instances in their experience when the prepositions were used. Clues to the form of the mental images for *under* and *underneath* came from children who, when asked by the experimenter to put Cookie Monster *under* or *underneath* the red box, said "I can't," or "it's stuck" (the red box glued to the shelf), or "He'll get squished" (Cookie Monster). These comments suggest that, for these children, under or underneath lies between the upper surface of the middle shelf and the bottom of the red box.

If you look at figure 9.2, you can see that, in the structure for the first experiment, there was only one correct location (6) to put Cookie Monster when the experimenter asked the child to put Cookie Monster under or underneath or below the red box. To be successful, the child had to have an analytic featural concept for each of the prepositions so that location (6) would be seen to be correct. That is, the child had to see that location (6) was the only location available in the structure which had the necessary locational feature, situated lower than the reference object (the red box). The comments of the children, like the ones quoted above, suggested that, if locations more like those designated *under* and *underneath* in the child's ordinary experience were provided, errors on these two prepositions would be reduced. Furthermore, the location *in* was the incorrect response made 40 percent of the time when an error was made on *under, underneath,* or *below.* Since the red box was glued to the middle shelf, *in* is the location (3, on figure 9.2) *under the top* of the red box. If children are accustomed to the locations under the table, under the chair, or under the bed, the child's concept (mental image) would correspond to location (3) provided the child ignored the bottom of the box glued to the middle shelf.

We carried out a second experiment with the children to check this reasoning. For the second experiment, we altered the blue structure (see figure 9.2, altered structure) by ungluing the red box, providing location (4) so that children could put Cookie Monster on the middle shelf and hold the red box on or over his head. We also added a new shelf just below the middle shelf, providing location (5). Using the new structure in the experiment was associated with 10 percent fewer errors. The children who had not responded correctly on the first experiment to *under* and *underneath,* but were correct on the second experiment used location (4), primarily, and held the red box on or over Cookie Monster's head. Some of the children who had missed *below* on the first experiment also used location (4) the second time, but they used locations (5) and (6) nearly as often as (4).

Having found that the altered structure with its new locations perhaps fit the children's mental images better, we were curious to see what the children would do who were correct the first time, who were able to use the necessary feature "lower in elevation than the reference object" to figure out that location (6) was the only possibility. Less than 5 percent chose location (6) for *under* and *underneath*

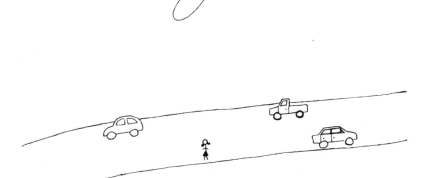

Erika is under/underneath the plane
The cars are all moving along below the plane

Figure 9.3 Picture showing the spatial relations of *under/underneath* and *below*

in the second experiment. Ninety-four percent chose location (4) for *underneath* and 71 percent for *under*, but 80 percent chose location (5) for *below*. Clearly *under*, *underneath*, and *below* had qualities of meaning for these preschoolers in addition to the abstract feature, "lower in elevation than the reference object." It is impossible to be sure what the distinction is for them, but it looks as though they have encountered *under* and *underneath* in situations where the objects to be related were very close to each other vertically and *below* where the vertical distance is greater. The dictionary distinction between *under* or *underneath* and *below* (for one object to be *under* another is, it must lie in the same vertical plane; this is not necessary for *below*), would probably not even be comprehensible to a preschooler. Figure 9.3 sketches the distinction.

Semantic Networks for Spatial Prepositions

In the first experiment the only correct place to put Cookie Monster for *under*, *underneath*, and *below* was location (6). The children who responded correctly to two or three of these prepositions were responding to them as *synonyms*, words that have the same meaning. Thirty-three percent of the children responded correctly on this experiment to all three prepositions, treating them as synonyms. In a related experiment (carried out in the same session), we asked the children to produce verbal concepts for *in, or, underneath, under*, and *below*; they were asked to tell a robot, who was just learning to talk, what the preposition meant. The children were successful most of the time. What was unexpected is that only three children produced verbal concepts like "underneath means the same thing as under" and "below and under mean the same." Instead, for example, they responded with "under is underground" and "the foundation is under the house." These latter expressions link the prepositions to the child's experience and the real world. Verbal concepts like "under means the same as underneath" link the prepositions to each other to form a semantic network. Even though *under* means the same as *underneath* or *below* is implied by using the same location for the three prepositions in the comprehension task, only 6 percent gave evidence of having, in their minds, semantic networks linking *under, underneath* and *below*. The other 94 percent of the children had verbal concepts that linked the words to the world and their experience rather than to other words (see figure 9.4).

Recall that in Moran's (1973) study of word associations of Japanese and North American preschoolers and adults he found that American adults gave mainly logical associations. "Means the same" is, in Moran's terms, a logical relationship. Our research on prepositions is consistent with Moran's in that our North American preschoolers did not give evidence of being able to directly relate verbal concepts, to have spatial prepositions semantically organized in terms of logical or abstract relations linking words.

Natural Categories

I have briefly discussed verbal concepts of children as prototypical mental images that are formed automatically and effortlessly. I contrasted them with analytic featural concepts that are the result of purposeful, effortful mental processing. I have mentioned that other animal species besides human beings are able to categorize stimuli (that is,

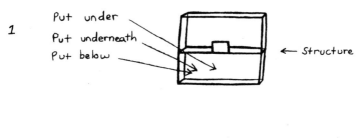

1
Put under
Put underneath
Put below
← Structure

2
Tell under ⟶ "underground where miners go"
Tell underneath ⟶ "underneath the bed"
Tell below ⟶ "They're below, we're over"

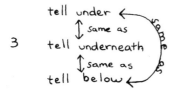

3
tell under
↑↓ same as
tell underneath
↑↓ same as
tell below

Figure 9.4 Levels of cognitive processing: the level of cognitive processing does not produce (3) in response to "tell" even though it is implied by (1)

select from a group of objects, pictures, and so on) subgroups that belong together. The categorizing abilities of apes and pigeons are mentioned in chapter 3.

Let me digress for a moment to relate categories to verbal concepts. Pigeons in Herrnstein et al.'s (1976) experiment discriminated slides of trees (or parts of trees) from other slides. The pigeons had been conditioned to peck when slides showing trees or parts of trees were shown and not to peck at other slides. The ability of the pigeons to respond to the category "trees or parts of trees" was measured by their success in discriminating new slides showing trees or parts from other new slides; the abilities of apes to categorize have been demonstrated analogously. In Jeremy Anglin's (1977) work on verbal concept development in young children, he named the category "animal" and asked his subjects if the pictures he showed them (without naming them) were animals. The children said of the butterfly, "It's not an animal, it's a butterfly." Responding to the picture of the wombat, they said it was an animal. His research indicated that, for his subjects, the concept "animal" that underlies and names the category was perceptually determined.

I described in chapter 7 how a syntactic operation, putting a word after an article to form a noun phrase, clues the child to a word's status as a common noun, the name for a class or category of "things." The question now is this: how is membership in the group named by the noun determined? Adults and older children have both mental images (perceptual concepts) and analytic featural verbal concepts for the same noun, concepts based on different rules for being an example of the concept. Some items that will be excluded from the child's mental image concept "animal," like butterflies and fish, will be included in the analytic featural concept.

Rosch (1975, 1978) has done a great deal of research to determine whether there are natural categories, based on characteristics of the real world, that influence the way human beings classify phenomena. Rosch has written that the notion that human classification schemes are arbitrary systems imposed on the real world is incorrect. The occurrence of the features wings, feathers, beaks, and two legs are highly correlated (tend to occur together), as are fur and four feet. At the same time, feathers and four feet, and wings and fur, are negatively correlated (do not occur together). If an animal has feathers, it will not have four feet. The animals that have the highly correlated features form a natural category of animals. We call the category with wings "birds" and the category with fur "mammal." Having called the category with fur "mammal," we are immediately made aware of another characteristic of natural categories; they have fuzzy boundaries. Whales, which look like fish, belong to the analytic *featural* category, mammals. Natural categories and analytic featural categories overlap but are not identical. Most mammals will fall into both the perceptually (mental image) and featurally defined categories. Whales, porpoises, and other ocean-dwelling mammals will fall into the featural but not the mental image category.

Rosch has proposed that natural categories have a core consisting of the best (prototypical) examples of the category surrounded by other members of the category of decreasing similarity to the prototypical examples. The more prototypical a member of the category is, the more features it has in common with other members of the category and the fewer with members of other categories. Thus, the whale is a mammal at the fuzzy boundary between mammals and fish. It has breathing, live birth, and nursing its young in common with the other mammals. It has its shape, absence of fur and feet, and its dwelling place in common with fish. The concepts based on mental images of young children appear to consist of the central (prototypical) examples of categories.

The mental image and the analytic featural concept are two different kinds of concept, or ways of organizing roughly the same contents of the mind in thinking and remembering. They are verbal concepts if the concept has a name so that, for example, hearing or seeing the word *dog* will retrieve from memory the mental image or verbal material about number of legs, warm-blooded or not, type of coat, type of vocalization, and other features organizable as an analytic featural concept. The featural concept is a *proper set*. Membership in a class or proper set depends on having the particular groups of features that define the class or set. The whale is a borderline animal with the defining features of the mammal but with other features that are characteristic of fish, particularly the shape, lack of legs, and dwelling place. The natural concept of the whale is as a fish. In the ordinary experience of most human beings, the whale is a fish. The concept of the whale as mammal is a learned concept. The system of classification of the Earth's animals is the product of the science of biology. Each species and animal class is defined in terms of features, not all of which affect the animal's appearance. The set of features has to be purposefully learned.

When children are first learning the meaning of a word, and developing a verbal concept from their ordinary experience, the concept will be a natural concept like the concept of the moon of the very young princess in James Thurber's fairy tale, *Many Moons*. The princess wanted the moon, and the wise men who know about the moon knew it could not be gotten for her. One of the court thought to ask the princess how big the moon was. She said that she knew it was quite small because when she held her thumb up between her eye and the moon, the moon was blocked from her view. This may seem an unusual and unlikely concept for the moon. But consider the concepts of the flat Earth and the conceptualization of the universe with the Earth in the center and the sun and the moon revolving around it. These were the prevailing concepts for centuries, and the heliocentric (sun-centered) concept of our solar system did not replace the

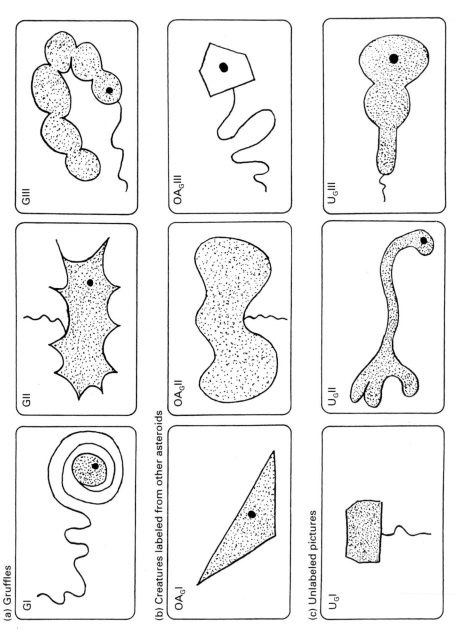

(a) Gruffles

GI GII GIII

(b) Creatures labeled from other asteroids

OA$_G$I OA$_G$II OA$_G$III

(c) Unlabeled pictures

U$_G$I U$_G$II U$_G$III

Figure 9.5   Stimuli for Gruffles identification task

Earth-centered concept as the scientifically accepted concept until the sixteenth century.

Even now, in my day-to-day life, although I "know" the Earth is round, I use my natural concept that the world is flat as I go about my business. The sun rises and sets in my everyday thinking in accordance with my natural concept of the Earth in relation to the sun and moon. When it was explained to me that the pictures of the moon taken by Luna 3 in 1959 showed the side of the moon that we on Earth had never seen, I had to use my learned concept of the solar system to understand.

Before children go to school they have not, for the most part, developed learned featural concepts. Some of their naturally occurring concepts are shortlived or at least go underground because they are corrected by others. But we all say, including the meteorologist on the nightly news telecast "Sunrise will be at 6:10 tomorrow morning." So we know that there are natural concepts that people hang on to for everyday use, even though all of us who have been through school also have learned concepts that organize the same contents of the mind but in the scientific way.

Verbal Concepts for Creatures from Outer Space

My students and I did an experiment several years ago to see how children and adults would categorize creatures from outer space. Our subjects were first graders, fifth graders, and college students. Our hypothesis was that first graders would use natural categories (like the classification of whales as fish) and fifth graders and college students would construct analytical categories based on features (like the classification of whales as mammals). We had three sets of creatures to classify called Snorbs, Gruffles, and Jexums. The pictures used for the Gruffles categorization task are shown in figure 9.5.

Children who decided whether an unlabeled picture was a Gruffle on the basis of a natural category looked at an unlabeled picture, then at the pictures of Gruffles, and then at pictures of creatures from the other asteroids until they found a picture that "looked like" the unlabeled picture. The two pictures that were most often seen as looking alike were UGII and GIII. Roughly a quarter of our subjects matched these two and said "It's a Gruffle (UGII) because it looks like this one," pointing at GIII.

Children who constructed analytical categories compared the Gruffles and the creatures from other asteroids to find the defining features for Gruffles (tails, dots, and round eyes), features that defined the proper set. We inferred this procedure from responses to UGII like, "Not a Gruffle, no tail," and to UGII, "A Gruffle it has an eye, freckles, and a tail."

In our subject sample 19 percent of first graders', 51 percent of fifth graders', and 88 percent of college students' responses were based on construction of analytical categories. (These differences were statistically significant, $P \leq 0.01$.)

Perceptual matching on the basis of natural categories should be an expected strategy for first graders. Its use is in keeping with Anglin's findings, and it is the natural first response of most people when confronted with a novel object. "What does it look like?" is the first question to ask in finding out what an object is. This first question may be the only question asked by the young and unschooled. What causes people to ask further questions is their becoming dissatisfied with the results of their conceptualizing. That has occurred frequently in our history. Concepts get reorganized, by scientists for example, when it becomes clear that there are facts that the old concept cannot explain. The shift from the concept of the Earth as flat to spherical came about because important predictions based on the flat Earth concept were false. Boats did *not* sail off the edge of the ocean, never to return.

Sometimes ordinary experience leads us to reconceptualize. It looks as though the railroad tracks come together in the distance, but by walking along the tracks a long way, we can verify that the point at which the tracks look as though they meet keeps receding. In the lives of most people who have grown up in societies where children are educated in schools, schooling is the most important agent fostering conceptual change and development in children. In school, children learn to monitor their thinking, to ask themselves if their mental processing is achieving a good result. It has been suggested that self-monitoring of thinking (meta-cognitive awareness) is the trait that differentiates the intellectual activity of schooled and unschooled persons and makes the cognitive functioning of educated people more effective than that of uneducated people. Semantic development, the subject of this chapter, is a component of cognitive development. Whenever the organization of the contents of the mind has a verbal aspect, it becomes not just a cognitive organization but more specifically a semantic organization, the development of which, through experience and/or maturation, is semantic development.

Partial Verbal Concepts for Times Past

This will be a very limited look at how children's language and communication regarding time is constrained by their cognitive development. There are many things people think about but are unable to put into words. All the mental processes of infants are non-verbal. Their thought processes are inseparable from their sensations and physical activity. As young children begin to learn words as names and to understand utterer's meaning of some of the sentences spoken to them, these verbal objects become part of their thought processes. But just because the child has the same word in his vocabulary as adults have, or produces a phrase or sentence adults use, does not mean that these verbal entities have the same meaning for the child as they have for an adult. Children's verbal concepts depend, in the first place, on their level of cognitive development. I overheard my 4-year-old daughter tell her father,

1 Yesterday, I saw a duck cross the street.

and her friend, Stephanie,

2 Last night we had bacon.

She had seen the duck about half an hour before she recounted the experience, and she had eaten the bacon at breakfast on the day she was talking to Stephanie.

Even though my daughter had the same words in her vocabulary as adults have, the words did not reflect the same verbal understanding as the adults. My daughter had had enough experience hearing *yesterday* and *last night* to induce part of their meanings but not enough experience to get the meaning precisely. Once she started a sentence to me with,

3   Last year before I was born . . .

I interrupted her to say,

4   Last year you were already born; you were three years old.

She replied indignantly,

5   I meant *very* last year.

She was gradually building up the meanings of the words, automatically associating the words to the experiences they accompanied and making assumptions about the range of experiences the words referred to. This works for the child so that her automatically acquired verbal concepts match the adult ones in so many instances that we notice and remember mismatches. They are not likely to be common, physical object names because the child receives negative feedback, as my daughter did one night as we looked up at the full moon, and she said, "See egg." In order for a child to understand the extension (range) of a term, she has to experience positive and negative instances. Many times we are not aware that the child's verbal concept is being brought into conformity with the conventional concept. The child does not always use a word inappropriately to name an object or experience. The child thinks, but does not say, that the object in the sky is an egg. Later, the child hears someone else say, "Oh, look at the moon."

Metaphor

One sunny Sunday afternoon the Holzman family was out for a sightseeing drive in the country. We passed a railroad yard in which several trains, engines with freight cars attached, were to be seen standing. They were not in service, perhaps because it was Sunday. My 3-year-old daughter said, plaintively. "I want to see a train walking along."

"What do they walk with?" I asked.
"They walk with their tires," she said.

Was Miriam speaking metaphorically? If I had been asked before I read Glucksberg and Keysar (1990) I would have said no, because I would have been sure that she didn't intend the similes:

(a)   Rolling along is like walking along.
(b)   Tires (wheels) are like feet.

You got credit for producing a metaphor if you understood that the literal meaning of the metaphor (trains do not walk with their wheels) is false but that the non-literal account provides meaning. How do people recognize when a metaphor is intended? The traditional view is that a metaphor is to be interpreted as an implicit simile. Trains are like people. They move and wheels are like legs in being used for moving. Glucksberg and Keysar's (1990: 4) position is that metaphors are "class inclusion assertions not implicit comparisons"; in other words, members of the same category. There is a superordinate category under which the movement of trains and the walking of people are both subsumed and another category subsuming feet and wheels. What will these categories be called? According to Glucksberg and Keysar (1990), one possibility is to use the name of a prototypical category member as the name of the superordinate category, itself. For a 3-year-old, walking is a good candidate for a prototypical kind of self-movement; that is, movement not caused by pushing, throwing, pulling, or gravity. Walking is prototypical movement in a human context compared to hopping, skipping, crawling, jumping, swimming, and flying. Walking is our most typical way of getting from place to place. It is a good candidate for name of the superordinate category subsuming the above categories because there is no one word superordinate like animal in relation to fish, birds, mammals, etc. Many natural languages use the name of a prototypical category member to name the superordinate.

Glucksberg and Keysar (1990) present a convincing argument for concluding that metaphors are class-inclusion assertions rather than implicit similes. Similes – a bird is like a butterfly (because they both fly) – are reversible. Metaphors are non-reversible because they are class-inclusion assertions.

Roger is (like) a big teddy bear.
*   A big teddy bear is (like) Roger.

Roger belongs to the class of large, fuzzy, lovable beings.

A dog is an animal.
*   An animal is a dog.

Miriam's metaphor, *I want to see a train walking along*, is a verb rather than noun metaphor. *He's slimy, she's hard-hearted* are adjective metaphors, members of the class of pejorative, non-literal, but meaningful descriptors of human characteristics.

I want to see a train walking along is a metaphor produced by a young child in the course of her ordinary experience. Most of the empirical data about young children and metaphor comes from experiments in which the experimenter investigates children's understanding of metaphors. Gentner (1988) cites Asch and Nerlove's (1960) finding that a 4-year-old asked, "Can a person be sweet?", takes the question literally, for example, "not unless he was made of chocolate." Not until they are in their early teens can children explain metaphors like, "The prison guard was a hard rock" (Gentner, 1988).

What we have is analogous to people's being able to use language grammatically and appropriately long before being able to explain the grammatical and social rules they are unconsciously applying. Young children have class-inclusion rules which they unconsciously apply to create metaphors. Older children can explain metaphors.

Experimental findings indicate that metaphors based on object structure are consciously understood by children before metaphors based on relational structure. In "If a tree had a knee where would it be?", Gentner (1977) found that preschool children could understand the structural analogy between a tree and a standing person: tree trunk – body, branches and leaves – head and hair. The knee of the tree should be about a third of the way up the trunk. They demonstrated understanding by pointing.

Gentner's research demonstrating that attributional metaphors can be explained by children before relational ones was carried out with 4–5-year-olds, 7–8-year-olds, and college students. She presented her metaphors as similes, so I made a quick check to see if they fit Glucksberg and Keysar's (1990) definition of metaphors as class-inclusion statements in being non-reversible. Even if I thought about Gentner's examples leaving the word "like" out, only a few seemed non-reversible to me (table 9.3). Tree bark is skin, a lake is a mirror, and grass is hair strike me as non-reversible. That is a small group, and I wouldn't be surprised if others disagree about their non-reversibility. Glucksberg and Keysar's conclusion that metaphors are class-inclusion statements succeeds for the metaphors they presented but not for the majority of Gentner's. Most of hers are analogic, based on shared attributes or functions of two disparate objects or on both attribute and relation for double metaphors (see table 9.4).

Gentner found no difference in her three groups of subjects on attributional metaphors. All three groups preferred attributional interpretations. However, the interpretations of relational and double metaphors evoked steadily increasing relational focus from age 6 to adulthood. Gentner attributes this to an increasing understanding of relational analogy with age, with earliest understanding in domains with which young children have great familiarity. Even a 3-year-old sees that a train

Table 9.3 Gentner's metaphors to judge reversibility

Metaphor type	Examples
Relational metaphors	The moon is (like) a lightbulb
	A camera is like a tape recorder
	A ladder is like a hill
	A cloud is like a sponge
	A roof is like a hat
	Treebark is like skin
	A tire is like a shoe
	A window is like an eye
Attributional metaphors	Jelly beans are like balloons
	A cloud is like a marshmallow
	A football is like an egg
	The sun is like an orange
	A snake is like a hose
	Soapsuds are like whipped cream
	Pancakes are like nickels
	A tiger is like a zebra
Double metaphors	A doctor is like a repairman
	A kite is like a bird
	The sky is like the ocean
	A hummingbird is like a helicopter
	Plant stems are like drinking straws
	A lake is like a mirror
	Grass is like hair
	Stars are like diamonds

Source: Gentner (1988)

Table 9.4 Gentner's sample metaphors and interpretations

Samples		Interpretations			
Relational metaphors					
A cloud is like a sponge	R1	Both can hold water	A1	Both are soft	
	R2	Both can give off water	A2	Both are fluffy	
A tire is like a shoe	R1	Both are used to move something	A1	Both are made of rubber	
	R2	Both cover the bottom of something	A2	Both can be black	
Double metaphors					
Plant stems are like drinking straws	R1	Both can be used to get water	A1	Both are long	
	R2	Both draw liquid up	A2	Both are thin	
Grass is like hair	R1	Both grow quickly	A1	Both are long	
	R2	Both cover and protect something	A2	Both are skinny	
Attributional metaphors					
Jelly beans are like balloons	R1	Both are fun at parties	A1	Both can be different colors	
	R2	Both can be tossed in the air	A2	Both are round	
A snake is like a hose	R1	Both squirt liquid	A1	Both are long	
	R2	Both can curl up	A2	Both are wiggly	

R1 and R2 denote relational interpretations; A1 and A2 denote attributional interpretations.
Source: Gentner (1988)

rolling along a railroad track is like a person walking down the street. But the analogy of drinking straws and plant stems would elude her because characteristic behavior in the botanical domain is beyond her ken.

Secondary Consciousness, the Sense of Self and Autobiographical Memory

We have seen that apes can learn to associate a referent and arbitrary auditory or visual signal and to remember the association so that perceiving the signal will call to mind the referent or at least the ape's sensation of the referent. Currently, researchers may describe the ape's mental processes somewhat differently. When the situation is a recurring one, the animal learns that one specific event is usually followed by another; for example, the ape pokes a blade of grass into a termite nest and when the ape pulls it out it is covered with termites which are good to eat. The ape learns and remembers this sequence and acquires "an adaptive function for guiding present action and predicting future outcomes," a script or event schema memory system (Nelson, 1993: 1).

Nelson, as well as others, attributes memory for events to animals. Nelson identifies scripts like "poke grass stem into termite nest, pull out grass stem covered with termites, eat termites" as generic memory for recurring situations, a mental capability of all mammals, not just primates and presumably not dependent on some simple kind of reward or punishment. Having scripts makes animals capable of limited anticipation of consequences of action. Nelson also attributes generic memory to young children. The memory ability which is limited to adult humans and older children is autobiographical memory, the memory of specific episodes involving one's self which may be retrievable over the entire life.

The earliest remembered events appear to occur between 3 and 4 years (Pillemer and White, 1989; cited by Nelson, 1993). Autobiographical memories are sparse for the early years in which individuals are just beginning to construct a self-system, the sense of themselves as persons existing in time located in a particular place with family, friends, and an ongoing life continuously available to be shaped into autobiographical memory. This is memory in which one is oneself the character from whose point of view the story is told. As the human infant develops, what begins as non-verbal generic event memory (in scripts) develops into autobiographical memory, for which secondary consciousness, the sense of self is required. The evolutionary development from just primary to primary and secondary consciousness is recapitulated in the human child's development.

Parents are amazed to find that their infants who were perfectly happy to visit the doctor for weighing, measuring, and listening with stethoscope shriek as the doctor approaches on the visit following their first innoculation. The shot becomes a defining element in the infant's generic memory or script for visit to the doctor. Nelson

(1993) points out that generic memory is highly useful. It makes prediction and planning for future occurrences of the scripted event possible. (This point was made also by Edelman, 1987; see chapter 4.) She points out that scripts have greater adaptive value than memory of particular episodes. However, she concludes from her research and that of others that generic memory and memory for particular episodes develop at about the same time. She attributes the development of memory for particular early episodes to the influence of adult talk. Has anyone ever said to you, about an event from childhood, "I'm not sure whether I remember this happening or if I remember being told it happened"?

Whether memory of a particular episode was adult talk scaffolded or self-generated, the memory contributes to the child's knowledge of the world rather than to the construction of a personal past or autobiographical memory. However, the personal past, autobiographical memory, may develop from generic memory and memory of specific episodes (Nelson, 1993: 8). Nelson asks what episodes children specifically remember and why. I have two memories of events that occurred in my life before I was 3 years old. I fell and burned my arm on a steam radiator. The memory is purely visual. My upper arm has a yellow sore place. My other memory is of our doctor saying to me as I lay in my bed, "We're going for a little ride." I know the little ride ended in the hospital and that I was there 10 days, but this knowledge is not part of my memory of the doctor episode. I was told. I believe these episodes stuck in my memory because they were traumatic. The burn is a memory fragment, but the hospital episode makes a little problem story. The doctor did a wrong to me. He misled me, and I have not forgotten nor, I guess, forgiven. I have a few other later memories, and they cohere as evidence in my memory of an unsympathetic physician, part of my developing knowledge of the world, but at the same time part of my autobiographical memory. Part of the organizing of the contents of the mind is cross-referencing.

In chapter 6, I described changes over the period in the way mothers responded to their infants' utterances. Even when the four children's utterances were just one word, mothers' utterances in response consisted much of the time, late in the one-word period, of sentences including the child's word rather than just a repetition of the child's word. I see this as parent talk contributing to the linguistic development of children as Nelson sees adult talk contributing to autobiographical memory. Nelson (1993) cites Engel's research finding of two styles of memory talk, pragmatic and elaborative, and Firush and Framhoff's similar finding of elaborative and repetitive styles. In both cases, children of elaborative mothers engaged in more extensive memory talk when children were 2 years old than the children of the pragmatic or repetitive mothers. However, neither study was designed so that the direction of conversation can be determined. Were the elaborative mothers responding to their more talkative 2-year-olds or were the 2-year-olds talking more because their elaborative mothers inspired them? Maybe some of both. In any event, Nelson's work gives evidence that the important organization of contents of the mind into autobiography uses material provided by the child's adults.

Notes

1   Children acquire noun and verb inflections before they attend school. These are part of the syntax of the language, dependent on innate linguistic capacity.
2   I have said "acceptable" because adults may censor words in a word association task if they find the first word that comes to mind unacceptable. In our culture, college students may feel constrained to make logical word associations.

Further Reading

Confen, J. and Glack, M. (1992) "Explaining basic categories: feature predictability and information," *Psychological Bulletin*, 291–303.
Dorfman, M. and Brener, W. (1994) "Understanding the points of fables," *Discourse Processes*, 17: 105–29.
Ebeling, K. and Gelman, S. (1994) "Children's use of context in interpreting 'big' and 'little'," *Child Development*, 65: 1178–92.
Gelman, S. A., Wilcox, S. A. and Clark, E. V. (1989) "Conceptual and lexical hierarchies in young children," *Cognitive Development*, 4: 309–26.
  Examines how linguistic form and conceptual level might affect acquisition. In their linguistic form, labels can be single nouns (for example, oak) or compound nouns (oak-tree). Conceptually, categories can be structured at the basic (tree), superordinate (plant), or subordinate (oak) levels. The most common error was to treat hierarchically related words as labeling mutually exclusive subjects.

Gentner, D. and Imai, M. (1994) "Further examination of the shape bias in early word learning," *Proceedings of the Child Language Research Forum.* Stanford University, April.

Gunnar, M. and Maratsos, M. (1995) *Modularity and Constraints in Language and Cognition* (Hillsdale, NJ: Lawrence Erlbaum).

Mervis, C. and Bertrand, J. (1994) "Acquisition of the novel name–nameless category, N3C, principle," *Child Development*, 65: 1646–62.

Mervis, C., Golinikoff, R. and Bertrand, J. (1994) "Two year olds readily learn multiple labels for the same basic level category," *Child Development*, 65: 1163–77.

Sell, M. A. (1992) "The development of children's knowledge structures: events, slots, and taxonomies," *Journal of Child Language*, 19: 659–76.

    Findings support Nelson's hypothesis that taxonomic knowledge structures are derived from event-based knowledge structures with the aid of slot-filler categories.

10

Reading

I came to the study of reading with the biases of the psycholinguist. I thought that learning to read was the same as learning to speak, except that the code was different: the reading code is orthographic (based on spelling and the alphabet) instead of phonemic (based on the speech sounds of language). In order to read the learner has to crack the orthographic code. Reading for meaning, the goal of reading, depends in part on having cracked the code. The child already knows from life experience the relation between word sounds and word meanings. When the child learns in first grade to crack the orthographic code, he is learning the relation between the orthographic and phonemic codes (table 10.1).

If there are no words in the reading material presented to the beginning reader that are not in the child's spoken vocabulary, and the words are used in the kinds of sentences that have occurred in the child's language experience, then the task for the child is just code

Table 10.1 Phonemic code, meaning, and orthographic code

Phonemic code[a]	Meaning	Orthographic code
/dɔg/	Four-legged animal that barks and chases cats	dog
/rʌn/	To move on foot at a fast pace	run
/hat/	Opposite of cold	hot

[a] I have written out the phonemic spellings, but what the child knows is just how the words sound.

cracking. It sounded to me, a psycholinguist, straightforward and not too hard.

The teacher teaches the children the names of the letters, to recognize them by sight and the common sound of each. I remember *Sesame Street* teaching W. "Witches who wash their wigs on windy, winter Wednesdays are wacky," was the sentence shown on the TV screen while a *Sesame Street* character said it.

A kindergartener I know named Aaron brought the words reproduced in figure 10.1 home from school for his mother. We can see that he has been taught to write his name and the word *stack*, and perhaps other correctly spelled words. *Like you*, spelled by Aaron as "LKU," *think you are a*, spelled as "FEKDAT URA," and *we went in the hay*, spelled "WE CAMT IN DA HA," and *we coming in*, spelled "WECAMTIN" include invented spellings based on how the words sounded to Aaron, the names of the letters, and what he knew as a kindergartener about phonemic orthographic correspondence.

Children have produced writing like Aaron's often enough that the process has been labeled "invented spelling." Phonetically driven spelling is a more precise description. Children are using the name of the letter or the way they hear it sound as the basis for spelling the word. In languages, like English, in which words are made up of linear strings of letters, speaking, reading, and writing could be acquired in parallel. Traditionally, we have thought acquisition is ordered. First, one acquires the sound–meaning correspondence, the string of speech sounds that names the object. "See the kitten," says mother to Jean, pointing at the small furry being. After some months, Jean says "kitten" when she sees the animal. In the preschool years, language is learned in relation to experience, the word–world match. Understanding precedes production, except for sound play where meaning doesn't matter or in certain brain malfunctions, like autism in which an individual has the ability to produce language without understanding it.

Part of preschool experience for many children is being read to: "The three little kittens lost their mittens and they began to cry." If it's a picture-story book with one line of the story or poem on a page paired with an appropriate picture, a child who has heard the story read to her enough times to memorize it, concurrently looking at the pictures, could crack the code. A significant number of American children enter kindergarten who are self-taught readers, and some are self-taught writers. It is the self-taught writers who motivate me, and

Figure 10.1 Invented spelling: (a) "I do not like you – poop-poop!"; (b) "I think that you are a poop-poop!"; (c) "We went in the hay stack. We coming in stack"

others, to rethink learning to read as one aspect of the acquisition of literacy. Rather than learning reading, writing, and spelling skills in the primary grades, children are acquiring literacy. Acquiring literacy is not based on learning skills. Literacy is acquired as a byproduct of accomplishing the goals of understanding and communicating with others using written language. This conception is being called *whole language* in contrast to separate reading, writing, and spelling skills.

Looking at figure 10.1, we can get some ideas about what kind of home environment and preliteracy activities are conducive to children's early acquisition of literacy. A current buzzword, really a buzz-phrase, is "print rich environment." Books, shopping lists, newspapers, magazines, and magnetic letters on the refrigerator door provide print. The unstated assumption seems to be that the print provides opportunities for children to become aware of printed material and its functions and to notice that their elders find the materials interesting and useful. Among the books, there may be *Mother Goose* or other nursery rhyme books which are read to infants and preschool children in the home. Preschoolers' learning of nursery rhymes turns out to be significant in early success in learning to read in school. Why should this be? It could be that knowing nursery rhymes as a preschooler and easily learning to read in school are both results of a child's high level of intelligence. It could be that both accomplishments are products of parental tutoring. Research reported by Goswami and Bryant (1989) provides evidence that it is enhanced phonological sensitivity from knowing the nursery rhymes that leads to early success in learning to read. The authors report longitudinal data beginning when the children were on average 3.4 years old to a time when they were on average 6.3 years old. Most had been in school for a year and had begun learning to read.

The children's knowledge of nursery rhymes at the start of the research was assessed by asking each child, "Can you say *Jack and Jill* for me? Or *Hickory Dickory Dock, Baa Baa Black Sheep, Humpty Dumpty, Twinkle Twinkle Little Star?*" Each child was asked to recite all five rhymes. Goswami and Bryant (1989) recorded whether the child knew the whole rhyme, part of it or none of it.

Children's ability to read at an average age 6.3 years was assessed in two ways. First, they were shown 15 pictures with four or five words beside each picture – for example, a picture of a car and the words *cake, camp, car, came* – and told to make a line under the word that goes with the picture. Secondly, they were asked to underline the word (one of six) that correctly finishes the sentence; for example, lemons are *you, yes, year, yet, yellow, yard*.

The test data were analyzed to control for effects of IQ, vocabulary, and mother's education. The resultant correlation between knowing nursery rhymes at 3.4 years and reading at 6.3 years is highly significant, $P < 0.001$. Further analysis indicates that early nursery rhyme knowledge enhances phonological sensitivity and that it is phonological sensitivity that is the key to reading. The child who has cracked the phonemic–orthographic code can look at the letters of a word and sound it out, reading it, and if it's in his spoken vocabulary, understand its meaning.

If a child is learning to read a completely phonetic language, like Polish or Korean, in which a letter always makes the same sound, once he cracks the code he can read anything. Of course, his understanding of what he reads will be limited by his knowledge of what the words mean. Learning to read English requires acquiring the understanding that the sounds letters make are influenced by neighboring letters: silent *e* causes a preceding vowel to "say its name," so that *bit* becomes *bite*; *hat, hate*. The sequence *tion* which occurs in many words – for example, *ration, damnation, national, arbitration, conversationally* – is pronounced like the phonetically predictable verb, *shun*. "When two vowels go walking the first one does the talking," as in *goal, hail*, and *hair*. These exceptions to phonetic regularity must be learned and, perhaps surprisingly, are mastered by English-speaking children learning to read English.

Children who learn to read as readily as they had learned spoken language do not remember how they learned to read. It is the ones, like me, who had trouble who remember. I remember sitting at my desk one day toward the end of first grade with my book open to a story. We were having "silent" reading, and our teacher was going from desk to desk looking over people's shoulders. She stopped at my desk and ran her finger under a sentence as she read the words. She made a comment, which I have forgotten. What I remember is a sinking feeling. The teacher's comment indicated that she thought I was actually getting meaning from the printing on the page. My problem was that I really did not understand how to read. I thought all I had to do was look at the printing on the page. I was a beginning reader in the days of the look–say method. The teacher had words printed on large cards (like flash cards for arithmetic). She would hold a card up for the class, say the word, and go on to the next card. Later in the year, she would ask a child the word when she held up the card. I had not been exposed to the alphabet. I do not remember being able to print my name.

My second memory is of sitting at home in the kitchen with my mother and my sister who was in kindergarten. I was looking at the word *grapes* in my reader and trying to sound it out. I said, "gur ay pus." I didn't understand blending speech sounds. My little sister said "grapes." I have no further memories, so I assume that after that it was smooth sailing. My problem cleared up when I learned that reading was an active process dependent on figuring out what the words on the page were, or as I would now say, cracking the orthographic–phonemic code. That is the beginning, but there are important differences between reading and talking besides the difference in code.

Top-down and Bottom-up Processes in Reading

In my experience as a psycholinguist studying reading, becoming acquainted with the distinction between *top-down* and *bottom-up* processes greatly clarified issues. In the early 1970s, I read in the report of a conference on reading, "Good readers are good guessers," which implies that good readers are figuring out words on the basis of their sentence contexts rather than by stopping and sounding out words they do not recognize by sight (if they are beginning readers) to see if the words are in their spoken vocabularies. About the same time a child I knew, a fourth grader, was beginning to experience grave problems in school. Her parents were told that their daughter had never really learned how to read. She had gotten along in the primary grades guessing at the meanings of words on the basis of sentence context and the pictures which accompany the text in early readers. Figuring out word meanings from sentence context is a *top-down* process; the reader is going from the higher level organization of sentence meaning to the lower level of word meaning. Getting at word meaning by sounding out the word is a *bottom-up* process. It is figuring out a word (a higher level of organization) from a sequence of phonemes (a lower level). If there are words and sentences rather

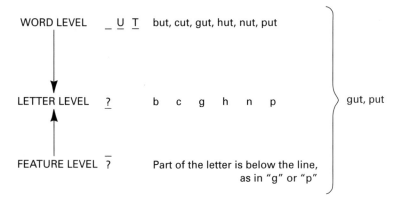

Figure 10.2 Top-down and bottom-up analysis to determine the letter in a word

than simply isolated letters from the beginning of learning to read, both top-down and bottom-up processes need to be used. It is clear why the bottom-up processes are needed: these provide the elements of the code. What we read are letters, words, and sentences. We need the top-down processes because what we read for and understand, and what carries us along in reading, is meaning. It is not present in the letters, and is barely glimpsed in the words, but it becomes more and more apparent as the sentences and paragraphs take shape.

The lowest level process specific to reading is letter perception. The model presented by Rumelhart and McClelland (1982) makes use of top-down and bottom-up processes to explain the perception of the letters in individual words. In their presentation, Rumelhart and McClelland (1982) make use of three levels of information used by the reader in perceiving the letters of a word. These are the levels of the word, letter, and feature (figure 10.2). The reader uses information from the feature and the word level in perceiving the letter. This comes about because the reader is acquiring information simultaneously at all three levels. It is partial information, but the letter perceived has to be consistent with this partial information, and this narrows the range of possibilities, perhaps to a single letter. In figure 10.2, for example, the barely perceived features suggest a three-letter word ending in UT. This ending is consistent with the word being *but, cut, gut, hut, nut,* or *put.* If the reader detects the feature, part of the letter extends below the line of type, the possibilities become limited to *gut* and *put*. Look at *but*, *cut*, *hut*, and *nut*. Their beginning letters do not have a part that extends below the line of type.

The interactional analysis (figure 10.2) has been applied to higher levels of processing involved in reading. (An excellent exposition is presented in Adams and Collins, 1979.) In perceiving a word, the reader makes use of information at the level of the letter and at the levels of syntax and semantics. I will carry on with the example of the perception of the letter to complete the three-letter word ending in *ut*. If the word were being perceived as a word by itself, or in a list, and therefore without context clues, the reader would have to continue examining the features of the letter for ones that differentiate *g* and *p*. The main one is that the part that extends below the line of type in *g* is on the right, in *p* on the left. But if the word is part of a sentence, the context of the rest of the sentence clues the reader. If *ut* is in the sentence, "That's my *ut* reaction," the missing letter is *g*. If *ut* is in the sentence, "Please *ut* your knife on the table," the missing letter is *p*.

Rumelhart's and McClelland's (1982) model predates the research demonstrating that the information being processed in reading is not just visual but auditory as well. The letters have a phonological as well as visual shape, and at least for people just learning to read the phonological input is crucial. For the skilled reader, word recognition has a high degree of automaticity, but word identification is not always automatic. Many words are not automatically identified (Perfetti et al., 1991). However, the skilled reader can identify words without requiring phonological input.

The reader acquires semantic context from the part of the text that she has already read and, in the case of primary grade readers, the pictures that accompany the text. From these, the reader will know in a general way what the text is about, or the *topic*. The reader will know, for example, whether it's about a trip to the moon, or Dick and Jane planting a vegetable garden. The reader will have vastly different expectations about what will appear on the printed page depending on whether the topic is a trip to the moon or planting a garden. All the top-down processes in reading are dependent on expectations derived from the context. Some are very low expectations concerning the letters of a word or the words in a sentence. But topic determines high-level expectations about the text and its content.

Topic Familiarity

Readers' expectations as to the characteristics of text are strongly influenced by topic, and reading efficiency is enhanced if the reader is knowledgeable concerning the topic. If the reader is familiar with the topic, he or she is able to fill in gaps in the text that make reading difficult for the person who lacks the knowledge of the world that the text takes for granted. I have made up a little story using vocabulary and sentence structure appropriate for second graders. I am including it to demonstrate the importance of topic familiarity to reading comprehension.

Summer Vacation Fun

Erika and Raymond woke up very early. They could hardly wait to go clamming with their father. He had told them that low tide would be at eight o'clock this morning, so they would have to be down at the flats by seven. Raymond pulled on his trunks and ran back out of the cottage to look for his rake. Just then father called,

"Hurry up, you two. I've got the pail and shovel." He came out the door and looked at Raymond and Erika.

"Erika, find your rake, and both of you put on your old sneakers." The children hurried with their shoes, Erika found her rake, and they ran down to the beach. This was the first day of the Vivante family vacation and it was starting off just right.

The reader's ability to understand and remember the story depends, in part, on knowing about clamming. Knowledge related to hunting clams is summarized as follows:

1   What are clams?
    Clams are shellfish that are good to eat.
2   Where found?
    Clams live in shallow ocean waters. Some live between the high and low tide lines, spending much of the time dug into the mud and sand.
3   When can they be hunted?
    They can be hunted during a period of time before and after dead low tide when the tide has gone out exposing the "flats," a muddy sandy area where clams may have dug themselves in.

4   How are clams hunted? (Clamming)
    Persons going clamming bring a pail, shovel, and rake to the flats
    at low tide. They look for a squirt of water coming out of the flats
    because squirts are made by clams. When they see a squirt, they
    dig up the sand and mud around it, pull the rake through the
    mud and sand, looking for clams. They put the ones they find in
    pails and continue looking for squirts and digging for clams until
    they have collected as many as they want.
5   Are there precautions to take?
    Because there are likely to be broken shells with sharp edges on
    the flats, it is wise to wear shoes.

If the reader is knowledgeable about family life in the United
States, then family summer vacations, father–children activities, and
appropriate clothing (swimsuits and tennis shoes) will be familiar. In
short, if you are a child whose life experience has included family summer vacations and activities like those in the little story, you will be
able to make sense of it. Otherwise, the story may be hard to understand even if you can read the words. The second graders whose life
experience has not included digging clams may not have *clamming*,
or *flats*, or even *low tide* in their spoken vocabularies.

Research on reading (Anderson, 1981) has shown that the reader's
knowledge of the subject of the reading is the principal determiner
of what will be understood and remembered. In his research, Anderson
found that topic familiarity was more important than vocabulary difficulty. Knowing the meaning of technical words like *clamming* and
flats is part of *topic familiarity*. *Vocabulary difficulty* refers to the
occurrence in the reading of less familiar words rather than more
familiar ones with the same meaning, such as *amicable* instead of
friendly. In other words, Anderson found that how much children
understood and remembered from what they had read depended
more on whether the topic was familiar or unfamiliar (for top-down
processing). Along with topic familiarity, topic interest is important
to children's reading comprehension. Children will be motivated to
make an effort to read when the topic is of consuming interest to them.

Currently, analyzing a narrative like "Summer Vacation Fun" might
be seen as an exercise in text comprehension (Graesser et al., 1994).
Readers are seen as constructing a situation model of what a narrative is
about on the basis of explicit content and what the reader fills in from

world knowledge (life experience including book reading, TV viewing, and so on). How elaborate the reader's situation model is depends on the reader's goals – what does he want to get from the reading? Why is he reading the story, poem, text that he is reading? Part of the reader's "search after meaning" is finding if the text is coherent. Does the narrative hang together and not violate the reader's world knowledge so that the text is comprehensible? The Tuck family in *Tuck Everlasting* (Babbitt, 1975) will live forever and each will remain the age she or he was the day they drank from the magic spring. This is a novel for 8–12-year-olds who like the idea of not growing old and dying. The only element of fantasy in the story is the Tucks' living forever, and children will "suspend disbelief" to get a view of immortality and to think about their family growing up, old, and dying while they stay forever 10 years old, for example. Understanding the story and its implications for real people is straightforward based on text and world knowledge of 8–12-year-olds.

The information-processing model of reading which I have been presenting deals largely with visual information. The ironic fact about reading is that much of the information needed and used is phonological, available from auditory input and memory. The phonemic–orthographic code relates speech sounds and letters. At least for the beginning reader, the bottom-up processes are phonologically anchored. The phonological features determine phoneme–orthographic letter pairs for the English-speaking (and hearing) child becoming English literate.

English Literacy and Deaf Children

What of the deaf child who has learned American Sign Language (ASL) instead of spoken English? She must crack the sign–orthographic code in order to become English literate, but ASL is not English in the visual mode. ASL and English are different languages, not the same language in different codes, so the deaf child attending school where the written materials are to be in English and books are in English is studying in a foreign language. Furthermore, the visual forms of the two languages – ASL signs, the only form for ASL – and written English have different basic units. Signs stand for words or concepts, and letters, the building blocks of written words, correspond for the most part to the phonemes of English.

English, like all languages in contact with other languages through history, has been affected by other languages, particularly languages spoken by conquerors of England. (We will return to second-language learning in chapter 11.) In English, all written words are made up of combinations of (some of) the 26 letters of the alphabet. Twenty-six letters and their common sounds must be learned by rote. But, then, thousands of words can be written or read, combinations of the 26 letters.

In some written languages, Chinese for example, the basic unit is not the written letter, but the word. The relation of a logograph (the word written) and its sound must be learned by rote. In other words, the relation of the written expression of the word and the spoken word (and meaning) must be memorized. The written word cannot be "sounded out" on the basis of phoneme–letter correspondence. In order to read a newspaper, a Chinese person must recognize and have memorized the meaning of 5,000 Chinese characters. Becoming literate in Chinese entails an enormous task of memorization. The path is eased for the beginning reader because the Chinese have a set of phonetic symbols for pronouncing characters. They are simpler than most characters but are not used for formal writing. For example, lower case Q, *q*, in the International Phonetic Alphabet is used to represent the voiceless uvular stop (not an English phoneme) but, in the Pinyan Transliteration of Mandarin, *q* stands for alveolo-palatal affricate (not an English phoneme) (Pullum and Ladusaw, 1986).

The advantage of the logographic writing system is that, no matter which dialect a Chinese person speaks, and these are many, unintelligible to speakers of other dialects, all Chinese share the same reading and writing system – which is totally unrelated to the spoken languages. The cost of the system is the great difficulty of becoming literate when phonology and orthography are unrelated.

It is ironic that becoming a reader, which looks like a visual accomplishment, is so greatly facilitated if one can hear, and the visual and auditory images of messages which form strings of symbols can be aligned. The difficulty deaf children encounter in school – most deaf children do not progress beyond the fourth grade – bears a resemblance to the Chinese situation. Because deaf children do not receive phonological input, they cannot sound out words as hearing children can. ASL, American Sign Language, is not English in the visual medium. It is a different language where signs symbolize concepts. Some English words are finger spelled so there is one-to-one correspondence between English and the language of the deaf, but most are not.

Greek was the first writing that informed readers what the words sounded like so that reading did not depend on knowing what the word meant (as does Chinese, for example). All later alphabets are modifications of the Greek alphabet, having the same structure, letters corresponding to speech sounds (Powell, 1991). Powell subscribes to the theory that the Greek alphabet was invented in order to transcribe the poetry of Homer about 800 BC. Powell's evidence that Homer's composition of the *Iliad* and *Odyssey* was contemporaneous with the invention of the Greek alphabet is the correspondence of the social and material world of Greece at that time and that of the *Iliad* and the *Odyssey*, subtracting out the "archaisizing and fantastic elements" of the poems incorporated to give them "epic distance" (Powell, 1991). Powell presents a detailed comparison of archeological finds with objects and customs that obtained in Greece around 800 BC. Peter Reid, Professor of Classics at Tufts University, dates the *Iliad* to 740 BC and the *Odyssey* to 700 BC (personal communication).

Reading Instruction

In addition to being mature enough to spend three or four hours sitting in a school room, being ready to learn to read means having had the experiences in life that give a child the vocabulary, grammatical knowledge, experience in making sense out of communications using language, and knowledge of the world that the school-reading program assumes children have as they begin reading. Most American middle-class children come to school ready to learn to read texts that have been prepared with an eye to their experience. Children whose life experience has been different may not be ready, and teachers need to be aware of reading difficulties arising because a child's background knowledge does not have the ingredients that the reading material assumes. There are, moreover, differences between spoken and written language that will affect children even if difference in life experience is not a factor.

Written Language Instead of Spoken

For the most part, spoken language is used in face-to-face conversation so that the people talking and listening have the time and place in common. They can observe each other's gestures and tone of voice. They share non-verbal information that clarifies verbal messages or indicates that clarification is needed, a quizzical look for example, and that generally makes communication easier. In communication by written language, much more depends on characteristics of the text. The use in books of charts, diagrams, and pictures indicates that the written word is often not sufficient by itself. The beginning reader has to learn to get information from written language that comes with very little effort from spoken language. The extensive use of pictures in primary readers helps the new reader, partly by providing information and partly by attracting the child's attention and getting him interested and motivated to do the sometimes difficult work of reading.

In addition to the difference in code (written rather than spoken) and the change from an interactive relationship (taking turns being both hearer and speaker to being just reader), the beginner is faced with further challenges in learning to read. A crucial aspect to the problem of moving from spoken to written language is interpreting sentence structure from written materials. Sentence structure does not present problems in spoken language because it is clearly communicated by the stress and pitch patterns in utterances. We know whether a speaker is looking for an English soldier or a new garment by the stress on *red* or *coat*. If the speaker says

 1   I'm looking for a r̄ed coat

it's the soldier.

 2   I'm looking for a red c̄oat

means the garment.

The same patterns pertain for *White House*, the President's residence, and *white house*, a house painted white. We usually do not mark stress and pitch patterns of written sentences. We get some clues from punctuation.

 3   You're going to school

is a question or a statement depending on whether it is punctuated with a question mark or a period. But the question of whether the *red coat* is a person or a garment is answered by contextual information, including the topic of the text in which the sentence appears.

Another syntactic problem for the beginning reader is the greater complexity of written sentences compared to spoken ones. Sentences like

4   I saw the little green man who wanted an egg for supper

do not present a problem for the skilled reader. A beginner, however, is likely to read

4a   I saw the little green man

and

4b   Who wanted an egg for supper?

as two separate sentences, (4a) and (4b). Sentence (4b) is a question that is a confusing non-sequitor if (4a) is read as a complete sentence. In a sentence such as

5   I want a cookie to eat with my ice cream

a beginning reader is likely to expect the sentence to end with

5a   I want a cookie

The reader may attempt to start a new sentence with

5b   to eat with my ice cream

and again be confused. If children have been read to from books that have complicated sentences, they will be prepared to meet complicated sentences in their own reading. Joy Adamson's book, *Born Free*, about Elsa, a lion cub whom she tamed and then returned to the African wild is such a book.

The Teacher's Role in Helping Children Acquire Literacy

This chapter is titled "Reading," but in recent years *literacy* has replaced *reading* as the name of the subject. Over the past decade, practitioners have changed their focus from, "Why Johnny can't read?"

(the question which Jean Chall, 1967, provided research findings to settle) to *Beginning to Read: Thinking and Learning about Print* (Adams, 1990). We have experienced a radical change in our perception and analysis of the ability to read and write and consequently how the ability is acquired. In the days when people wondered about Johnny, the debate concerned teaching beginning reading by phonics as opposed to teaching beginning readers to recognize whole words in context. Phonics is bottom-up processing to figure out words. Recognizing words in context is top-down processing. Today, it is well understood that cracking the phonemic–orthographic code is the essential first step in becoming a reader of an alphabetic written language. Some children do this on their own, others need varying amounts of experience, like learning the alphabet and words that begin with each letter.

The most important research finding of the past decade is the role of phonological coding and memory in becoming a reader and the fact that phonological sensitivity in children can be developed after they have entered school and will contribute to their becoming skilled readers.

The history of research on skilled reading for the past 20 years or so reveals researchers strongly committed to the importance of bottom-up processes that lead to automaticity of word recognition on the basis of letter recognition (Vellutino, 1991). During this same period, top-down processes have had strong adherents (for example, Goodman et al., 1979; Smith, 1971), culminating in the text, task, meaning perspective of the whole language approach to literacy acquisition. But, as an adherent of the whole language approach to literacy acquisition, I would say that it does not proscribe learning bottom-up processing. Whenever the person acquiring literacy by the whole language way feels the need to improve his spelling or "hear" a particular grammatical construction he has not acquired, he should be helped to do so. He will need to "monitor" or review his performance and practice the correct way, a bottom-up process. In sum, when the goal is to facilitate acquisition of literacy, a balanced approach that is learner centered is most useful.

Further Reading

Adams, M. J. (1990) *Beginning to Read: Thinking and Learning about Print* (Cambridge, Mass.: MIT Press).

Chaney, C. (1994) "Language development, metalinguistic awareness and emergent literacy skills of 3 year old children in relation to social class," *Applied Psycholinguistics*, 15: 371–94.

Importance of family literacy experiences and maternal education.

Grasser, A., Singer, M. and Trabasso, T. (1994) "Constructing inferences during narrative text comprehension," *Psychological Review*, 101: 371–96.

Krashen, S. (1989) "We acquire vocabulary and spelling by reading: additional evidence for the input hypothesis," *Modern Language Journal*, 73: 440–64.

Reviews research in vocabulary and spelling and suggests that results of this research are, so far, consistent with a central hypothesis that subjects acquire language by understanding messages.

Olson, D. (1994) *The World on Paper: the Conceptual and Cognitive Implications of Writing and Reading* (Cambridge: Cambridge University Press).

Paratore, J. (1994) "Parents and children sharing literacy," in D. Lancy (ed.), *Children's Emergent Literacy* (Westport, Conn.: Praeger).

A difficulty frequently confronted in the US is teaching the children of low literate parents to read. Paratore describes a project to help parents as well as their children acquire literacy. Many of the families are poor immigrant families so that this suggested reading is appropriate also to chapter 11.

Perfetti, C., Stankovich, K., Vellutino, F. and Calher, R. (1991) "How Johnny learns to read: review of *Beginning to Read* by M. Jager," *Psychological Science*, 2: 70–85.

Weaver, C. (1990) *Understanding Whole Language* (Portsmouth, NH: Heinemann).

11

Bilingualism and Second-language Learning

Every few months since the early 1980s, I have seen newspaper articles or received mail about the language policy "problem" faced in the United States. Unlike many other countries (for example, France, Israel, and Iceland), the US has not had a language policy – laws about the grammar of the language or borrowing words from other languages. Nor has an official language been established in the US as in Canada. English and French are the official languages of Canada and all government documents, including ballots for voting, must be available in both languages. In Boston I have noticed, in the airport and in hospitals and other public buildings, signs printed in English and Spanish. I have received mail advocating the passage of legislation declaring English and only English the official language of the US. There is evidence of an emerging language policy issue. Spanish is the mother tongue of the largest segment of the US population who are not native English speakers. The southern border of the US is with Mexico whose southern border leads to Central and South America where Spanish is the language of every country except Brazil whose language is Portuguese. By far the largest number of immigrants to the US in 1992 were from Spanish-speaking countries. Of the total 973,977 immigrants, 281,972, or 29 percent, were from Mexico, the Dominican Republic, and El Salvador, all Spanish-speaking countries (US Immigration and Naturalization Service, 1993). There is every reason to believe that the migration from south of the border to the US will be continuing. Should the US become a bilingual country like Canada, or a country with an English-only legal policy, or should it continue as it is with no language policy and increasing *de facto* English–Spanish bilingualism?

This is not an issue to be settled only on the basis of effectiveness and efficiency in matters requiring language use for thinking and communicating. Psychosocial and political variables are involved. There was a time when the metaphor of melting pot was appropriate for the US. Today, the talk is of stews or salads as the pre-1960s goal of assimilation has given way to pride in ethnic identity and cultural diversity. Life is more interesting since people have been opening restaurants which feature the – Italian, Thai, Ethiopian, Indian, Korean – cuisine of the country from which they emigrated. Folk festivals take place and we see the dances and hear the music immigrants have brought with them. This is the bright view, but some have a much dimmer view of the effect of cultural diversity. They worry about the divisive effects of multiculturalism. Emphasizing that many Americans, technically almost all Americans, are hyphenated Americans – Italian-American, African-American, Korean-American – may lead people to become so rooted in their ethnicities that their sense of being, all of them, American, loses its power to bond them together. Emphasizing the ethnicity that precedes the hyphen may perhaps involve old ethnic rivalries, like that troubling Serbs, Croats, and Muslims in the former Yugoslavia.

In many parts of the world at various times, an informal language and a formal language have existed together. When a number of separate communities speaking different languages have political, religious, or other reasons for communicating with each other, they need a language for these purposes. In Europe until the middle of the seventeenth century, Latin was the formal language. English, French, and German, for example, were spoken in local regions, but Latin was the language of the church, government, courts, and for conducting relations between political units. During the Middle Ages, the church, whose language was Latin, was the institution which prevented the total collapse of civilization. Most people could not read or write and spoke only the language of their speech communities. Only a very few people, mainly the clergy, some scholars, and a few of the nobility, learned to read and write as well as speak Latin. By the middle of the seventeenth century, France had become the dominant political and economic power of Europe and the French language replaced Latin as the *lingua franca* (language used as a medium of communication between people of different languages) for official, formal purposes in Europe.

When a group of separate states, principalities, or tribal groups speaking different languages form a nation, they have to adopt a common language. In Tanzania, Swahili has become the national language. In China, the government of Mao made Mandarin the national language and the language of instruction in the schools. Pilipino, a version of Tagalog, has been established in the Republic of the Philippines as the national language. Russian was the *lingua franca* of the USSR, a nation in which 130 different languages were spoken in its 15 republics. Many people in the USSR did not speak Russian, and, especially after 1970, the central government sought to have Russian taught in school as the second language in the non-Russian speaking parts of the Soviet Union. Early in the history of the United States, there were Spanish-, French-, and Dutch-speaking communities. These languages were superseded by English as political domination of the country fell to Britain.

When a nation is formed and a national language is established without the willing compliance of local language/culture communities, the resistance of the communities to the political development is frequently expressed by an intense interest in the local language and customs. The identity of the people as members of a particular group is maintained by speaking and teaching their children the "old" language and keeping up the old customs. Is this analogous to what is going on in the US right now, even though the US is not a new nation?

Over the period of the great migrations to the United States before the First World War, the goal of most immigrants was to become Americans, not "hyphenated Americans" but "melting pot Americans", not to be distinguished ethnically from other Americans. "Greenhorn," a term meaning recent immigrant, was a term of derision. Everyone wanted to look, talk, and act as though he or she had been born in America and preferably to educated parents. Today, all newcomers to the US may not share this goal.

Learning a Second Language

France, a nation intent on preserving its language, has been the new land for many immigrants and "guest workers," a euphemism meaning people permitted to live and work in a country but not become its citizens. All of these immigrants have been taught French, if it was not their mother tongue, beginning with their arrival in France. In the mid-1960s I remember seeing Yugoslavs, Spanish, and Turkish workers at the Alliance Française, the French language school, devoted to bringing about immigrant and sojourner fluency in French. (A *sojourner* is a person temporarily living, not settling in a country.)

Starting in the public primary school system in Paris, there is one school in each district (*arrondissement*) that has a class for each grade to initiate all foreign school students in the French language. Children are from many different countries and their only means of communicating with each other is their emerging French. This provides a powerful social motivation for learning and at the same time makes it unintimidating since everyone in the class is just learning French. As soon as they are fluent, the children are moved into the regular class. In 1979, a third grader and fifth grader (both boys) attended such a class in the 16th *arrondissement* in Paris. The fifth grader was placed in grade *huitième* in January. The third grader remained in the adaptation class the entire year. His parents were told that he also could have been placed in the regular class in January but the class was too crowded. The boys' father told me that by the end of the school year both boys were culturally integrated, knew the French slang, and socialized with the French children. The younger boy's English, however, was beginning to slip a little through lack of use.

In my reckoning, a person has truly acquired a second language when she can think in the language – which means when the person does not need to mentally translate into English to understand or to consciously construct an utterance in the second language in order to say something. This happens to Americans who live in a foreign country, associate mainly with speakers of the target language, read and write the target language, and avoid having anything to do with English speakers, books, and so on. Two college-age women described this experience to me, one with French and the other with Italian. After six months of total immersion in the language, schooling, and life of the foreign country – a difficult, tiring, and wearing time when they had to concentrate on forming their utterances and on listening to others – one day, each found she didn't have to work at it anymore. She didn't have to think out what she was going to say. It came naturally, just like English. This must be the experience of all those who become fluent in a second language, including all of the adult immigrants to the

United States who learn to speak, read, and write English, even though they always speak English with an accent. The processing becomes automatic, and the speaker can concentrate on what she wants to say and not on how to say it.

When a person is fluent and literate in two languages, he is bilingual. He may be a balanced bilingual, equally fluent and literate in his two languages. American college students who become bilingual in the course of spending their junior year abroad do not usually return to the United States balanced bilinguals. Even if they love the country, its language and literature, they've had a 20-year head start on English. The balanced bilingual has a long time experience with both languages. A student who looked "American" and spoke in unaccented American English one day spoke to an immigrant Chinese student in fluent (I was told) Mandarin. I hadn't recognized that her last name was Chinese, but it was. She is the daughter of a Chinese father and an American mother and has spoken both Chinese and English since she began to talk. I don't know whether she is literate in Chinese or whether she is bicultural. I would have had to ask her and I didn't. Children growing up in Canada with one French–Canadian and one English–Canadian parent are likely to grow up bilingual–bicultural.

Today, bilingualism is common in many parts of the world where countries (or speech communities) are small and where in day-to-day life, members of one speech community are in contact with members of another community. Italian, German, and French are the languages of the different cantons (states) of Switzerland. People who do business throughout the country acquire a certain fluency in the two languages that are not the principal language of their canton. I say a certain fluency because I do not want to make a claim that the Swiss become equally fluent in all languages. That depends on the extent of their use of the non-mother tongues (languages not their first language). Do they use the non-native languages only for business purposes? Do they read and write the non-native languages? The answers to these questions tell a great deal about how bilingual or trilingual a person is.

In addition to bilingualism based on speech communities in day-to-day contact, there is also the bilingualism based on learning. Second languages are acquired in the course of education and scholarly work. People become bilingual in order to work in the foreign service of their countries. They learn second languages in order to study the work of foreign scholars, poets, and scientists.

In the United States, second-language familiarity based on learning has been more widespread than bilingualism based on day-to-day contact. Typically, students in American secondary schools, and to a lesser extent in primary schools, are taught foreign languages. Foreign-language teaching has been more successful for purposes of reading and writing than for day-to-day living. When a foreign language is learned for reading and writing, the emphasis is on translation from the foreign language to English (reading) and from English to the foreign language (writing).

English as a Second Language

The foreign language concern in the US in the 1990s is the tide of non-English speakers coming to settle. The US needs to prepare to enable about a million immigrants per year to acquire English fluency and literacy. For adult immigrants who are well educated in their native language, and for children educated as well as American children of their age, prospects are good. People appropriately literate in their native language are able to transfer their literacy skills to English. Being literate in one language makes it possible to become literate in another. The great number of immigrants who are poor and poorly educated have a much less favorable educational prognosis. Those who are totally illiterate and have reached puberty will never become literate in English or any language.

All other immigrants whose literacy is low in comparison with native English speakers with comparable occupational and educational goals have the problem of "catching up" as well as acquiring English fluency and literacy. Is it better to help immigrant children:

1 Become fluent and literate in English as a first step in a level two years behind the children's grade level and then to help them catch up?
2 Tackle English in a transitional bilingual education program at the grade level appropriate for American children of the same age?
3 Tackle English at the appropriate grade in an English-speaking

class room with "pull out" English in second-language (ESL) tutoring sessions one or more times a week?

The main programs in United States public schools are (2) and (3). The program at some private schools in Paris, France, has been (1). It is not an option in confronting the problems of American public schools coping with the influx of immigrant children.

Transitional bilingual education (TBE) is, in principle, a three-year program for pupils from Haiti, Vietnam, Spanish-speaking countries, or any other linguistic group in a school district with 20 or more children eligible to be in a class. A class may have children from two grades to have the required number of students. The first year, children are to be educated three-quarters of the school day in their native language and one-quarter in English; second year, half in English and half in their native language; third year, three-quarters in English and one-quarter in their native language; fourth year, students move to a regular classroom in which English is the language of instruction.

Why is it that immigration to the United States since the 1980s is attracting such worried attention? If we look at the immigration totals for the decades of the 1880s (5,246,613) and the 1980s (7,338,062) and compare them with total US population in 1890 and 1990, we see that in 1890, when the US population was 62.9 million, almost 10 percent of the population were immigrants, and in 1990, with a total population 249.9 million, less than 1 percent were immigrants. So it is not that the US has recently been overwhelmed with a vast immigrant population. In the 1880s, 4,735,484 were from Europe, 69,942 from Asia, and of the 426,967 from America, 393,304 were from Canada, and 1,913 from Mexico. In the 1980s, 761,560 were from Europe, 2,738,157 from Asia, and of the 3,615,225 from America, 156,938 were from Canada and 1,655,643 were from Mexico. I believe it is not the numbers but rather the radical shift in the countries of origin that gives the new look to immigration (see table 11.1).

Part of the reason why the influx of non-English speaking immigrants is a source of concern is worry about jobs and taxes. In California, a law (probably non-constitutional) has been enacted which denies to some immigrants benefits like welfare and medicare, for example. California is feeling the financial pinch brought on by downsizing of the aircraft and other defense industries occasioned by the end of the Cold War. California is the destination of an unknown, but

Table 11.1 Patterns of US immigration in the 1880s and 1980s

Region and country of last residence	1881–90	1981–90
All countries	5,246,613	7,338,062
Europe	4,735,484	761,550
Austria-Hungary	353,719	24,885
Austria	226,038	18,340
Hungary	127,681	6,545
Belgium	20,177	7,066
Czechoslovakia	–	7,227
Denmark	88,132	5,370
France	50,464	32,353
Germany	1,452,970	91,961
Greece	2,308	38,377
Ireland	655,482	31,969
Italy	307,309	67,254
Netherlands	53,701	12,238
Norway-Sweden	568,362	15,182
Norway	176,586	4,164
Sweden	391,776	11,018
Poland	51,806	83,252
Portugal	16,978	40,431
Romania	6,348	30,857
Soviet Union	213,282	57,677
Spain	4,419	20,433
Switzerland	81,988	8,849
United Kingdom	807,357	159,173
Yugoslavia	–	18,762
Other Europe	682	8,234
Asia	69,942	2,738,157
China	61,711	346,747
Hong Kong	–	98,215
India	269	250,786
Iran	–	116,172
Israel	–	44,273
Japan	2,270	47,085
Korea	–	333,746
Philippines	–	548,764
Turkey	3,782	23,233

Table 11.1 Cont'd

Region and country of last residence	1881–90	1981–90
Vietnam	–	280,782
Other Asia	1,910	648,354
America	426,967	3,615,225
Canada & Newfoundland	393,304	156,938
Mexico	1,913	1,655,843
Caribbean	29,042	872,051
Cuba	–	144,578
Dominican Republic	–	252,035
Haiti	–	138,379
Jamaica	–	208,148
Other Caribbean	29,042	128,911
Central America	404	468,088
El Salvador	–	213,539
Other Central America	404	254,549
South America	2,304	461,847
Argentina	–	27,327
Colombia	–	122,849
Ecuador	–	56,315
Other South America	2,304	255,356
Other America	–	458
Africa	857	176,893
Oceania	12,574	45,205
Not specified	789	1,032

A dash indicates no separate data available.
Source: US Immigration and Naturalization Service (1993)

assumed to be very large, number of undocumented immigrants seeking to settle, work, and raise families. Undocumented immigrants are welcomed by some employers because they can be hired at below the minimum wage and/or do not receive the benefits that US citizens and documented immigrants receive. Texas, Florida, and New York, large coastal states, like California, are also the destinations of disproportionately (to other states) large numbers of immigrants, documented and not. If finding employment is difficult for US citizens, immigrants will be seen as stealing their jobs, even though immigrants take jobs like healthcare aides, dishwashers, and hospital orderlies that others will not take.

Since *Brown* v. *Board of Education*, 1964, the Bilingual Education Act of 1968, 1984 (August, 1986), and other federal and state initiatives, *de jure* (by law) discrimination in education is no longer a legal instrument of repression of ethnic (including black) minorities. This does not mean that there is equal educational opportunity for all children in the United States. In this chapter, we focus on immigrant children but notice that conditions that may negatively affect their educational prospects impinge at times on certain groups of native born Americans, in particular, lower-class Hispanics and African–Americans.

When my 12- and 14-year-old sons, with no experience or instruction in French, attended a *lycée* in a Paris suburb where French was the language of instruction, they became fluent in about two and a half months and literate to the standard of their classes, *sizième* and *troisième*, by spring. They had been well schooled in English in the United States. They had simply to transfer their educational capabilities to a new language and were motivated to do so by all the attractions of Paris for middle-class Americans which one had to acquire French to enjoy. This is the ordinary course of events when a school-aged child or young person moves to a country where a language not her mother tongue is spoken and is the language of instruction in school. As long as the child is motivated to become fluent and literate in the new language and is fluent and literate (at appropriate grade level in her mother tongue) this will be the case.

Non-native languages, like mother tongues and father tongues in bilingual families, are acquired rather than learned, if they come to function for communication like a native language. We know that acquisition comes about "naturally" in prepubescent children in the course of their daily lives if they interact in a friendly way with speakers of the target language, and it is the language of instruction in school. Adults, people in secondary school and older, may consciously strive to master the target language. Immersing oneself in the community of speakers, reading material in the target language, going to movies and plays in which the dialogue is in the target language are useful. What about studying the grammatical rules of the language and memorizing words in the language? The only words one will remember are words one uses and is interested in, just like words in one's first language. If I go to the dictionary or thesaurus to look up a word, it's because I want to use it and either it's not a word of whose meaning I feel sure or I am searching for a way to express an idea or feeling that I can't readily verbalize. I am extending or making my semantic knowledge more precise in whichever language I am working.

Sometimes people speaking a second language continue to use a grammatical form from their first language, not grammatical in the second language. For example, Russian does not have the definite article *the*. The grammatical rule is to use the definite article for a referrent, i.e. *the ball*, when the audience can be assumed to know what ball is being referred to. If I say, "John caught a fly but then he dropped the ball", the hearer knows what ball is being referred to. If I say, "I was crossing the street and a ball rolled in front of me," the hearer is being informed that this ball's appearance is to be regarded as unanticipated by me.

Russian has only one present tense which is used for the timeless present, "I know the rule" and the historical present, the present progressive, "I am learning to play." A native Russian speaker I know who acquired English as an adult has opted for always applying the rule, absent in Russian. He always uses the definite article and the present progressive in speaking English, even though he converses generally with native English speakers. If he wanted to improve his English grammar, he would need to monitor his speech, to consciously apply the English rules, easier to do when one is writing or preparing a speech, rather than conversing (Krashen, 1982).

Acquisition of English and Cultural Integration of Immigrants

Why does the United States have a strong commitment to bilingual education programs for immigrant school children to help them make the transition from their native language to English? It might make it easier for children to become adjusted to life in a new country who may feel uprooted and unhappy with a change they do not understand or wish had not happened. It might be that until their English fluency and literacy are similar to American children of their age, immigrant children will not understand what transpires in their classes and will not learn what is being taught. Both of these reasons have contributed to the establishment of transitional bilingual education programs in the US.

In a *New York Times* article (October 24, 1994), it was reported that the New York City Board of Education had released a report concluding that immigrant students, even recent immigrants, in bilingual programs do not do as well as immigrant students educated primarily in English. There are currently 154,000 "limited English proficient" (LEP) students in New York in either bilingual programs, conducted largely in their native languages, or English as a second-language programs in which instruction is in English, with special individual or small group English tutoring sessions in addition. Different ethnic groups place different emphasis on children's learning of English. Chinese, Russian, and Korean parents want their children to learn English as a second language as rapidly as possible. Other parents, in New York Puerto Rican parents, want their children to maintain their Spanish. The report documents that about 9 of 10 Korean- or Russian-speaking students who enter either ESL or bilingual education in kindergarten learn English well enough after three years to be placed in ordinary classrooms. About 8 of 10 Chinese- and 6 of 10 Haitian Creole-speaking students and only 5 of 10 Spanish-speaking students do so. Further, at all grade levels, students in ESL programs exited the program faster than students in bilingual education programs. Children entering these programs in higher grades are less likely to be ready to be mainstreamed after three years. Although 79 percent who entered an ESL class in kindergarten, and 51 percent who began a bilingual program in kindergarten, are mainstreamed in three years, only 33 percent in ESL and 7 percent in bilingual education are mainstreamed after three years if they began in sixth grade.

The *New York Times* report doesn't explain these results but it is possible to offer explanatory variables, studied in other research, as suspects. If English is the only language used in a classroom, it becomes necessary to learn English to understand at all. In a classroom in which half of the lessons are in the student's native language this part is available to the students without their knowing English. Assuming the students are not selected into ESL rather than bilingual education because they are smarter, more motivated to succeed, we can conclude that program difference, ESL *v.* bilingual education, is the operative variable.

The *Times* states that Chinese, Korean, and Russian parents want their children to acquire English rapidly while Puerto Rican parents want their children to maintain their Spanish. Cultural and parental values affect children, their values, and motivation. Native language maintenance is a value for many immigrants and may interfere with the acquisition of English.

As more data on the success of bilingual and ESL programs becomes available, a better evaluation of relative merit can be made and the hard decisions taken. In order to best do this, educational goals must be agreed upon and the associated costs determined. One educational goal should be that each student complete his public school education and get a high school diploma. That immigrant children in bilingual classes are less likely to drop out of school than those in English-only classes is a claim made for bilingual education. Olsen reports that one of 20 students, K–12, in US schools are "limited English proficient" (Olsen, 1991, cited in Freeman and Freeman, 1992) and one in six in California (Olsen, 1991, cited in Freeman and Freeman, 1992). According to Kollars (1988), nearly 45 percent of Hispanics fail to complete high school. In the 1990s the outlook for education of disadvantaged immigrants and low-literate Hispanics and blacks is poor, and it is not clear how improvement will come about (Fox, 1990).

Whole Language for Second-language Acquisition

The whole language philosophy which has been gaining adherents as the method of choice for first-language learners can be investigated for second-language learners as well. It is called *whole language* because listening, talking, reading, and writing are undertaken as they are naturally needed to address the students' goals. All aspects of language are viewed as acquired rather than as separate skills. This perspective is highly appropriate for second language learners in school. They have acquired some competence in their native language to be transferred to English. Since they are old enough to be attending school, whole language principles are appropriate.

1   Lessons should be learner centered because "learning is the active construction of knowledge by the student" (Freeman and Freeman, 1992: 7).

2 Learning should relate to students' goals.
3 Acquisition procedes from whole to part: meanings are what powers and motivates learning. Skills are developed so the learner can use the meanings.
4 Learning takes place in social interaction.

Whether it is hard or easy to learn a second language partly depends on how the learner feels about the people who speak the language and their culture in relation to him or her. If the person (a) likes and admires the people who speak the target language; (b) wants to be friends with them; and (c) feels that they will like him or her and his or her people and be friendly, learning the target language will be easier than if the language learner has reservations about (a), (b), or (c).

When people learn a new language because they are refugees from their native lands, either because of war, persecution, or political unrest they may have mixed feelings about the country in which they settle. The customs, values, and way of life may be very different from those of their native countries. They may be homesick and unsympathetic to the ways of the people of the new country. The longing for one's native land, the feeling that one's human identity is as an Argentinian, Hungarian, and so on, creates a psychological barrier to becoming a proficient speaker of a new language. A friend who became a citizen of the United States after leaving Poland to escape the Nazis, once said to me, "If I lost my accent I wouldn't be Polish anymore. I would lose my identity." She has lived in the United States for 40 years and yet her sense of self is still tied to being Polish. However, people who choose to emigrate and become citizens of a new country may be eager for an identity as citizens of their chosen country. They may not have nostalgic feelings creating a psychological barrier to learning the new (target) language. (This will be true for many refugees also.)

Social barriers arise from factors that prevent good relations between the group who speak the target language and the group learning it. For example, there are strong, negative social attitudes separating English-speaking Americans from Spanish-speaking immigrant workers in the south-western United States. According to John Schumann (1978), a bad situation for acquiring a second language exists when the immigrant group and the population in the new country (a) have conflicting cultures; (b) have negative attitudes toward each other; and (c) do not want to see the immigrant group assimilated in the new country. Acquiring a second language is hampered further when (d) the immigrant group is large and cohesive, and (e) it does not plan to remain in the new country over a long period of time. Any one of these factors will raise a social barrier to the learning of the new language by the immigrant group.

Further Reading

Kurahachi, J. (1994) "Individual differences in learning a second language," *Japanese Journal of Education Psychology*, 42: 227–39.
   Reviews the English-language and Japanese literature on individual differences in second-language acquisition.
Letts, C. A. (1991) "Early second language acquisition: a comparison of the linguistic output of a preschool child acquiring English as a second language with that of a monolingual peer," *British Journal of Disorders of Communication*, 26: 219–34.
   Recorded linguistic behavior of two preschool children at regular intervals over a nine-month period while they were playing freely together. One subject was acquiring English as a second language; the other was a monolingual English speaker. The sociolinguistic domain was such that the subjects were likely to be motivated to communicate with each other in English. The subject for whom English was a second language was well able to interact on equal terms with his partner, despite being somewhat less advanced in some aspects of English language development by the end of the sampling period. While this subject appeared to be consolidating language skills during this time, the monolingual subjects appeared to be developing rapidly.
Magiste, E. (1992) "Second language learning in elementary and high school students. Special Issue: multilingual community," *European Journal of Cognitive Psychology*, 4: 355–65.
   Compares the developmental changes in picture naming and number naming of 77 high school and 74 elementary students (aged 6–19 years) who came from Germany to Sweden. Results provide evidence that elementary school students achieved a balanced form of bilingualism two years earlier than high school students on the picture-naming task. Naming two-digit numbers was shown to be a relatively difficult task for elementary school children. After about four years of residence in Sweden, both groups reached language balance on this task.

12
Sociolinguistics

The final chapter of this book provides a brief consideration of socio-linguistics, how cultural construction of social reality is reflected in language use. In the 1960s and into the 1970s, the Whorfian hypothesis (Whorf, 1956) was influential in sociolinguistics. B. L. Whorf proposed that the way language cuts up the world determines the reality for societies. Suppose there is a culture that labels the part of the color spectrum that we label green and blue, by one word, *grue*, will it be the case that the people of this culture see only one color rather than two? Research done by Eleanor Rosch (1973) with members of a technologically undeveloped culture in New Guinea, the Danai, who had only two color terms in their vocabulary, words meaning black and white, or more accurately, dark and light, responded with a behavior that indicated that they saw differences in colors. What had mislead researchers was their asking research subjects to respond verbally with the names of colors. A subsequent study done at the Yale Medical School with infants who had no language yet, showed sensitivity to color difference, indicating that color perception is innate or acquired very early.

The meanings we associate with colors is a cultural decision. In Western countries, brides wear white for purity, funerals require black for sadness and mourning. In Japan, brides and corpses wear white because weddings and funerals both mark endings (Dalby, 1993).

In Western culture we put objects or people in the same category on the basis of similarity defined by agreed-upon "objective" grounds, such as biological, geological, familial, or class membership in an arti-factual category like furniture, vehicles, media, etc. In other cultures, not as technologically oriented as ours, the basis for categorization may be very different. Looking at the non-Western language, Diurbal, we see a four-way classification of nouns. Each noun must be preceded by a classifier, a grammatical marker, telling which category it belongs to. In English, in most uses nouns are preceded by determiners which depend on syntax. *A* and *an* precede an indefinite singular NP like *a* monkey, *an* unexpected storm. *Some* and *any* precede plurals or mass nouns like *some* marbles or *any* snow, but in Diurbal classifiers reflect cultural values. Nouns fall in one of four categories. The *bayi* class includes men, kangaroos, possums, bats, most snakes, the moon, and so on. The *balan* class includes women, bandicoots, dogs, anything connected with fire or water, the sun, stars, and so on. The *balam* class includes all edible fruits and the plants that bear them, ferns, honey, cigarettes. The *bala* class includes body parts, meats, bees, most trees, mud, stones. What determines class membership? The first class includes human males and animals; the second, human females, birds, water and fire; the third, non-flesh food; and the fourth, everything else. Fish are in the class with men because they are seen as animals and fishing lines and *spears* because they are used to fish. Birds are not associated with animals and go in the second class because they are regarded as the spirits of dead human females. The Diurbal myth has the moon and sun as husband and wife so the sun belongs in the category with human females. If a member of an object class differs from others in an important way, usually because it is dangerous, it is put in another category. Thus the stone fish and the garfish, which are harmful, and potentially dangerous, are put in the second category along with women, water, and fire (Romaine, 1994). What can we infer about Diurbal culture from their noun classification system? A first look suggests that it is a male-dominated society with an ambivalent attitude towards women. They are important in the society, like fire, water, and sun and beautiful like the stars, but potentially dangerous like the poisonous fish.

Values reveal themselves in the sayings or proverbs of a society. We say "good as gold" when we mean an entity is valuable. In many societies, not as affluent as ours, the corresponding saying is "Good as bread." In English, we ask a person, "How old are you?" In many other countries, like France, one asks, *"Combien des ans avez vous?"* (How many years have you?) avoiding the word old. In China, "How old are you?" can be asked because old people are respected. Wisdom comes with age. In the West, we have a youth culture: growing old is a disgrace. Despite our having the question "How old are you?," we use it selectively. It's fine to ask children this question. They are proud of becoming more grown up. But sometime around the age of 30, earlier for women than men, "How old are you?" becomes a sensitive question, not frequently asked. Language use provides a window through which to view culture.

Politeness Markers

Suppose that you heard a business-like but pleasant male voice coming from an office with its door partly closed so you could not see the speaker or the person(s) to whom he was speaking. You heard the voice say,

1   Get ready to take a letter, Mary.

and several minutes later,

2   Would you mind taking this letter down to the mail room when you take yours down?

Could you guess who was being addressed in (1) and (2)? There is a reason to believe that different persons were being addressed in the two cases because (1) lacks the politeness markers that (2) has. A business man might address (1) to his secretary, and she might reply.

3   Yes, Mr Jones.

If the reponse to (2) is,

4   No problem, Chuck.

regardless of whether the voice responding is that of a man or a woman, the status relationships of Chuck Jones to the person responding with (3) and with (4) are quite different. There are tell-tale signs of the difference in the language used in the two interchanges. I have mentioned politeness markers; the other sign is the use of first names (or nicknames) as opposed to Ms and Mr plus the last name.

The situations in which politeness markers are most likely to be significant because of their presence or absence are just those of (1) and (2). One person wants a second person to do something for him or her. "Get ready to take a letter" is an *imperative*, a syntactive sentence form in English and other languages. Using the imperative form is expressing what you want done as an order or directive. Parents do this with their children. "Wash your hands," "Clean up your room," "Come to supper," "Stop that," are all imperatives frequently directed at children. And children speak this way to each other: "Get out of my way," "Help me," "Run faster," "Catch the ball."

It is offensive to adults to be addressed in the way an adult might address a child. Who does it to whom and why is it tolerated? The imperative form is used by persons of higher status and greater power when addressing persons of lower status and less power. Imperatives seem to be used less frequenty now than a generation ago. It would make an interesting study of the United States' changing social customs and beliefs reflected in language to chart the history of imperative use to request behavior of another person. I cannot provide the history of the development of polite ways of guiding other people's behaviors; instead I will give a brief analysis of the change.

How and Why the Imperative Becomes Polite

The imperative is a form of command. Its use indicates that the user expects to be obeyed. When father says, "Stop that," or the commanding officer says, "Halt," they expect the persons addressed to do as they are told. Their expectation is based on their having the power to control the behavior of the persons addressed.

5   Would you mind mailing my letter?
6   Could you please mail my letter?
7   If it's not out of your way, would you mail my letter?

Each of these implies that the control of his or her behavior is in the hands of the addressee. For the most part, this is true of adults in the United States, but there are exceptions. Soldiers have to obey their commanding officer, and if a policeman says to a person, "Pull over," "Get in the police car," "Hand it over (the gun)," the person typically does as he or she is told. Commanding officers and policemen can back up their imperatives with the power to compel obedience. Furthermore they do not view themselves as being in a friendly relationship to the person they are ordering around that will be spoiled by the imperatives.

Politeness markers get attached to imperatives because, in many instances, the person requesting behavior does not have the power to compel it; therefore, phrasing a request in a way that acknowledges that the addressee is in control of his or her own behavior is appropriate and reflects the social reality of the situation. But even in the instances where there is considerable inequality in power, politeness markers may be in evidence to foster a spirit of friendliness and cooperation. People respond differently when they are treated as equals than when treated as inferiors.

Language use reflects the values of the speech community, and in the United States polite forms of the directive are preferred to the imperative, not just in adult–adult interchanges but also when adults are speaking to children. For example, teachers say, "Do you want to collect the papers?"; "Can you shut the door?"; "Please pass the books in." "Please," "can you," and "do you want to" are ways of introducing a requested behavior while implying that the child has control over her behavior and could answer no rather than comply. Until rather recently in human history, the law has been that children are under the control of their parents and do not have the same rights as adults. It was possible for parents to behave with impunity toward their children in ways that would get them put in jail if the behavior was directed at someone outside their family. An adult may take a switch or a belt to his or her child. If the same adult hit another adult with a belt, he or she could be arrested for assault and battery.

Language use is an interpersonal behavior, and it will be consistent with other interpersonal behaviors. Socially appropriate language use is determined by the social beliefs and conventions of society. The effects of the variables, social status, age, and sex on language use have been widely studied. Power differences are implicated in the effect of each. Social interaction between persons of high and low social status, older and younger persons, and a man and woman typically reflect the dominance–submission relationship between the higher status, the older person, or the male and the lower status, the younger person, or female in Western society and in most others.

In English when a person is talking to someone, the pronouns, I, me, and you are sufficient. *I want you to marry me* is appropriate whether "I" is a worker in a factory or CEO of the company, and "you," the president's daughter or a high school drop out. German, Italian, Spanish, and French have a formal and a solidary or intimate form of *you*. In German, the formal you is *sie*, third-person singular and the solidary, *du*, second-person singular. In French, the formal *you* is the plural form, *vous*. Spanish and Italian both have formal and familiar forms for the second-person singular pronoun. In Spanish, the familiar is *tu*, the formal, *usted*. In Italian, the forms are *tu* and *Lei* (Martin and Vincent, 1988). The formal plural you, *loro*, has almost completely gone out of use. Why the plural? Because kings and heads of state tend to identify themselves with their country and consider that when they speak they speak for all, creating the royal "we." I remember an anecdote about Queen Victoria in which she is reported to have said, "We are not amused." If kings and queens call themselves "we," they must be addressed as "you," plural. The use of plural *you* as the formal term of address is a trickle down effect, not just royalty or heads of state but any high-status individual. Brown and Gilman (see Brown, 1970) have made a study of the use of the familiar and formal pronouns by speakers of French, German, and Italian. There are three different possibilities:

1   Persons exchange the formal pronoun (reciprocal use).
2   Persons exchange the familiar pronoun (reciprocal use).
3   One person uses the familiar to the other person who returns the formal pronoun (non-reciprocal use).

Relaxation of the sociolinguistic code in France began with the French Revolution. The non-reciprocal use of the *tu* and *vous* was not consistent with the *egalité* (equality) of the revolutionary motto, nor reciprocal use of *vous* with *fraternité* (brotherhood) and for awhile universal use of *tu* was advocated. This usage did not continue long after the revolution, and the pre-revolutionary pattern of usage again became prevalent until well into the nineteenth century, when, once again, non-reciprocal use of *tu* and *vous* began to give away to reciprocal use of *vous* between people who did not have affiliative relationships, and reciprocal use of *tu* for those who did. The same general pattern prevailed in Germany and Italy. But differences existed in who was seen as having affiliative relationships, according to the subjects of the research, French, German, and Italian students studying in the US, questioned about their own country.

1   In Germany, the extended family members exchange the familiar pronoun.
2   In France, peers like fellow male students but not young and elderly members of an extended family.
3   In Italy, both peers and extended family.

Brown and Gilman feel that once usage becomes largely reciprocal, there is a tendency for the scope of reciprocal use of familiar address to expand at the expense of mutual use of the formal. Does this mean that eventually all speakers of languages with a familiar and formal *you* will abandon the formal, or perhaps abandon the familiar form as has actually happened with *thee* and *thou*, the archaic, familiar, nominative and accusative forms of you in English? A student of historical linguistics might want to venture a response to the question.

Terms of Address

Another way of studying how power relationships and societal values are reflected in language use is to look at terms of address, touched on earlier in this chapter. If, for example, you read in a novel that a 9-year-old girl said to a grown man,

8   Fetch me my coat, Jim.

and the grown man answered,

9   Yes, Missy Angela.

you can figure out that Jim is a servant in a household in which Missy Angela is a child of the family that Jim serves. Further, the interchange took place in a highly stratified society in which the social gap between servant and master's family was wide and carefully respected. We can use terms of address to look at social change in the US in the same way as Brown and Gilman used the formal and familiar forms of *you*. We can see these same patterns in the use of a title (Mr, Ms, and so on) plus last name, corresponding to the formal, and first names, corresponding to the familiar.

1 Persons call each other by title plus last name (reciprocal use).
2 Persons call each other by first names (reciprocal use).
3 One person calls the other by title plus last name and is called by first name in return (non-reciprocal use).

For developmental psycholinguists, it is interesting to observe how language use by upper-class and lower-class males in conversation with one another mirrors language use by adults and children involved in discourse with each other. That is, prior to the 1960s, newly acquainted adults or adults who had only business dealings addressed each other with title plus last name; children addressed each other with first names. Adults addressed children with first names, and children addressed adults with title plus last name.

There has been a relaxation of the formality of address among adults, particularly younger adults, in the United States since the late 1960s so that a large proportion of the adult population expects to be on a first-name basis with other adults. In this relaxation of formality in address among adults, we see how social change brings about change in language use. The disillusionment of the American people with the Vietnam War manifested itself, in part, in an abandonment of former standards of appropriate formality of dress and behavior, including language usage. This change was not uniform throughout the society. Some people adhered to old standards but, since the 1970s, it has been possible to go to a theatrical or musical performance in the most prestigious theater or concert hall in the large cities of the eastern United States and see some people in formal dress and others, male and female, probably young, informally attired, some even wearing jeans. It was no longer necessary when going to the opera to "dress up," and along with relaxation of the dress code came relaxation of the sociolinguistic code.

This change is not necessarily all to the good because it obscures differences in status or role that continue and mean that some people are in positions of power and responsibility toward others. Everyone in a business being on a first-name basis does not change the fact that hiring and firing still take place at the discretion of the people in authority. A colleague told me about observing in a sixth-grade classroom where the teacher had told the students to use his first name. The teacher was hugely discomfitted when a boy in the class told him an offcolor joke. Certain expectations that go with first-name use do not match the reality of business and school.

Language and Social Class

10   I have no intention of leaving.
11   I ain't goin' nowhere.

The way we talk pretty much, not absolutely, classifies us. Looking at (6) and (7) we pick out (7) as the utterance of a person of low SES (socioeconomic status). How do we make that judgement? "I ain't goin' nowhere" lacks the syntax of standard English. It has a double negative, one of which is the non-standard *ain't*, and dropping the final *g* in *going* marks the speaker's pronounciation as non-standard. This is the utterance of a person who acquired non-standard English, indicating a low SES home, and whose schooling failed to standardize his or her speech, indicating little educational opportunity or little desire to become educated or to sound "middle class." In the United States, there are different dialects spoken in different regions, social classes, and age groups. We recognize that the speech of people living in the southern US, and some people from Brooklyn, NY, and Boston, MA, sound different from the way Ted Koppel, Diane Sawyer, Connie Chung, and other TV news anchor persons speak. TV news anchors, whatever the country, use the standard version of the speech of their country, be it American English, British English, French, or Hebrew. TV anchor person speech tends to homogenize the speech of a country. Younger, urban, educated persons are most likely to speak the standard dialect.

A path-breaking study (Labov, 1966) established the social-class pattern of the occurrence of post-vocalic *r* (*r* sounded after vowels) in Manhattan. The research is path breaking because of its clever method for getting empirical data. Labov picked three department stores which he ascertained from their prices and advertisements catered to upper SES (Saks Fifth Avenue), middle SES (Macy's), and lower SES (Klein's) customers. His subjects were clerks working on the first floors of the stores. He approached each research subject (clerk) and asked for the location of a department he knew to be on the fourth floor. He asked again after the clerk had responded, "Fourth floor," to get two samples from each respondent. The second would be the subject's careful speech since Labov feigned that he had not understood the first response.

He was investigating the occurrence of the sound /r/ in *fourth* and *floor*. His hypothesis was that stores would employ clerks whose dialect matched the store's customers' and that occurrence of postvocalic *r*, *fourth* rather than *fɔth* and *floor* rather than *flɔ*, would be higher in ascending order of SES. His data confirmed the hypothesis, the percentages of occurrence of post-vocalic /r/ were 12, 20, and 32 in ascending order of SES.

The Effect of Social Class on Language Use in Schools

It has been proposed that use of the imperative to direct or guide behavior is linked to social class (Bernstein, 1975; cited in McConnell-Ginet, 1984). Specifically, Bernstein, a British sociologist, has stated that the frequent use of short commands, that is, simple imperatives, is one of the features that characterizes lower socioeconomic status (SES) language use. The public school in the United States is predominately a middle-class institution; American teachers and administrators in the latter part of the twentieth century are primarily from middle SES backgrounds and have been educated in the colleges of the United States, which are also predominately middle-class institutions. There is a preference on the part of middle SES persons not to order other persons around, and this extends to the treatment of school children. This means not using simple imperatives to guide the children's behavior. In my observations of the interaction of preschool children and teachers, I have rarely heard a simple imperative from teacher to child except when there was immediate physical danger; even then, there typically followed an explanation of the danger and how the child was involved. "Come here, Bill," followed by, "That was a dangerous place to stand. Mary Ann's swing could have knocked you over," said a teacher as she and Bill watched Mary Ann's swinging. Usually children's behavior is guided by teacher's speech acts in which the behavior the teacher desires from the child is politely and indirectly specified. For example, a preschool teacher said to a girl riding a tricycle, "Jean, it's about time to put the bikes away," meaning: put your bike away. To another child who was beginning to climb up the slide instead of going up by way of steps, she said, "That's a one-way slide," meaning: go up the steps. I think that children whose home experience has not included the use of politeness markers and indirect directives to guide their behavior may be confused by these in school. They may not understand that "Would you like to clean up now?" or "Isn't it about time to work on your spelling?" mean "Do it," even though they sound as though they mean, "You decide."

A study of children's responses to questions about how they would get another child or their teacher to return something that belonged to them provides data on middle socioeconomic status children's use of directives (Montes, 1978). The children were kindergarteners and preschoolers, and first, second and third graders. They were interviewed individually to find out how they would get a person to return something that belonged to them. Most of the children would say something to get back their ruler or dog or whatever the object was. However, a few said that they would grab it or use some other non-verbal means to secure the return of their paint brush or hammer. Montes (1978) categorizes the responses of the children who responded with a verbal means of getting back their property into direct, indirect, and inferred means. Direct and indirect correspond quite well to imperatives and to interrogatives that begin, "Would you mind," "Can you," and so on. The inferred category is made up of rights and reasons. Rights are responses based on ownership ("That's my pencil"), permission ("Teacher said I could keep the hammer until Monday"), and turntaking ("You've had your turn"). Reasons are responses like, "The longer you keep her (subject's dog) the hairier you'll get," as the child said to the teacher to secure the return of his dog. The preschool examples, "It's about time to put the bikes away," and "That's a one-way slide," would fall into the reasons category of this research and be inferred directives.

The middle SES children who were the subjects in Montes' (1978) research responded with a small percentage of direct directives (simple imperatives) as the means they would use in getting another person to return something that belonged to them. Since this was true for even the preschool and kindergarten children, it appears that avoiding the direct directive is learned in middle SES homes from the way the children's behavior is guided by their parents. Use of indirect and

Table 12.1 Frequency (%) of directive strategies by type and grade

	Grade				
	PS	*K*	*1*	*2*	*3*
Direct	9	13	4	16	15
Indirect	36	48	56	43	31
Inferred	54	39	37	37	52
Total children	78	80	111	110	85

PS = preschool; K = kindergarten.
Source: Montes (1978)

inferred directives seem to be about equally favored means for getting property returned. There are no comparable data for lower SES children to make a comparison of frequency of type of directive strategies. Thus I cannot say whether lower SES children would propose imperatives (direct directives) with greater frequency than middle SES children as implied by Bernstein's (1975) theories. It should be remembered that Montes' research is not a naturalistic study of the actual use of directives by children but rather a study of the frequency of directives the children said to the experimenter that they would use to get their property returned. It could be argued that all table 12.1 tells us is that middle-class children as young as preschoolers know what the socially desirable directives are in an environment in which middle SES adult standards of politeness prevail. Actual behavior may differ from the socially desirable with a higher percentage of direct directives, like "gimme back my doll," spoken than the children in this study say they use. What may be crucially important is knowing what the socially desirable directives are so that, when the teacher says "Do you want to pick up the crayons?" the child spoken to knows what is expected of him. Will lower SES children know this?

I have some evidence that leads me to say that they will. In doing a study of middle and lower SES children and mothers called "The verbal environment provided by mothers for their very young children" (Holzman, 1974), I found no class-linked differences in use of indirect, inferred, and direct directives. But I had only two mother–child pairs representing each class.

I have more compelling indirect evidence that lower SES children may not have had the home experience necessary to understand indirect and inferred directives. In a comparative study of language use by white, lower SES and middle SES preschoolers, Landau (1970) found significant differences in language use by the two groups of children. Landau studied 13 matched pairs of children, seven female and six male pairs, each pair-matched on IQ (Stanford–Binet) and age. IQs ranged from 100 to 130, ages from 3 years and 4 months to 5 years and 1 month. There were no significant mean differences in sex, age, or IQ between the middle and lower SES groups. The lower SES preschoolers had been in a suburban Head Start program in Massachusetts and the middle SES preschoolers in a university-affiliated preschool in the same geographic area. Landau obtained a 20-minute spontaneous speech sample from each child, sampled across the variety of free activity periods in each class. Samples were taped and hand recorded by Landau. She states that she had been the assistant teacher in the Head Start group all year so that whatever inhibition young children experienced from the presence of a strange adult in their classroom would have affected the middle SES rather than the lower SES children.

Landau's findings comparing characteristics of the children's spontaneous speech are presented in table 12.2. Even though the children are matched for sex, age, and IQ, middle SES children's spontaneous

Table 12.2 Spontaneous speech: characteristics of lower and middle SES preschoolers

	Lower SES	Middle SES	Significance level
No. of responses	63	70	n.s.
No. of words	241	297	0.05
Mean of five longest responses (no. of words)	8	9	0.02
No. of prepositions, adverbs and adjectives	21	27	0.05
No. of personal pronouns	34	40	n.s.
No. of complex sentences	4	7	0.02

SES = socioeconomic status.
Source: Landau (1970)

speech is more complex and better developed than that of lower SES children. Middle SES children's syntactic development is also in advance of that of lower SES children.

Landau attributes her findings mainly to differences in maternal behavior and in home environment. Landau was able to observe the interaction of middle SES mothers and children when mothers picked their children up from preschool at noon. Mothers greeted children, asked what they had done at school, and talked about different afternoon plans. Landau observed lower SES mothers as they took turns helping out in the Head Start class. "Even though mothers were supposed to be helping with the whole group, they primarily watched their own children's behavior and verbally jumped on them if they made a movement unacceptable to the mother, even though it was permitted by the teacher. Giving no explanation, a mother would say, 'Stop it,' or 'Be quiet'" (Landau, 1970: 38).

Landau was unable to visit any middle SES homes, but I think we can go along with the assumption that the middle SES homes would provide better settings for language development than the lower SES homes. In the lower SES homes she visited, Landau noticed

> an unusually high noise level. These homes were in a housing project and, in addition to a lot of noise in each apartment (that of television, many siblings, birds, and other animals), there was a tremendous noise level from the neighboring apartments and the street outside. In general, there appeared to be at least one argument of some sort sifting in through the walls or windows. (Landau, 1970: 37)

In my judgment, the differences Landau found in mother–child interaction and noise level of the homes, which adversely effected language use by her sample lower SES children, would also interfere with learning about indirect and inferred directives. It is not SES itself, but the quality of experience, that fosters or impedes development of language use. Experience in school with indirect and inferred directives, with time, will bring about their understanding by children who have not had experience with them at home. But initially, lack of understanding contributes to the feeling of not being at home in the strange, new world of school. In my house, we kept up the custom of my German-speaking ancestors of saying *gesundheit* (to your health) to a person who had sneezed. The person would respond with *danke schön* (thank you). When I started kindergarten, I rapidly found out that nobody except me said *gesundheit* and *danke schön*, and I assumed that nobody said "please" and "thank you" either. This is another difference in language use, not SES linked, but linked to ethnicity.

Sex as a Sociolinguistic Variable

Language use in English and many other languages has had a pervasive sexist bias. We have been known as "mankind" rather than "humankind" over the centuries. Our language is so locked into sexist usage that we have to consciously avoid the pronouns *he, his,* and *him* in referring back to an unspecified human being – the baby, the child, the adult. We say automatically, "When the child starts school, he may miss his afternoon nap." Since the 1970s we have become increasingly sensitive to sexist language; *mankind* has become *humankind; chairmen* have become *chairpersons,* and in the psycholinguistic literature, many writers consistently use *she,* hers, and her where *he, his,* and *him* would formerly have been used. In addition to the bias resulting from referring to human beings as mankind, vocabulary, grammars, and style of discourse have female and male characteristics, which may be given sexist interpretations. Vocabulary reflects differences between the man's world and the woman's world; or, more prosaically, differences in female and male vocabularies are reflections of differences in sex roles, occupations, and interests. We might be surprised to hear a man call his 12-year-old son "honey" or even "hon." It's all right for a father to call his baby boy "honey" but some people might worry that a father's use of "honey" to a 12-year-old son might interfere with the son's developing manliness. It's all right for mothers to call their sons "honey" because it's a cross-sex relationship, and in this relationship males may continue to be called "honey" all their lives. In years past, we would have expected women's vocabularies to be replete with cooking, sewing, child-rearing, and housekeeping terms. As Conklin (1978) points out, a man whose vocabulary has a large complement of any of these sets of terms will be assumed to be a professional in his field. If he has a large cooking vocabulary, he must be a chef; a large child-rearing vocabulary, a pediatrician. Until the 1970s, women, for the most part, were not professionals, and thus a large complement of profession-related terms in a woman's vocabulary would be unexpected and perhaps viewed negatively.

In the 1990s, women have become much more visible in former bastions of male provenance. There is still a glass ceiling keeping women from the top echelons of corporate America and the armed forces, but women direct films, head non-profit foundations, are Supreme Court Justices, senators, and a woman was chief prosecutor in the O. J. Simpson case. Even so, we have not yet achieved true social parity of the sexes. Even though the unidentified individual is no longer typically *he*, we can see from discourse in which men and women and boys and girls participate that men tend to dominate. In cross-sex conversations, men interrupt women, initiate conversation, and introduce new topics more frequently than women. This occurs because women more than men reliably respond to men in conversation rather than introducing a new topic or interrupting. Men and women have different orientations in conversations. Men strive to make points, to take the conversation in the direction of their interests. Women respond to others in a conversation, contributing to the established topic. Swacker (1979, cited in McConnell-Ginet, 1984) and Zimmerman and West (1975) found men's questions from the floor after a conference paper much more likely than women's to introduce new material and women's more likely to offer corroborating evidence or to ask a question to clarify what the speaker had said. In women's conversations, the group collaborates on a topic. Do these findings indicate that it's a man's world – men have taken control – or do the findings suggest that the psychosocial makeup of males and females is very different, as those who propose that biology is destiny imply.

Leeper (1991) studied the effect in samples of 138 5- and 7-year-olds, of own gender, partner's gender, and age on occurrence of collaborative and controlling speech acts as dyads interacted. He found that collaborative speech acts and cooperative exchanges were the most common discourse strategies in all dyads, for example, "I'll help you with that," "I need your help," rather than "You jerk," "I don't care." Older females used them proportionately more than any other group. This reflected an increase in collaborative speech for female dyads but not for mixed or male dyads.

Controlling speech acts were more common in male than in female dyads at 7 years and domineering exchanges more common in male dyads at both ages. Collaborative speech acts and cooperative exchanges for girls and controlling speech acts and domineering exchanges for boys were more likely in same gender than in mixed gender dyads. In mixed gender dyads, girls became more controlling, boys more collaborative at the age of 7. The interpersonal styles of boys and girls are consistent with the traditional socialization processes that emphasize separation and independence training for boys and closeness and interpersonal cohesion for girls.

In Leeper's (1991) research, the findings suggest that the foundations for adult discourse are laid in young children's socialization experience, not in biology. As they grow older, their behavior becomes more distinct because the girls become more affiliative. At 5, they were more like the boys.

Ethnic Stereotyping

In Paris, I sat in a café with a French Canadian couple who had just left Quebec to live in France. The young woman told me she had left Quebec because the anglophones were so disparaging of the francophones. One had said to her after she had said something in her French Canadian dialect of French, "Talk white." In Quebec in the late 1950s, 80 percent of the population were francophones, 20 percent anglophones who had the high social status. Francophones usually worked for anglophones who were not interested in learning French. One way, bilingualism prevailed and francophones spoke English with varying degrees of skill. The situation appalled a McGill professor who launched a research program to find ways to change the prevailing lack of community feeling of the two groups (Lambert, 1991). To demonstrate that ethnic stereotyping of the francophones was involved, Lambert devised the "matched guise" research technique. Listeners hear a short passage first in one of their languages, say English, and subsequently in the other, say French. The passages are read by the same perfectly bilingual speaker, a fact that the listeners are not told. Listeners are then asked to evaluate personality characteristics of the person reading each passage, using voice cues. We do this as a matter of course. We hear a person speaking whom we do not know and we get impressions of what she is like from the way she looks and the way she sounds. If we can't see her, we have only her voice and what she is saying as clues.

Lambert (1991) based his research on this. He asked various groups of people to judge the personalities of male and female perfect bilinguals reading various short passages in English, Parisian French, and French-Canadian French. Both English-Canadian and French-Canadian respondents evaluated the English-Canadian guise more favorably than the French-Canadian. The English-Canadian guise samples were rated as being better looking, taller, more intelligent, more dependable, more ambitious, and having more character. Although English-Canadians rated English-Canadian guise speech as kinder, French-Canadians rated French-Canadian guise as kinder and also more religious. English-Canadians had not been asked to rate the latter. This research revealed a widely held stereotype in Quebec, held not only by the English-Canadian community, but by the French-Canadian as well. This research was carried out in the 1950s, but unhappily in a follow-up study (Genesse and Holobow, 1989) the findings were confirmed. In the 1990s and beyond, the issues arising from multi-cultural multi-lingualism in most countries of the world must be resolved.

Further Reading

Anderson, A. H., Clark, A. and Mullin, J. (1994) "Interactive communication between children: learning how to make language work in dialogue," *Journal of Child Language*, 21: 439–63.
    Investigates the development of interactive communication skills. Success is found to relate to the active involvement of both participants: asking/ answering questions, volunteering information, and responding sensitively to contributions from partners.
Jespersen, O. (1956) *Growth and Structure of the English Language* (Garden City, NY: Doubleday).
    How English developed over time as the result of invasions and the Latin influence, especially during the Renaissance.
McCrum, R., Cran, W. and MacNeil, R. (1986) "Black on white," *The Story of English*, ch. 6 (New York, Viking).
    How American English has been given vividness by the African-Americans in the United States.
Neuman, S. and Roskos, K. (1992) "Literacy objects as cultural tools: effects on children's literacy behaviors in play," *Reading Research Quarterly*, 27: 203–25.
    Looking at emergent literacy in early childhood.

Glossary

androgenous having both male and female characteristics.

anglophone English speaker.

aphasia loss or impairment of the ability to use or understand speech.

cognitive having to do with mental processes; knowing and thinking.

comment a verbalization that is a remark concerning a topic; a discourse as opposed to a syntactic category.

conditioning a procedure by which an individual is caused to produce (or refrain from) a behavior by the association of the behavior with a reward (positive reinforcement) if the behavior is being encouraged or with a punishment (negative reinforcement) if the behavior is being discouraged.

corpora several collections of utterances.

corpus a collection of utterances.

critical period a biologically determined period in which an organism is capable of acquiring a particular behavior. Certain aspects of human language appear to have to be acquired before puberty.

discourse a sequence of utterances by one or more persons in which communication of thought takes place in a more or less orderly way.

documented, undocumented immigrants people seeking to establish residence in a country where they lack citizenship, with or without appropriate legal documents.

ESL English as a second language.

ethnic identity, ethnicity largely self-defined membership in a cultural, religious, national group.

francophone French speaker.

gene complex a group of functional hereditary units.

gloss define, explain, provide a running commentary for.

grammar all the rules (phonological, semantic, and syntactic) for a language. Rule systems based on what speakers of a language do are called *descriptive grammars*.

grammatical speech or writing in accord with the rules of the language.

holophrase one-word sentence.

hominoid a primate species of which modern man, *Homo sapiens*, is the only extant representative.

illocutionary force utterer's meaning or what the person means by his or her utterance; the function of the utterance.

linguistic ellipsis an utterance that leaves out some of the words necessary for a complete sentence, but which is linguistically well formed because the syntactically correct sentence can be constructed from the linguistic ellipsis and the preceding sentence in the discourse, using the rules of English grammar. Example:

1 Previous utterance: *I want a cookie.*
2 Linguistic ellipsis: *I do too.*
3 Correct sentence based on (1) and (2): *I want a cookie too.*

linguistics the study of language as a rule-governed system, including its rules governing speech sounds (phonological rules), sentence structure (syntactical rules), and use and meanings of words and sentences (pragmatic and semantic rules).

mean length of utterance (MLU) the number of words per utterance for a group of utterances; for example, a sample of utterances by a 2-year-old child. MLU is frequently used as an indicator of grammatical complexity of utterances because more grammatically complex utterances require more words than less grammatically complex utterances.

meta-cognitive awareness self-monitoring of thinking.

module, modular separate mental domain, brain structure and process specifically governing, e.g. language.

morpheme smallest meaning-bearing unit in a language. In English, the morpheme is usually a word, but suffixes like *ed* marking the past tense (*walk, walked*) or the plural *s* (*apple, apples*) are also morphemes.

morphological evolution   evolution of structure and form of an organism, excluding function.

mother tongue   one's native language.

occasion meaning   the circumstance or activity to which a particular verbalization becomes linked; for example, "bye bye" becomes linked to leave-taking.

orthographically   spelled in the written (English) alphabet.

performatives   acts that are accomplished simply by saying the words appropriate to the occasion, as when a judge says to the prisoner at the conclusion of the trial, "I sentence you to ten years in prison."

phonemic   the speech sounds that are contrastive in a language. For example /lut/ and /rut/ are different words in English because /l/ and /r/ are different phonemes. Japanese does not have separate phonemes /l/ and /r/, so a native Japanese speaker hearing *loot* and *root* would not know from the sound of the words said, without clues provided by context, that they were different words.

phonetic   relating to speech sounds.

phonology   having to do with the sound pattern of a language, its phonemic structure, and the stress and pitch patterns that mark its syntactic structure.

phylogenetic order   order of evolutionary development.

presyntactic   verbalizations that are not syntactically well formed (grammatically correct).

proposition, propositional content   specifies an idea, person, or object and makes a comment (says something) about it.

psycholinguistics   study of language as a psychological as well as a linguistic topic.

referential meaning   a word or phrase has referential meaning if it names an object.

reinforcement   the reward, in the case of positive reinforcement, or the punishment, for negative reinforcement, used to condition a behavior of an animal (including human beings).

secondary consciousness   the capacity to take one's thoughts, feelings, goals, etc. as objects of thought as well as the thoughts, feelings, etc. of others.

semantic   having to do with the linguistic meaning of words and sentences.

sociolinguistics the study of language use as it is affected by variables that influence social behavior, such as sex, age, and social status.

speech act a way of analyzing verbalizations, which contrasts with linguistic analysis.

syntactic markers (1) the variable parts of words, like suffixes, that indicate the plural of nouns, the past tense of regular verbs, and so on; (2) order of words in a sentence that, in English for example, indicates which noun is the subject of the verb and which the object.

syntactic–semantic meaning the meaning of a sentence in the English language as opposed to utterer's meaning, or what the person means by his or her utterance, the function of the utterance.

syntactic system rules for generating grammatically correct word strings.

syntax the set of rules that determines the way linguistic units, like words, can be combined to produce other linguistic units, like noun phrases, verb phrases, and sentences.

taxonomic system of principles for classifying into categories.

theory of mind currently used to describe development of secondary consciousness in children.

topic some languages do not have grammars whose basic unit is the sentence which requires a verb as English does. Well-formed utterances in these languages may not contain verbs. The linguistic unit in these languages analogous to subject in English – what the utterance is about – is called the *topic*.

utterance a word or words spoken one after the other to form a group; an utterance is not necessarily syntactically well formed.

whole language method of teaching reading and writing (literacy) not as separate skills but in relation to functions of language use.

References

Adams, M. J. (1990) *Beginning to Read: Thinking and Learning about Print.* Cambridge, Mass.: MIT Press.

Adams, M. J. and Collins, A. (1979) "A schematic view of reading," in R. O. Freedle (ed.), *New Directions in Discourse Processing.* Norwood, NJ: Ablex.

Anderson, E. (1986) "Acquisition of register variation by Anglo-American children," in B. Schieffelin and E. Oehs (eds), *Language Socialization across Cultures.* Cambridge: Cambridge University Press.

Anderson, R. (1981) "The role of knowledge in reading comprehension," paper presented to the National Institute of Education, Reading Synthesis Meeting, Washington, DC, September 23–26.

Anglin, J. (1977) *Word, Object and Conceptual Development.* New York: Norton.

Anglin, J. (1993) "Vocabulary development: a morphological analysis," *Monographs of the Society for Research in Child Development*, no. 158 (10): 238.

August, D. (1986) "Bilingual Education Act, Title II of the education amendments of 1984," *Washington Report*, SRCD 1, no. 5.

Austin, J. L. (1962) *How to do Things with Words.* London: Oxford University Press.

Babbitt, N. (1975) *Tuck Everlasting.* New York: Bantam Books.

Bates, E. and MacWhinney, B. (1987) "Competition, variation, and language learning," in B. MacWhinney (ed.), *Mechanics of Language Acquisition.* Hillsdale, NJ: Lawrence Erlbaum.

Bates, E. and MacWhinney, B. (1989) "Functionalism and the competition model," in B. MacWhinney and E. Bates (eds), *The Crosslinguistic Study of Sentence Processing.* Cambridge: Cambridge University Press.

Bates, E., Camaioni, L. and Volterra, V. (1975) "The acquisition of performatives prior to speech," *Merrill-Palmer Quarterly*, 21: 205–26.

Bates, E., Bretherton, I. and Snyder, L. (1988) *From First Words to Grammar*. Cambridge: Cambridge University Press.

Berko, J. (1958) "The child's learning of English morphology," *Word*, 14: 150–77.

Berkoff, M. (1977) "Social communication in canids: evidence for the evolution of a stereotyped mammalian display," *Science*, 197: 1097–9.

Bernstein, B. (1975) *Class, Codes and Control*. London: Routledge and Kegan Paul.

Bickerton, D. (1990) *Language and Species*. Chicago: University of Chicago Press.

Bloom, P. (1991) "What does language acquisition tell us about language evolution," *Behavioral and Brain Sciences*, 14: 553–4.

Bonner, J. T. (1980) *Evolution of Culture in Animals*. Princeton, NJ: Princeton University Press.

Bower, T. (1966) "The visual world of infants," *Scientific American*, 215: 80–9.

Bowlby, J. (1969) *Attachment*. New York: Basic Books.

Brown, R. (1970) *Psycholinguistics*. New York: Free Press.

Brown, R. (1973) *A First Language: the Early Stages*. Cambridge, Mass.: Harvard University Press.

Carrier, J. and Leet, H. (1972) "Effects of context upon children's referential development," unpublished paper, Tufts University.

Carter, A. L. (1975) "The transformation of sensory-motor morphemes into words: a case study of the development of 'more' and 'mine'," *Journal of Child Language*, 2: 233–50.

Chall, J. (1967) *Learning to Read: the Great Debate*. New York: McGraw-Hill.

Chandler, M., Fritz, A. and Hala, S. (1989) "Small scale deceit," *Child Development*, 60: 1263–77.

Chomsky, N. (1965) *Aspects of the Theory of Syntax*. Cambridge, Mass.: MIT Press.

Conklin, N. F. (1978) "The language of the majority," in M. A. Lowrie and N. F. Conklin (eds), *A Pluralistic Nation: the Language Issue in the United States*. Rowley, Mass.: Newbury House.

Cook, V. J. (1988) *Chomsky's Universal Grammar*. Oxford: Basil Blackwell.

Cosmides, L. and Tooby, J. (1992) "Cosmic adaptations for social exchange," in J. Barker, L. Cosmides and J. Tooby (eds), *The Adapted Mind*. New York: Oxford University Press.

Crabtree, M. and Powers, J. (comp.) (1991) *Language Files: Materials for an Introduction to Language*. Columbus, Ohio: Ohio University Press.

Crook, J. H. (1980) *The Evolution of Human Consciousness*. Oxford: Oxford University Press.

Cross, T. G. (1977) "Mother's speech adjustments: the contribution of selected child listener variables," in C. Snow and C. Ferguson (eds), *Talking to Children: Language Input and Acquisition*. Cambridge: Cambridge University Press.

Dalby, L. (1993) *Kimono: Fashioning Culture*. New Haven, Conn.: Yale University Press.

Darwin, C. (1871) *The Descent of Man*. New York: Modern Library, 1982.

Darwin, C. (1895) *On the Origin of Species by Means of Natural Selection*. Franklin Center, PA: Franklin Library, 1975.

Denes, P. and Pinson, E. (1973) *The Speech Chain: the Physics and Biology of Spoken Language*. Garden City, NY: Anchor Press/Doubleday.

Diamond, J. (1992) *The Third Chimpanzee*. New York: Harper Collins.

Donahue, M. (1986) "Phonological constraints in the emergence of two-word utterances," *Journal of Child Language*, 13: 209–31.

Dore, J. (1978) "Cognition and communication in language acquisition and development," paper presented at Boston University Conference on Language Development.

Edelman, G. (1987) *Neural Darwinism*. New York: Basic Books.

Edelman, G. (1989) *The Remembered Present: a Biological Theory of Consciousness*. New York: Basic Books.

Eilers, P. D. (1980) "Infant speech perception: history and mystery," in *Child Psychology, vol. 2: Perception*. New York: Academic Press.

Eimas, P. D. (1985) "Perception of speech in early infancy," *Scientific American*, 252: 46–62.

Entwistle, D. (1969) "Subcultural differences in children's language development," *International Journal of Psychology*, 3: 13–32.

Erreich, A. (1980) "The acquisition of inversion in 'wh' questions: what evidence the child uses?," unpublished doctoral dissertation, City University of New York.

Ferguson, C. (1977) "Baby talk as a simplified register," in C. Snow and C. Ferguson (eds), *Talking to Children: Language Input and Acquisition*. Cambridge: Cambridge University Press.

Fernald, A. (1992) "Human maternal vocalizations to infants as biologically relevant signals," in J. Barkow, L. Cosmides and J. Tooby (eds), *The Adapted Mind*. New York: Oxford University Press.

Fernald, A., Traute, T., Dunn, J., Papansek, M., Boysson, B. and Fuleni, I. (1989) "A cross language study of prosodic modifications in mothers' and fathers' speech to preverbal infants," *Journal of Child Language*, 16: 477–501.

Fox, B. (1990) "Antecedents of illiteracy," *Social Policy Report*, SRCD, IV, no. 4.

Freeman, Y. S. and Freeman, D. E. (1992) *Whole Language for Second Language Learners*. Portsmouth, NH: Heinemann.

Fromkin, V. and Rodman, R. (1978) *An Introduction to Language*, 2nd edn. New York: Holt, Rinehart and Winston.

Gallup, G. G. (1970) "Chimpanzees: self-recognition," *Science*, 167: 86–7.

Gallup, G. G. and Suarez, S. R. (1986) "Self-awareness and the emergence of minds in humans and other primates," in J. Sues and A. G. Greenwald (eds), *Psychological Perspectives on the Self*, vol. 3, pp. 3–26. Hillsdale, NJ: Lawrence Erlbaum.

Gardner, B. T. and Gardner, R. A. (1971) "Two-way communication with an infant chimpanzee," in A. M. Schrier and F. Stolnitz (eds), *Behavior of Non-human Primates*, vol. 4. New York: Academic Press.

Gardner, H. (1983) *Frames of Mind*. New York: Basic Books.

Gardner, R. A., Gardner, B. T. and van Canfort, T. E. (eds) (1989) *Teaching Sign Language to Chimpanzees*. Albany: State University of New York Press.

Genesse, F. and Holobow, N. (1989) "Change and stability in intergroup perceptions," *Journal of Language and Social Psychology*, 8: 17–38.

Gentner, D. (1977) "If a tree had a knee where would it be?," *Papers and Reports on Child Language Development*, 13: 157–64.

Gentner, D. (1978) "What looks like a jiggy and acts like a zimbo?," *Papers and Reports on Child Language Development*, 15.

Gentner, D. (1988) "Metaphor as structure mapping: the relational shift," *Child Development*, 59: 47–59.

Gentner, D. and Imai, M. (1994) "A further examination of the shape bias in early naming," paper presented at Child Language Research Forum, Stanford University, April 16.

Gessell, A. (1940) *The First Five Years of Life*. New Haven, Conn.: Yale University Press.

Gleason, J. (ed.) (1993) *Development of Language*. New York: Macmillan.

Gleitman, L. (1990) "The structural sources of verb meaning," *Language Acquisition*, 1: 3–35.

Glucksberg, S. and Keysar, R. (1990) "Understanding metaphorical comparisons: beyond similarity," *Psychological Review*, 97: 3–18.

Goldner, J. (1981) "Four mother–infant dyads: turn taking and the role of rising intonation in infant language acquisition," unpublished master's thesis, Tufts University.

Goodall, J. (1971) *In the Shadow of Man*. Boston: Houghton Mifflin.

Goodman, K., Goodman, Y. and Flores, B. (1979) *Reading in the Bilingual Classroom: Literacy and Bi-literacy*. Rosslyn, VA: National Clearing House for Bilingual Education.

Goswami, V. and Bryant, P. (1989) *Phonological Skills and Learning to Read*. Hove, East Sussex: Lawrence Erlbaum.

Gould, S. J. (1980) *The Panda's Thumb*. New York, Norton.

Graesser, A. C., Singer, M. and Trabasso, T. (1994) "Constructing inferences from narrative text comprehension," *Psychological Review*, 101: 371–96.

Greenfield, P. (1991) "Language tools and brain: the ontogeny and phylogeny of hierarchically organized sequential behavior," *Behavioral and Brain Sciences*, 14: 531–95.

Greenfield, P. and Smith, S. (1976) *Structure of Communication in Early Language Development*. New York: Academic Press.

Grice, H. P. (1957) "Meaning," *Philosophical Review*, 66: 377–88.

Grice, H. P. (1968) "Utterer's meaning, sentence-meaning and word-meaning," *Foundations of Language*, 4 (3): 225–42.

Grice, H. P. (1989) *Studies in the Way of Words*. Cambridge, Mass.: Harvard University Press.

Halliday, M. (1975) *Learning How to Mean*. New York: Elsevier.

Hatcher, P. J., Halme, C. and Ellis, A. W. (1994) "Ameliorating early reading failure by integrating the teaching of reading and phonological skills: the phonological linkage hypothesis," *Child Development*, 15: 41–57.

Herrnstein, R. J. (1982) "Stimuli and the texture of experience," *Neuroscience and Biobehavioral Reviews*, 6: 105–17.

Herrnstein, R. J. (1990) "Levels of stimulus control," *Cognition*, 37: 133–66.

Herrnstein, R. J., Loveland, D. and Cable, C. (1976) "Natural concepts in pigeons," *Journal of Experimental Psychology, Animal Behaviour Processes*, 2: 285–311.

Holzman, M. (1973) "The use of interrogative forms in the verbal interaction of three mothers and their children," *Journal of Psycholinguistic Research*, 1: 311–37.

Holzman, M. (1974) "The verbal environment provided by mothers for their very young children," *Merrill-Palmer Quarterly*, 20: 31–42.

Holzman, M. (1981) "Where is under? From memories of instances to abstract featural concepts," *Journal of Psycholinguistic Research*, 10: 421–39.

Holzman, M. (1984) "Evidence for a reciprocal model of language development," *Journal of Linguistic Research*, 13: 119–48.

Ingram, D. (1989) *First Language Acquisition*. Cambridge: Cambridge University Press.

Ingram, D. and Tyack, D. (1979) "Inversion of subject NP and auxiliary in children's questions," *Journal of Psycholinguistic Research*, 8: 333–41.

Jackendoff, R. (1983) *Semantics and Cognition*. Cambridge, Mass.: MIT Press.

Jusczyk, P. W. (1992) "Developing phonological categories for the speech signal," in C. A. Ferguson, L. Menn and C. Stoel-Gammon (eds), *Phonological Development*. Parkton, MD: York Press.

Keller, H. (1961) *The Story of My Life*. New York: Dell reprint.

Kenender, K. R. (1990) "Lessons from the study of speech perception," *Behavioral and Brain Sciences*, 13(4): 139–40.

Klima, E. S. and Bellugi, U. (1966) "Syntactic regularities in the speech of children," in J. Lyons and R. J. Wales (eds), *Psycholinguistic Papers: the Proceedings of the 1966 Edinburgh Conference.* Edinburgh: Edinburgh University Press.

Kollars, D. (1988) "State school reform leaves disadvantaged behind," *Fresno Bee*, December 18.

Krashen, S. D. (1982) *Principles and Practice in Second Language Acquisition.* Oxford: Pergamon Press.

Labov, W. (1966) *The Social Stratification of English in New York City.* Washington, DC: Center for Applied Linguistics.

Lambert, W. (1991) "Challenging established views on social issues: the power and limitations of research," invited address, APA Convention, San Francisco, CA, August 16–21.

Landau, D. E. (1970) "A comparative study of the language use of matched groups of lower-class and middle-class preschool children," unpublished master's thesis, Tufts University.

Lashley, K. (1950) "In search of the engram," *Symposium of the Society for Experimental Biology, 4: Physiological Mechanisms in Animal Behaviour.* London: Cambridge University Press.

Leeper, C. (1991) "Influence and involvement in children's discourse: age, gender and partner effects," *Child Development*, 62: 787–811.

Leger, D. (1992) "Contextual sources of information and responses to animal communication signals," *Psychological Bulletin*, 113: 295–304.

Lempert, H. and Kinsbourne, M. (1985) "Possible origin of speech in selective orienting," *Psychological Bulletin*, 97: 63–73.

Lenneberg, E. (1967) *Biological Foundations of Language.* New York: Wiley.

Leslie, A. (1987) "Pretense and representation: the origins of theory of the mind," *Psychological Review*, 94: 412–26.

Levin, H. and Snow, C. (1985) "Situational variation within social speech registers," in J. Forgas (ed.), *Language and Social Situations.* Hamburg: Springer Verlag.

Lewontin, R. C. (1990) "How much did the brain have to change for speech?," *Behavioral and Brain Sciences*, 13(4): 740–1.

Lillard, A. (1993) "Young children's conceptualization of pretense: action or mental representational state?," *Child Development*, 64: 372–87.

Locke, J. (1983) *Phonological Acquisition and Change.* New York: Academic Press.

Lorenz, K. (1970) *Studies in Animal and Human Behavior*, vol. 1. Cambridge, Mass.: Harvard University Press.

McClelland, J. and Rumelhart, D. (eds) (1986) *Parallel Distributed Processing*. Cambridge, Mass.: MIT Press.

McCloskey, R. (1941) *Make Way for Ducklings*. Boston, MA: Puffin.

McConnell-Ginet, S. (1984) "Origins of sexist language in discourse," in S. White and V. Tulley (eds), *Discourse in Reading and Linguistics*. New York: Academy of Sciences.

Maratsos, M. (1973) "Nonegocentric communication abilities in preschool children," *Child Development*, 44: 697–701.

Markman, E. (1989) *Categorizing and Naming in Children: Problems of Induction*. Cambridge, Mass.: MIT Press.

Markman, E. (1992) "Constraints on word learning: speculations about their nature, origins, and domain specificity," in M. Gunnar and M. Maratsos (eds), *Modularity and Constraints in Language and Cognition*. Hillsdale, NJ: Lawrence Erlbaum.

Markman, E. and Hutchinson, J. (1984) "Children's sensitivity to constraints on word meaning: taxonomic vs. thematic relations," *Cognitive Psychology*, 16: 1–27.

Marler, P. (1957) "Specific distinctiveness in the communication signals of birds," *Behavior*, 11: 13–39.

Marler, P. (1976) "Organization, communication and graded signals: the chimpanzee and the gorilla," in P. P. G. Bateson and R. A. Hinde (eds), *Growing Points in Ethology*. Cambridge: Cambridge University Press.

Marshall, J. C. (1970) "The biology of communication in man and animals," in J. Lyons (ed.), *New Horizons in Linguistics*. Harmondsworth: Penguin.

Martin, H. and Vincent, M. (eds) (1988) *The Romance Languages*. New York: Oxford University Press.

Masur, E. F. (1978) "Preschool boys' speech modifications: the effect of listeners' linguistic levels and conversational responsiveness," *Child Development*, 49: 924–8.

Menn, L. (1976) "Pattern, control and contrast in beginning speech: a case study in the development of word form and function," unpublished doctoral dissertation, University of Illinois.

Miller, G. and Wakefield, P. (1993) "Commentary on Anglin, 'Vocabulary development: a morphological analysis'," *Monographs of the Society for Research in Child Development*, no. 158(10).

Montes, K. (1978) "Extending a concept functioning directively," in P. Griffin and R. Shuy (eds), *Children's Functional Language and Education in the Early Years*. Washington, DC: Center for Applied Linguistics.

Moran, L. (1973) "Comparative growth of Japanese and North American cognitive dictionaries," *Child Development*, 44: 862–9.

Morgan, J. and Newport, E. (1981) "The role of constituent structure in the induction of an artificial language," *Journal of Verbal Learning and Verbal Behavior*, 20: 67–85.

Nelson, K. (1973) "Structure and strategy in learning to talk," *Monographs of the Society for Research in Child Development*, no. 149.

Nelson, K. (1993) "The psychological and social origins of autobiographical memory," *Psychological Science*, 14: 7–14.

Nelson, K. and Seidman, S. (1984) "Playing with scripts," in J. Bretherton (ed.), *Symbolic Play*. London: Academic Press.

Newsome, J. (1978) "Dialogue and development," in A. Lock (ed.), *Action, Gesture and Symbol*. London: Academic Press.

Nice, M. (1925) "Length of sentences as a criterion of child's progress in speech," *Journal of Educational Psychology*, 76: 370–9.

Olsen, R. (1991) "Results of a K-12 and adult ESL survey," *TESOL Matters*, 1(5): 4.

Perfetti, C. A., Stankovich, K., Vellutino, F. and Calher, R. (1991) "How Johnny learns to read: review of *Beginning to Read* by M. Jager," *Psychological Science*, 2: 70–85.

Perner, J., Leckham, S. and Wimmer, H. (1987) "Three year olds' difficulty with false belief: the case for a conceptual deficit," *British Journal of Developmental Psychology*, 5: 125–37.

Pfungst, O. (1911) *Clever Hans (the Horse of Mr van Osten)*. New York: Holt, Rinehart and Winston, reprinted 1965.

Piaget, J. (1962) *Comments on Vygotsky's Critical Remarks*. Cambridge, Mass.: MIT Press.

Piatelli-Palmarini, M. (ed.) (1980) *Language and Learning: the Debate between Jean Piaget and Noam Chomsky*. Cambridge, Mass.: MIT Press.

Pinker, S. (1984) *Language Learnability and Language Development*. Cambridge, Mass.: Harvard University Press.

Pinker, S. (1989) "Language acquisition," in M. Posner (ed.), *Foundations of Cognitive Science*. Cambridge, Mass.: MIT Press.

Pinker, S. (1991) "Rules of language," *Science*, 253: 530–5.

Pinker, S. (1994) *The Language Instinct*. New York: Morrow.

Povinelli, D. J. (1993) "Reconstructing the evolution of the mind," *American Psychologist*, 48: 493–509.

Powell, B. P. (1991) *Homer and the Origin of the Greek Alphabet*. Cambridge: Cambridge University Press.

Premack, A. and Premack, D. (1972) "Teaching language to an ape," *Scientific American*, 227: 92–100.

Premack, D. (1971) "On the assessment of language competence in the chimpanzee," in A. M. Schrier and F. Stolnitz (eds), *Behavior of Nonhuman Primates*, vol. 4. New York: Academic Press.

Pullum, G. and Ladusaw, W. (1986) *Phonetic Symbol Guide*. Chicago: University of Chicago Press.

Richards, M. (1978) "The biological and the social," in A. Lock (ed.), *Action, Gesture and Symbol*. London: Academic Press.

Ristan, C. (1991) *Cognitive Ethology*. Hillsdale, NJ: Lawrence Erlbaum.

Romaine, S. (1994) *Language in Society: an Introduction to Sociolinguistics*. New York: Oxford University Press.

Rosch, E. (1973) "Natural categories," *Cognitive Psychology*, 4: 328–50.

Rosch, E. (1975) "Basic objects in natural categories," University of California, Berkeley, Language Behavior Research Laboratory.

Rosch, E. (1977) "Human categorization," in N. Warren (ed.), *Studies in Cross-cultural Psychology*. London: Academic Press.

Rosch, E. (1978) *Cognition and Categorization*. Hillsdale, NJ: Lawrence Erlbaum.

Rumbaugh, D. and Rumbaugh, S. (1977) "Chimpanzee language research: status and potential," *Behavior Research Methods and Instrumentation*, 10: 119–39.

Rumelhart, D. E. and McClelland, J. L. (1982) "An interactive activation model of context effects in letter perception: part 2," *Psychological Review* 89: 60–95.

Rymer, R. (1993) *Genie: an Abused Child's Flight from Silence*. New York: Harper Collins.

Savage-Rumbaugh, E. S., Murphy, J., Sevcik, R., Brakke, K., Williams, S. and Rumbaugh, D. (1993) "Language comprehension in ape and child," *Monographs of the Society for Research in Child Development*, no. 58, (3–4).

Schank, R. and Abelson, R. (1977) *Scripts, Plans, Goals, and Understanding: an Inquiry into Human Knowledge Structures*. Hillsdale, NJ: Lawrence Erlbaum.

Schumann, J. (1978) *The Pidginization Process: a Model for Second Language Acquisition*. Rowley, Mass.: Newbury House.

Scollen, R. (1976) *Conversations with a One Year Old*. Honolulu: University of Hawaii.

Searle, J. (1965) "What is a speech act?," in M. Black (ed.), *Philosophy in America*. New York: Cornell University Press.

Searle, J. (1969) *Speech Acts*. Cambridge: Cambridge University Press.

Sebeok, T. (1961) "A natural history of language," *Semiotica*, 65: 343–58.

Shattuck, R. (1980) *The Forbidden Experiment: the Story of the Wild Boy of Aveyron*. New York: Washington Square Press.

Shatz, M. (1978) "The relationship between cognitive processes and the development of communication skills," in C. B. Keasey (ed.), *Nebraska Symposium on Motivation 1977*. Lincoln, NE: University of Nebraska Press.

Shotter, J. (1978) "The cultural context of communication studies: theoretical and methodological issues," in A. Lock (ed.), *Action, Gesture and Symbol*. London: Academic Press.

Smith, F. (1971) *Understanding Reading: a Psycholinguistic Analysis of Reading and Learning to Read*. New York: Holt, Rinehart and Winston.

Snow, C. (1977) "The development of conversation between mothers and babies," *Journal of Child Language*, 4: 1–23.

Snow, C. and Ferguson, C. (eds) (1977) *Talking to Children: Language Input and Acquisition*. Cambridge: Cambridge University Press.

Snow, C., Shonkoff, F., Lee, K. and Levin, H. (1986) "Learning to play doctor: effects of sex, age and experience in hospital," *Discourse Processes*, 9: 461–73.

Terrace, H. (1985) "In the beginning was the name," *American Psychologist*, 40: 1011–28.

Terrace, H., Petito, R. and Sanders, J. (1979) "Can an ape create a sentence?," *Science*, 206: 892–902.

Tinbergen, N. (1951) *The Study of Instinct*. London: Oxford University Press.

Trehub, F. (1976) "Discrimination of foreign speech contrasts by infants and adults," *Child Development*, 47: 466–72.

US Immigration and Naturalization Service (1993) *Statistical Yearbook*. Washington, DC: US Government Printing Office.

Vellutino, F. R. (1991) "How Johnny learns to read, commentary," *Psychological Science*, 2: 81–3.

Veneziano, E., Sinclair, H. and Bertclous, J. (1990) "From one word to two words: repetition patterns on the way to structured speech," *Journal of Child Language*, 17: 633–50.

Vygotsky, L. (1962) *Thought and Language*. Cambridge, Mass.: MIT Press.

Watson, M. and Amgott-Kwan, T. (1983) "Transitions in children's understanding of parental roles," *Developmental Psychology*, 19: 659–66.

Wellman, H. (1990) *The Child's Theory of the Mind*. Cambridge, Mass.: MIT Press.

Werner, H. and Kaplan, E. (1950) "The acquisition of word meanings: a developmental study," *Monographs of the Society for Research in Child Development*, no. 15.

West, M. and King, A. (1988) "Female visual displays affect the development of male song in the cowbird," *Nature*, 334: 244–6.

Whorf, B. (1956) *Language, Thought and Reality*. Cambridge, Mass.: MIT Press.

Wijner, E. (1990) "The development of sentence planning," *Journal of Child Language*, 17: 651–75.

Wilcox, S. and Palermo, D. (1975) "'In,' 'on' and 'under' revisited," *Cognition*, 3: 245–54.

Wilson, E. O. (1972) "Animal communication," *Scientific American*, 227: 52–72.

Woodruff, G. and Premack, D. (1979) "Intentional communication in the chimpanzee: the development of deception," *Cognition*, 7: 333–62.

Zimmerman, D. and West, C. (1975) "Sex roles, interruptions and silences in conversation," in B. Thorne and W. Henley (eds), *Sex Differences and Dominance*. Rowley, Mass.: Newbury House.

Index